Nginx HTTP Server

Adopt Nginx for your web applications to make the most of your infrastructure and serve pages faster than ever

Clément Nedelcu

BIRMINGHAM - MUMBAI

Nginx HTTP Server

First published: July 2010

Production Reference: 1140710

Published by Packt Publishing Ltd.
32 Lincoln Road
Olton
Birmingham, B27 6PA, UK.

ISBN 978-1-849510-86-8

www.packtpub.com

Cover Image by Vinayak Chittar (vinayak.chittar@gmail.com)

Credits

Author

Clément Nedelcu

Reviewers

Pascal Charest

Manlio Perillo

Acquisition Editor

Usha Iyer

Development Editor

Wilson D'souza

Technical Editor

Kartikey Pandey

Copy Editor

Leonard D'Silva

Indexers

Hemangini Bari

Tejal Daruwale

Editorial Team Leader

Aanchal Kumar

Project Team Leader

Lata Basantani

Project Coordinator

Jovita Pinto

Proofreader

Lynda Sliwoski

Graphics

Geetanjali Sawant

Production Coordinator

Aparna Bhagat

Cover Work

Aparna Bhagat

About the Author

Clément Nedelcu was born and raised in France, and studied in U.K., French, and Chinese universities. He is now a computer science teacher at Jiangsu University of Science and Technology in Zhenjiang, a southwestern city of China. He also works as technology consultant in France, specialized in web and Microsoft .NET development as well as Linux server administration. Since 2005, he has been administering a major network of websites in his spare time. This eventually led him to discover Nginx: it made such a difference that he started his own blog about it. One thing leading to another…

The author's blog can be visited at `http://cnedelcu.net` and contains articles about Nginx and other web development topics.

I would like to express my gratitude to my girlfriend, my family and my friends who have been very supportive all along the writing stage. This book is dedicated to Martin Fjordvald for originally directing me to Nginx when my servers were about to kick the bucket. Special thanks to Maxim Dounin, Jérémie Bertrand, Shaun James, Zhang Yichun, Brendan, and all the folks on the #Nginx IRC channel on Freenode.

About the Reviewers

Pascal Charest works as senior principal consultant for Les Laboratoires Phoenix—an information system performance consulting firm based in Canada. Working with leading-edge algorithms and free software, he is called as subject matter expert to manage infrastructure projects, lead operations, and execute process validation.

Over the last year, sample mandates includes redesigning storage system (glusterfs) for a large North American investment group and managing the carrier-grade, international network of a prominent member of the telecommunication industry. He is also leading operations for quite a few local startups and answers their scalability needs through custom cloud computing solution / network infrastructure.

He is also a free software/society advocate and often speaks in conference about scalability issues in information systems.

He can be reached at pascal.charest@labsphoenix.com.

> Thanks to Catherine, my love, for everything you've done so I did not have to do it.

Manlio Perillo lives in Italy, in the Irpinia region, near Naples.

He currently works as a freelance programmer, mainly developing web applications using Python and Nginx.

In 2008, he began working on a WSGI (Python Web Server Gateway Interface) implementation for Nginx. It is available on http://bitbucket.org/mperillo/, along with some other open source projects.

Table of Contents

Preface

It is a well-known fact that the market of web servers has a long-established leader: Apache. According to recent surveys, as of October 2009 over 45 percent of the World Wide Web is served by this fifteen years old open source application. However, for the past few months the same reports reveal the rise of a new competitor: Nginx, a lightweight HTTP server originating from Russia— pronounced "engine X". There have been many interrogations surrounding the pronounced newborn. Why has the blogosphere become so effervescent about it? What is the reason causing so many server administrators to switch to Nginx since the beginning of year 2009? Is this apparently tiny piece of software mature enough to run my high-traffic website?

To begin with, Nginx is not as young as one might think. Originally started in 2002, the project was first carried out by a standalone developer, Igor Sysoev, for the needs of an extremely high-traffic Russian website, namely Rambler, which received as of September 2008 over 500 million HTTP requests per day. The application is now used to serve some of the most popular websites on the Web such as WordPress, Hulu, SourceForge, and many more. Nginx has proven to be a very efficient, lightweight yet powerful web server. Along the chapters of this book, you will discover the many features of Nginx and progressively understand why so many administrators have decided to place their trust in this new HTTP server, often at the expense of Apache.

There are many aspects in which Nginx is more efficient than its competitors. First and foremost, speed. Making use of asynchronous sockets, Nginx does not spawn as many times as it receives requests. One process per core suffices to handle thousands of connections, allowing for a much lighter CPU load and memory consumption. Secondly, ease of use—configuration files are much simpler to read and tweak than with other web server solutions such as Apache. A couple of lines are enough to set up a complete virtual host configuration. Last but not least, modularity. Not only is Nginx a completely open source project released under a BSD-like license, but it also comes with a powerful plug-in system—referred to as "modules". A large variety of modules are included with the original distribution archive, and many third-party ones can be downloaded online. All in all, Nginx combines speed, efficiency, and power, providing you the perfect ingredients for a successful web server; it appears to be the best Apache alternative as of today.

Although Nginx is available for Windows since version 0.7.52, it is common knowledge that Linux distributions are preferred for hosting production sites. During the various processes described in this book, we will thus assume that you are hosting your website on a Linux operating system such as Debian, Fedora, CentOS, Mandriva, or other well-known distributions.

What this book covers

Chapter 1, Preparing your Work Environment provides a basic approach of the Linux command-line environment that we will be using throughout this book.

Chapter 2, Downloading and Installing Nginx guides you through the setup process, by downloading and installing Nginx as well as its prerequisites.

Chapter 3, Basic Nginx Configuration helps you discover the fundamentals of Nginx configuration and set up the Core module.

Chapter 4, HTTP Configuration details the HTTP Core module which contains most of the major configuration sections and directives.

Chapter 5, Module Configuration helps you discover the many first-party modules of Nginx among which are the Rewrite and the SSI modules.

Chapter 6, PHP and Python with Nginx explains how to set up PHP and other third-party applications (if you are interested in serving dynamic websites) to work together with Nginx via FastCGI.

Chapter 7, Apache and Nginx Together teaches you to set up Nginx as reverse proxy server working together with Apache.

Chapter 8, From Apache to Nginx provides a detailed guide to switching from Apache to Nginx.

Appendix A, Directive Index lists and describes all configuration directives, sorted alphabetically. Module directives are also described in their respective chapters too.

Appendix B, Module reference lists available modules.

Appendix C, Troubleshooting discusses the most common issues that administrators face when they configure Nginx.

What you need for this book

Nginx is free and open source software running under various operating systems—Linux-based, Mac OS, Windows operating systems, and many more. As such, there is no real requirement in terms of software. Nevertheless in this book and particularly in the first two chapters we will be working in a Linux environment, so running a Linux-based operating system would be a plus. Prerequisites for compiling the application are further detailed in Chapter 2.

Who this book is for

This book is a perfect companion for both Nginx beginners and experienced administrators. For the former, it will take you through the complete process of setting up this lightweight HTTP server on your system and configuring its various modules to get it to do exactly what you need, in a fast and secure way. For the latter, it provides different angles of approach that can help you make the most of your current infrastructure. As the book progresses, it provides a complete reference to all the modules and directives of Nginx. It will explain how to replace your existing server with Nginx or configure Nginx to work as a frontend for your existing server.

Conventions

In this book, you will find a number of styles of text that distinguish between different kinds of information. Here are some examples of these styles, and an explanation of their meaning.

Code words in text are shown as follows: "We can include other contexts through the use of the include directive."

A block of code is set as follows:

```
[default]
exten => s,1,Dial(Zap/1|30)
exten => s,2,Voicemail(u100)
exten => s,102,Voicemail(b100)
exten => i,1,Voicemail(s0)
```

When we wish to draw your attention to a particular part of a code block, the relevant lines or items are set in bold:

```
[default]
exten => s,1,Dial(Zap/1|30)
exten => s,2,Voicemail(u100)
exten => s,102,Voicemail(b100)
exten => i,1,Voicemail(s0)
```

Any command-line input or output is written as follows:

```
# cp /usr/src/asterisk-addons/configs/cdr_mysql.conf.sample
    /etc/asterisk/cdr_mysql.conf
```

New terms and **important words** are shown in bold. Words that you see on the screen, in menus or dialog boxes for example, appear in the text like this: "clicking the **Next** button moves you to the next screen".

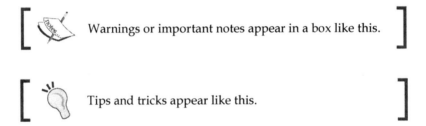

Warnings or important notes appear in a box like this.

Tips and tricks appear like this.

Reader feedback

Feedback from our readers is always welcome. Let us know what you think about this book—what you liked or may have disliked. Reader feedback is important for us to develop titles that you really get the most out of.

To send us general feedback, simply send an e-mail to feedback@packtpub.com, and mention the book title via the subject of your message.

If there is a book that you need and would like to see us publish, please send us a note in the **SUGGEST A TITLE** form on www.packtpub.com or e-mail suggest@packtpub.com.

If there is a topic that you have expertise in and you are interested in either writing or contributing to a book on, see our author guide on www.packtpub.com/authors.

Customer support

Now that you are the proud owner of a Packt book, we have a number of things to help you to get the most from your purchase.

Errata

Although we have taken every care to ensure the accuracy of our content, mistakes do happen. If you find a mistake in one of our books—maybe a mistake in the text or the code—we would be grateful if you would report this to us. By doing so, you can save other readers from frustration and help us improve subsequent versions of this book. If you find any errata, please report them by visiting http://www.packtpub. com/support, selecting your book, clicking on the **errata submission form** link, and entering the details of your errata. Once your errata are verified, your submission will be accepted and the errata will be uploaded on our website, or added to any list of existing errata, under the Errata section of that title. Any existing errata can be viewed by selecting your title from http://www.packtpub.com/support.

Piracy

Piracy of copyrighted material on the Internet is an ongoing problem across all media. At Packt, we take the protection of our copyright and licenses very seriously. If you come across any illegal copies of our works, in any form, on the Internet, please provide us with the location address or website name immediately so that we can pursue a remedy.

Please contact us at copyright@packtpub.com with a link to the suspected pirated material.

We appreciate your help in protecting our authors, and our ability to bring you valuable content.

Questions

You can contact us at questions@packtpub.com if you are having a problem with any aspect of the book, and we will do our best to address it.

1
Preparing your Work Environment

In this first chapter, we will guide you through the steps to preparing your work environment on both your work computer and the server that you will use to host the websites. There are a number of things that you will have to understand in order to establish a fully functional Nginx set up, particularly if you are working with a computer running a Microsoft Windows operating system.

This chapter covers:

- Setting up a terminal emulator for using the command-line interface of your remote server
- Basic Linux command-line tools that you will be using at different stages
- Introduction to the Linux filesystem structure
- System administration tools
- Managing files and permissions

Setting up a terminal emulator

For all of us working under a Microsoft Windows operating system on a daily basis for the past fifteen years, the idea of going back to a good old command-line interface may seem somewhat primitive, but it is nevertheless a reality—even a necessity for most server administrators. The first step of your preparatory work will consist of downloading and installing an SSH client. **Secure SHell (SSH)** is a network protocol that allows two devices to communicate securely by encrypting exchanged data. It is notably used for connecting to a system shell remotely. In other words, you will be able to take control of your server without compromising its security.

Finding and downloading PuTTY

PuTTY is by far the most widely used terminal emulator for SSH access under Windows. As such, you may find a large amount of articles and other documents on the web explaining the various features offered by this program. We will only be covering the aspects that directly concern our subject—configuring PuTTY to connect to your server, entering text, and using the copy and paste commands. But you should know that there is much more that this free and open source tool can do—creating SSH tunnels, connecting to a Telnet, rlogin, even raw TCP communication, and so on.

PuTTY can be downloaded directly from its author's website:

```
http://www.chiark.greenend.org.uk/~sgtatham/putty/
```

It comes as a standalone .EXE program and does not require any external files. All its data is saved in the Windows registry, so it will not be filling up your system with configuration files.

Creating a session

Before reading on, make sure you are in possession of the following elements:

- The host name or the IP address of the server you will connect to.
- The port on which the SSH daemon is running. Unless you were told otherwise, the service should be running on port 22.
- A user account on the system.
- A password for your account.

Let us take a quick peek at the main PuTTY window.

PuTTY saves your settings in *sessions*. So when you finish configuring the assortment of parameters, make sure to give a name to your session and click on the **Save** button, as highlighted in the preceding screenshot.

On the default PuTTY screen, you will need to enter a **Host Name (or IP address)** for the server you want to connect to. Then configure the port on which the SSH service is running on the remote server, 22 being the default port for SSHD. Here are a couple of additional settings that are optional but may be useful to you:

- In the **Window** setting group, you may adjust a few parameters such as the size of the terminal window and scroll back behavior.

- In the **Window | Appearance** setting group, you can change the font size in the terminal window as well as cursor options.

- In the **Window | Translation** setting group, you are given the possibility to enable a different character set. This is particularly useful if you work with servers that make use of the UTF-8 character set.

- In the **Connection** setting group, you may want to enable the **TCP keepalives** feature, which allows you to prevent disconnections due to TCP timeouts.

- In the **Connection | Data** setting group, you can enter your system account username. However, PuTTY will not allow you to store passwords for obvious security reasons.

Once you have finished configuring your session, remember to save it, and then initiate the connection by clicking on the **Open** button on the main window. When you connect to a server for the first time, you are required to validate its authenticity by accepting the server fingerprint. If you connect to the same server in the future, you shouldn't be seeing the confirmation again, unless the server settings such as hostname or port have been changed or security has been compromised and you are connecting to an intermediate server (man-in-the-middle attack). Eventually, you should be prompted for a login (unless you enabled the auto-login option) and a password. Please note that when typing the password, it will not appear on the screen at all — not even as asterisks, so make sure to enter it carefully, then press the *Return* key.

```
alex@ns304584:~                                                    _ □ ×
login as: alex
alex@example.com's password:
CentOS release 5.2 (Final)
Linux ns304584.ovh.net 2.6.28.1-xxxx-std-ipv4-32 #2 SMP Fri Jan 30 09:55:02 UTC
2009 i686 i686 i386 GNU/Linux

server    : 84119
ip        : 94.23.213.166
hostname  : ns304584.ovh.net

[alex@ns304584 ~]$
```

Working with PuTTY and the shell

If you have never worked with PuTTY or with a system shell before, there are a couple of details you may want to know regarding the behavior of the main terminal emulator window.

- Text that you select with the mouse cursor in the terminal window will automatically be copied to the clipboard when you release the left button.

- Pasting text to the terminal is done by a simple right-click anywhere on the window area.

- Pressing *Ctrl+C* does not copy text to clipboard. It is instead a shortcut used for interrupting the execution of a program. If you accidentally run a command that takes longer to execute than you imagined, then this shortcut will allow you to take control of the shell again.

- In case of a disconnection from the server, a right-click on the title bar of the terminal window will open a menu and allow you to restart the session.

- When typing a filename in the command line, pressing the *Tab* key will attempt to auto-complete the filename. If you hear a beep noise when doing so, it may be due to two reasons—either the segment you entered does not correspond to any file on the system, or there are multiple files found. In the last case, quickly press *Tab* twice to see the list of files matching your input. Note that this feature may be unavailable on your shell, depending on the operating system that your server is running.

Basic shell commands

Connecting to your server and opening up a terminal window is one thing, being able to actually make use of it is another. If you have never worked with Linux before, you may find this section particularly helpful as it will help you get started by describing some of the most basic and useful commands. All the commands that we will be using in later sections are covered here, but you will soon realize that there is a lot more that you can do with the shell in general.

File and directory management

There are a lot of similarities between common shells such as **BASH** (Bourne-Again SHell, default shell for GNU/Linux distributions) and the Microsoft Windows command-line interface. The main resemblance is that we use the notion of *working directory*. The shell prompts you for a textual command; the said command will be executed in the current working directory.

When you first log in to your shell account, you should land in your *home directory*. This folder is generally used to contain your personal files; it is a private space that no other users on the system should be able to see (unless specific access rights are granted).

Here is a list of the most useful basic commands for file and directory management:

Command Name	Description
pwd	Print working directory
	`[alex@example.com ~]$ pwd`
	`/home/alex`
cd	Change directory
	`[alex@example.com ~]$ cd images`
	`[alex@example.com images]$ pwd`
	`/home/alex/images`
	`[alex@example.com images]$ cd /tmp`
	`[alex@example.com tmp]$ pwd`
	`/tmp`
	Here are some useful shortcuts that can be used with cd as well as any other shell command:
	• Typing cd or cd ~ always takes you to your home directory.
	• More generally, ~ (tilde character) is a reference to your home directory, which allows you to use commands such as cd ~/images.
	• Typing cd .. takes you to the upper level in the directory tree. Note the space between cd and ..
	• cd . has no effect; however, note that the dot refers to the current working directory. For example, cd ./images.
ls	List all files in the current working directory (or a specified directory)
	`[alex@example.com ~]$ ls`
	`images  photo2.jpg  photo.jpg  shopping.txt`
	Try ls -l for a more detailed view. The -a switch reveals hidden and system files.

Command Name	Description
mkdir	Create a new directory
	`[alex@example.com ~]$ mkdir documents`
	`[alex@example.com ~]$ cd documents`
	`[alex@example.com documents]$ mkdir /tmp/alex`
	`[alex@example.com documents]$ cd /tmp/alex`
	`[alex@example.com alex]$ pwd`
	`/tmp/alex`
	Command-line applications in general do not output any text in the case of a successful operation. They will only display a message if an error occurred.
cp	Copy files.
	Command syntax: `cp [options] source destination`
	`[alex@example.com ~]$ cp photo2.jpg photo3.jpg`
mv	Move or rename files.
	Command syntax: `mv [options] source destination`
	Renaming a file:
	`[alex@example.com ~]$ mv photo3.jpg photo4.jpg`
	Moving a file to another folder:
	`[alex@example.com ~]$ mv photo4.jpg images/`
rm	Delete a file or a directory. The `-r` switch enables recursion.
	`[alex@example.com ~]$ rm photo.jpg`
	`[alex@example.com ~]$ ls`
	`images photo2.jpg shopping.txt`
	`[alex@example.com ~]$ rm -r images/`
	`[alex@example.com ~]$ ls`
	`photo2.jpg shopping.txt`
	Proceed with extreme caution with this command, especially if you are logged in as the Superuser (system administrator). Files cannot be recovered and a simple call to `rm -rf /` suffices to initiate a complete wipe of your filesystem.

Command Name	Description

locate	Locate the specified file on the entire filesystem. This command is directly related to the updatedb command below:
	
	`[alex@example.com ~]$ locate photo2.jpg`
	
	`/home/alex/photo2.jpg`
	
	`/home/jesse/holiday_photo2.jpg`
	
	Note: The locate command completely relies on indexes. If you create a new file, you will not be able to find it until you perform a database update with the command below.

updatedb	Updates the file database. Note that this command requires administrative permissions. For that reason, it is generally set to be executed on a daily basis via a "cron job" (the equivalent of *tasks* in Microsoft Windows operating systems) with administrative-level rights.
	
	`[alex@example.com ~]$ mkdir "Holidays in France"`
	
	`[alex@example.com ~]$ locate France`
	`No file found: a database update is required.`
	
	Once logged in with an administrator account:
	
	`[root@example.com ~]# updatedb`
	
	`[root@example.com ~]# locate France`
	
	`/home/alex/Holidays in France`

man	Displays documentation on a specified command `[alex@example.com ~]$ man ls` See the screenshot below. `[alex@example.com ~]$ man ls`

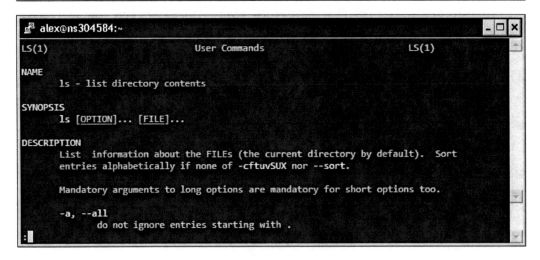

Eventually, you can use the `clear` command to erase all text on your screen and start afresh.

User and group management

The first obsession an administrator should have is who has access to which resources on their system. In that extent, Unix-based operating systems provide an elaborate user and group management mechanism.

Superuser account

Each and every operating system comes with a Superuser account, often required for performing administrative-level tasks. This account is usually called **root**, although on some systems it can be named otherwise ('admin' or even 'toor'). The Superuser has access to all files and directories of the system and has the right to read, edit, and execute all files as well as change file attributes and permissions.

Although an administrator should always have the possibility to access the root account, it is not recommended to constantly connect as the machine Superuser. In fact, some operating systems such as Ubuntu do not even allow you to do so. One of the great principles of computer security is *least privilege* — you should never be allowed to do more than what you need to do. In other words, why give a user the possibility to access your system configuration folder if they are only going to use your computer for surfing the web and writing documents with Open Office? Granting more privileges than one requires can only lead to situations where the system security and integrity get compromised. For that reason, it is highly recommended that you create user accounts, not only for physical users of your machine but also for applications to run in a secure environment with clearly defined boundaries.

User accounts

One particular file in the system configuration directory holds the list of system users: `/etc/passwd`. Contrary to what the name suggests, it does not usually contain user passwords; they are, in most cases, stored using the *shadow format* in a separate file `/etc/shadow` for security reasons. It, however, does come with certain bits of information for each user. One line of the `passwd` file representing one user, the following syntax should be respected:

```
Name:password:ID:group ID:comment:home directory:login shell
```

In practice, the *password* bit is replaced by 'x' indicating that the actual password is stored in the /etc/shadow file.

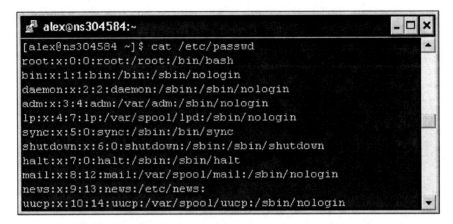

Adding a new user account can be as simple as adding a line to the /etc/passwd file. However, you might find the manual process somewhat bothersome, and rest assured—you are not alone. In that extent, you will be pleased to learn that a program automating the operation is available on most distributions—**useradd**.

The most basic syntax for this command is useradd username. This creates a new user account with the default settings (which can be customized)—a home directory for the user located in /home, no expiration date, the default group for users, and Bash as a login shell. If you add an account destined to be running a service such as Nginx, it is recommended that you do not grant the user account shell access; consequently, you should make sure that the login shell is set to nologin (usually found in /sbin/nologin). The command would then be:

```
useradd --shell /sbin/nologin nginx
```

You can also define the location of the home directory to the folder where you have installed Nginx:

```
useradd --shell /sbin/nologin --home-dir /usr/local/nginx nginx
```

The trailing *nginx* indicates the name of the user account to be created.

If you wish to edit some of these parameters after the account creation process is complete, you may use the **usermod** command. It allows you to rename the account name, change the account password, move the home directory along with its contents to another location, and much more. Eventually, you might want to delete a user account. This is done via the simple **userdel** command as in userdel username. The -r switch allows you to delete the home directory along with the user account.

Remember that for each of these commands, you have the possibility to consult more detailed information using **man**, for example, `man useradd`.

Group management

In addition to user accounts, Unix-based systems provide an even more advanced resource management mechanism—*user groups*. The purpose of a group is to have its own access permissions on files and directories; all users belonging to the group will then inherit the group permissions. A user account has to belong to at least one group—the user's primary group—although it may also belong to secondary groups.

In practice, the list of groups on the system is stored in the `/etc/group` file. Each line of the file represents one group, respecting the following syntax:

```
Group name:password:group ID:user list
```

The group password is rarely used; instead it is replaced by 'x' to indicate that the group has no password. At the end of each line, you will find the list of users belonging to the group. Here is an example of a group file on a production server:

```
alex@ns304584:~
[alex@ns304584 ~]$ cat /etc/group | grep ,
bin:x:1:root,bin,daemon
daemon:x:2:root,bin,daemon
sys:x:3:root,bin,adm
adm:x:4:root,adm,daemon
lp:x:7:daemon,lp
psaadm:x:2521:psaadm,sw-cp-server
psaserv:x:2522:apache,psaftp,psaadm
[alex@ns304584 ~]$
```

Again, if you wish to create a new group on your system, you have two options: either add a new line to the `/etc/group` file, or use the dedicated **groupadd** command. Its syntax is simple—`groupadd groupname`. There are some optional parameters to the command, which you can discover by running `man groupadd`.

Similar to the user management system, you will also find **groupmod** and **groupdel** commands for respectively editing group settings and deleting a group. More importantly, how to add a user to a group? It is done by either editing the `/etc/group` file to append the username at the end of the line corresponding to the group you wish to add the user to, or by using the following command:

```
usermod --append --groups groupname username
```

You may specify one or more groups. Skipping the --append option would have the effect to replace the user's group list by the specified groups. Eventually, the **groups** command shows the list of groups the current user belongs to.

Programs and processes

Running a program in the shell is not as simple as entering its filename. There are a couple of subtle details that you should understand about the way Bash handles the execution of binaries and scripts.

Starting an application

There are three different situations that you may face when you want to execute a program or a script from the shell:

- The program you want to execute is located in the current working directory.

  Solution: Prefix the filename with ./ (dot slash), which forces the shell to look for files in the current working directory only.

  For example:

  ```
  [alex@example.com ~]$ cd programs
  [alex@example.com programs]$ ./my-app
  ```

- The program you want to execute is not located in the current working directory, but you already know the file path.

  Solution: Enter the complete file path.

  For example:

  ```
  [alex@example.com ~]$ /home/alex/programs/my-app
  ```

- The program you want to execute is located in one of the folders of the PATH environment variable.

  Solution: Enter the filename without its path.

  For example: Starting a text editor called **nano**, which is usually found in the /usr/bin system directory (/usr/bin being in the PATH).

  ```
  [alex@example.com ~]$ nano
  ```

Note that when running a shell command, the prompt will be unavailable until the execution is complete. This can be problematic in the case of a lengthy operation, so you may want to start a program and have it running in the background instead of blocking the shell completely. This is done by appending a simple & at the end of the line.

```
[alex@example.com tmp]$ cp home.avi ~/movies/ &
[6] 2629
[alex@example.com tmp]$ [6]    Done      cp home.avi ~/movies/ &
```

As soon as you send the command, the pid (*Process Identifier*—a number identifying a running process on your system) will show up and the prompt will return. Once the execution terminates, a message appears to indicate its completion, along with the original command used to start the process.

System services

Most of the applications running in the background (often referred to as **services)**, are not started via a simple command followed by the & character. There are actually complex scripts that manage their startup and shutdown. Those scripts can be placed in several directories, the most common one being /etc/init.d.

Some Linux distributions such as Red Hat, Fedora, CentOS, or Mandriva come with a script called **service** that (among other things) allows you to control a service by using the service name command syntax, where script is the name of the service you want to start and command is one of the options from the table below. Distributions that do not have the service script installed may also control services using a similar syntax: /etc/init.d/name command. Note that init.d scripts do not always provide implementations for all of these common commands.

Command	Description
start	Starts the specified service
stop	Stops the specified service in a *clean* way
restart	Stops the specified service and starts it again
reload	Reloads the configuration of the specified service
status	Displays the status of the specified service

 Try service --status-all for listing all system services along with their current status.

Process management

As mentioned before, the system allocates a number to each and every process running on the computer. This number is called the Process Identifier (**pid**). Knowing the pid is important in various situations, some of which you are about to discover.

Finding the pid

Firstly, how does one find the pid of a process? Although there are a number of ways you could do that, most of them rely on a single tool—**ps**. Its many options (combined with the piping mechanism) will allow you to retrieve various details about a process.

```
 alex@ns304584:~                                                    _ □ ✕
[alex@ns304584 ~]$ ps aux | grep sshd
root      11757  0.0  0.1  11808  3052 ?        Ss   16:26  0:00 sshd: alex [priv]
alex      11820  0.0  0.0  11968  1744 ?        S    16:26  0:00 sshd: alex@pts/0
alex      12167  0.0  0.0   4156   660 pts/0    S+   16:27  0:00 grep sshd
root      32243  0.0  0.0   7036   992 ?        Ss   Oct29  0:00 /usr/sbin/sshd
[alex@ns304584 ~]$ 
```

The ps aux | grep sshd command can be dissected into three components:

1. ps aux is a command that lists all processes currently running on the system.

2. | (pipe) redirects the output of the command placed before the pipe to the command placed after it. Running ps aux generally returns a long list of processes, so you will only want to display the one process you are looking for.

3. grep sshd receives data from the ps aux command and only outputs lines containing the specified words. In other words, grep acts as the filter, retaining lines containing sshd.

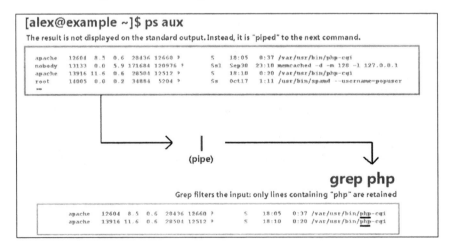

An administrator's best friend—top

Another tool that you will find particularly useful if you run a high traffic website is **top**. This program lists all the processes currently running on the system with their pid, which is sorted by their CPU usage. On top of that, the list refreshes every second until you interrupt the execution flow (with *Ctrl+C*, for example) or stop the application by pressing the *Q* key. This allows you to keep track of the most resource-hungry processes.

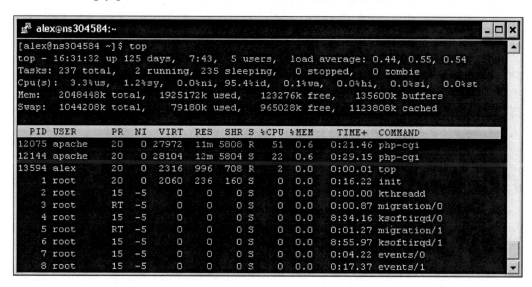

The upper part also provides loads of useful statistics on the current resource usage such as system uptime, active users, load average, memory and processor load, and more.

Killing processes

If a command ever turns out wrong and the prompt does not return, one of your possible solutions is to press *Ctrl+C* to interrupt the execution flow of the application. The equivalent operation can be applied to background processes by using the **kill** command. There is a subtle detail here—you cannot kill a process by specifying its name; you need to provide its pid. The reason, obviously, is that one program may be executed more than once; consequently, a program name does not always correspond to a unique process.

```
[alex@example.com ~]$ kill 12075
```

Again, if the command does not output any result, there is nothing to worry about. Actually, if there is one thing that `kill` may tell you, it would be something along the lines of `no such process` in case you entered an invalid pid. The kill command simply sends a signal to the specified process, which does not necessarily mean that the said process will have successfully stopped. If the program is locked, for example, it will not respond to the signal and thus will still be running. You will be reassured to know that there is a simple way to force a process to terminate—the `-9` option specifies that the system should immediately stop the execution.

```
[alex@example.com ~]$ kill -9 12075
```

Finally, as you can imagine, you may, at some point, need to terminate multiple processes at a time. For instance, you could kill all the processes that Apache spawned. In that case, we would use a slightly different command—**killall**. It differs from kill in the extent that it accepts a process name as argument instead of a pid.

```
[alex@example.com ~]$ killall httpd
```

Discovering the Linux filesystem

Linux-based operating systems have their files organized in a very specific way that follows more or less closely the long-established Filesystem Hierarchy Standard (FHS). According to the official FHS documentation, this standard enables:

- Software to predict the location of installed files and directories
- Users to predict the location of installed files and directories

Although the original standard specification was published in 1993, it is still used by modern distributions, but in a slightly revised version.

Directory structure

Unlike Microsoft Windows operating systems where all file paths begin with a drive letter (what happens if you have over twenty-six drives on your system?), FHS-based filesystems have a common parent. This parent is called the root directory, also known as / (the slash character). All files and directories (regardless of the device, drive, or partition, they are located on) are children of the root directory. Consequently, all absolute paths that you will find in this book start with a slash.

Let us now run `cd /`, followed by `ls` in order to discover the many subdirectories defined by the FHS. Please note that this directory structure is purely conventional; nothing actually prevents you from placing your own files in any of these folders or creating more directories at the root.

Path	Description
/	**The root directory**: Not to be confused with /root. No files are usually placed at the root, although nothing really prevents you from doing so.
/bin	**Binaries**: Common executable binaries and scripts available for all users of the system. This is where essential programs such as ls, cp, or mv are found.
/boot	**Boot**: Critical files used at system boot time.
/dev	**Devices**: Device and special files, more information in the next section.
/etc	**Et cetera**: System-wide configuration files for services and applications. You will often need to browse this directory, for example, when you will need to edit the Nginx server settings and virtual hosts.
/home	**Home directories**: This directory contains home directories for all users on the system except the *root* user. In the examples we studied before we used /home/alex, the home directory for the *alex* user.
/lib	**Libraries**: System-wide shared libraries and kernel modules, required by binaries found in the /bin and /sbin folders.
/media	**Removable media**: A directory that allows you to easily access removable media using mount points for devices such as CD-ROMs, USB devices, and so on.
/mnt	**Temporarily mounted filesystems**: This directory is a suitable placeholder in case the administrator wishes to mount a filesystem on a temporary basis.
/opt	**Optional software packages**: In theory, this directory should host application files and add-on packages that do not come with the default operating system installation. In practice, it is hardly ever used.
/proc	**Kernel and process information virtual filesystem**: This directory provides access to a virtual filesystem containing a variety of statistics and details about all running processes.
/root	**Root user home directory**: The root user, also known as **Superuser**, does not have its home directory stored in the same folder as regular users (/home). Instead, its personal files are stored in the /root. directory. The slash-root (/root) directory is not to be confused with the root directory (/).
/sbin	**System binaries**: Utilities dedicated to system administration, thus generally accessed by the root user only. Programs such as **ifconfig**, **halt**, **service**, and many others can be found here.
/srv	**Service data**: A placeholder for data coming from services hosted on the system. Like many others, this directory is rarely used.
/tmp	**Temporary files**: Files that do not need to be conserved beyond program execution should be stored here. Many operating systems actually clear the contents of this directory on reboot.

Path	Description
/usr	**Read-only user data:** This directory provides a secondary hierarchy for *shareable* read-only user data. The /usr directory should contain the following:
	• /usr/bin: Non-essential command binaries and scripts for all users (such as wget, gzip, firefox, and many more)
	• /usr/include: Header files from C libraries for inclusion at compile time
	• /usr/lib: Libraries used by program binaries found in /usr/bin and /usr/sbin
	• /usr/sbin: Non-essential system command binaries and scripts for all users (such as useradd, ntpdate, and so on)
	• /usr/share: Architecture-independent data files
	• /usr/src: Source code for kernel and installed applications
	• /usr/X11R6: X Window System (v11 release 6)-related files
	• /usr/local: A third hierarchy level for local data only
/var	**Variable files:** Files that are expected to be modified by running applications or services, for example, logfiles, cache, spool, and more. It comes with a hierarchy of its own:
	• /var/lib: Variable state information related to an application or more generally the operating system. Note that MySQL database files are usually stored in /var/lib/mysql.
	• /var/lock: Lock files used for synchronized resource access between applications.
	• /var/log: Logfiles generated by programs, services, or the system kernel.
	• /var/mail: User e-mail-related files. On most systems, /var/mail is now a simple shortcut to the actual location of the files in /var/spool/mail.
	• /var/run: Runtime variable data. Cleared when the system reboots, this directory provides information about the state of the system since it was started.
	• /var/spool: A directory in which files that are expected to be processed are placed such as e-mails and print jobs.
	• /var/tmp: A placeholder for temporary files that should not be deleted when the system reboots.

Special files and devices

As you may have noticed in the directory structure, Linux operating systems have a reserved directory for "device files" (/dev). As a matter of fact, this folder contains elements referred to as **nodes**, each node representing a different device on the system. They can be actual hardware devices or pseudo devices; either way, the purpose of having them listed as part of the filesystem is to facilitate input and output interactions with programs and services—software developers can access devices as simply as they would read or write to a file. You will learn that device files are used in a number of situations and you should sooner or later have a use for them.

Device types

There may be a large variety of devices available in the /dev directory, unfortunately all of them usually bear an obscure name making it nearly impossible for you to understand their purpose. Device files are named according to conventions in use in Linux operating systems. Since there is a potentially infinite amount of devices, we will only identify the most common ones. A device filename is composed of a prefix, conventionally defined according to the driver type, and optionally a number (or letter) if there is more than one device of that type present on the system.

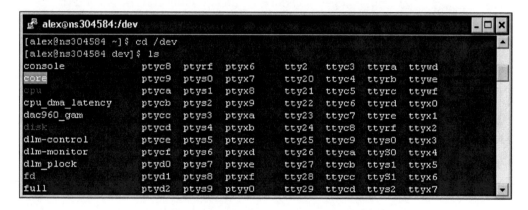

Device file conventional prefixes for the most common types:

- **cdrom**: CD and DVD-ROM drives
- **fd**: Floppy disk drives
- **hd**: IDE-connected devices such as hard drives and CD-ROMs
- **md**: Metadisks and RAID devices such as hard drives
- **ram**: RAM disks
- **sd**: SCSI-connected mass-storage device
- **usb**: USB-connected devices

Pseudo devices

Some of the devices listed in the /dev directory do not correspond to actual
hardware devices. Instead, they are here for the sake of providing administrators and
developers with simple input and output access to specific resources. For that reason,
we call them "pseudo devices". Here is a brief description of the most commonly-
used pseudo devices:

Pseudo Device	Description
/dev/null	**Null device**
	This pseudo device is often nicknamed *black hole* as its purpose is to disregard all data that is being sent to it. When written to, it always reports the write operation as successful. When read from, the device returns no data.
	This is particularly useful if you want to redirect the output of a program to nowhere; in other words, if you want to make sure a command executes but outputs no text on the screen.
	`[alex@example.com ~]$ cat shopping.txt > /dev/null`
/dev/random	**Random number generators**
/dev/urandom	Streams that generate flows of random numbers. /dev/random generates *true random* numbers, whereas /dev/urandom provides *pseudorandom* numbers. These streams can be written to in order to feed the pool.
	Since they generate binary data, numbers coming from /dev/random and /dev/urandom cannot be displayed to the console terminal (they would look like a flow of garbage data). These devices are mostly used by developers wishing to collect *reliable* random numbers.
/dev/full	**Full device**
	This pseudo device is a stream that returns an error when written to as it is always considered full. When read from, it returns an infinite stream of null characters.
	The purpose of /dev/full is to provide programmers and administrators with an operation that will always trigger an error:
	`[alex@example.com ~]$ echo Hello! > /dev/full`
	`~bash: echo: write error: No space left on device`

Pseudo Device	Description
/dev/zero	**Zero data**
	Much like /dev/null, the *zero* pseudo device always provides successful return codes when written to. However, when read from, it outputs an infinite stream of null characters.
	There is a variety of cases where reading from /dev/null can prove useful, such as providing data as input to a program that will generate a file of a given size or writing to a storage device in order to format it.

Mounting a storage device

As you may have noticed in the previous sections, some of the devices available in the /dev directory are storage devices, such as hard disk drives, solid-state drives (SSD), floppies, or CD-ROMs. However, accessing the content that they serve is not as simple as browsing them with the cd command. Storage devices need to be **mounted** to the filesystem. In other words, devices need to be attached to a fixed directory.

```
[alex@example.com ~]$ cd /dev/md1
~bash: cd: /dev/md1: is not a directory.
[alex@example.com ~]$ mount /dev/md1 /mnt/alexdrive
[alex@example.com ~]$ cd /mnt/alexdrive
[alex@example.com alexdrive]$ ls
Documents Music Photos Videos boot.ini
```

The mount command allows you to attach a device (first argument, /dev/md1 in the previous example) to an *existing* directory on your system (second argument). Once the drive is mounted, you are able to access the drive like you would access any other directory of the filesystem.

 In modern Linux distributions, CD-ROMs and other common devices are automatically mounted by the system.

If you want to obtain information about currently mounted devices, a simple call to mount does the job—it tells you where each device is mounted, as well as the filesystem in use:

```
alex@ns304584:~
[alex@ns304584 ~]$ mount
/dev/md1 on / type ext3 (rw,errors=remount-ro)
/dev/proc on /proc type proc (rw)
/dev/sys on /sys type sysfs (rw)
/dev/devpts on /dev/pts type devpts (rw,gid=5,mode=620)
/dev/md2 on /var type ext3 (rw,usrquota,grpquota)
/dev/shm on /dev/shm type tmpfs (rw)
none on /proc/sys/fs/binfmt_misc type binfmt_misc (rw)
tmpfs on /var/usr/local/psa/handlers/before-local type tmpfs (rw)
tmpfs on /var/usr/local/psa/handlers/before-queue type tmpfs (rw)
tmpfs on /var/usr/local/psa/handlers/before-remote type tmpfs (rw)
tmpfs on /var/usr/local/psa/handlers/info type tmpfs (rw)
tmpfs on /var/usr/local/psa/handlers/spool type tmpfs (rw,mode=0770,gid=31)
```

If you wish to have a drive automatically mounted on system startup, or to simply set a directory to be used as the default mount point for a device, you will need to edit the /etc/fstab file logged with administrator privileges. It is a simple text file and thus can be opened with a text editor such as nano. The file, however, respects a specific syntax, and making some changes unknowingly could cause a lot of damage to your system. More details on the **fstab** syntax can be found online on websites such as tuxfiles.org.

Eventually, if you need to remove a device while the computer is in use (for instance, remove a USB storage drive) you should always unmount it first. Unmounting a device is done using the umount command:

[alex@example.com ~]$ umount /dev/usb1

Note that the first argument of the command may either be the device filename or the mount point, producing the same result.

Files and inodes

There is a common misconception of the notion of "filesystem" when it comes to Unix-based operating systems in general. Since those systems respect the FHS, they use a common directory hierarchy regrouping all files and devices. However, storage devices may have their independent disk filesystem. A disk filesystem is designed for the organization of files on a mass storage device (hard disk drives, CD-ROMs, and so on). Microsoft Windows operating systems favor the FAT, FAT32, and NTFS specifications; whereas the default and most recommended one for working under Linux is the EXT3 filesystem. EXT3 comes with a number of characteristics, and it is essential for administrators to master them in order to fully understand the operating system they work with.

EXT3 filesystem specifications

Unlike Microsoft's antique FAT32 file system that only allows files up to 4 gigabytes, the size restriction with EXT32 is 16 terabytes (depending on the block size). Moreover, the maximum storage space that can be used by EXT3 on a device is 32 terabytes, so you should have no trouble using it for a number of years, unless storage drive capacities suddenly skyrocket. One of the interesting features of EXT3 is that it lays out the data on the storage device in a way that file fragmentation is kept to a minimum and does not affect system performance. As a result there is no need to defragment your drives.

Filenames

The EXT3 filesystem accepts filenames up to 256 characters. Filename extensions are not required, although they are usually present and correspond to the content offered by the file—a .txt file should contain text, a .mp3 file for music, and so on. An important fact, however, is that filenames are case-sensitive—you may find, in the same directory, files named "SHOPPPING.TXT", "Shopping.txt", or "shopping. txt"; all three are different files.

Inodes

With Linux disk filesystems such as EXT3, a large variety of information is stored for each and every file. This information is separated both logically and physically from the actual file data and is stored in a specific structure called **inode** (index node). Some of the data contained in the inode indicates to the OS how to retrieve the contents of the file on the device. But that is not all—to the inode includes file permissions, user and group ownership, file size, access and modification times, and much more. Note that it does not contain the actual filename.

Inodes each have an identifier that is unique to the device. This identifier is called *inode number* or *i-number* and can be used in various situations. It can be retrieved by using the ls -i command:

```
alex@ns304584:~
[alex@ns304584 ~]$ ls
Holidays in France   photo2.jpg   photo.jpg   shopping.txt
[alex@ns304584 ~]$ ls -i
1048590 Holidays in France   1048591 photo.jpg
1048592 photo2.jpg            1048593 shopping.txt
[alex@ns304584 ~]$
```

Atime, ctime, and mtime

Among the metadata contained in an inode, you will find three different timestamps concerning the file. They are referred to as *atime*, *ctime*, and *mtime*.

Timestamp	Description
atime	**Access time**
	The date and time the file was last accessed. Every time an application or service reads from the file using a system call, the file access time is updated.
mtime	**Modification time**
	The date and time the file was last modified. When a change in the file *content* occurs, the file modification time is updated.
ctime	**Change time**
	The date and time the file was last changed. This timestamp concerns changes on both the file attributes (in other words, alteration of the file's inode) and the file data.

Make sure to understand the difference between modification time and change time. The first one concerns the file data only, whereas the latter tracks modifications of both file attributes and data. Here are some common examples illustrating all three mechanisms:

File access time (atime):

```
[alex@example.com ~]$ nano shopping.txt
```

The file is opened in a text editor; its content is accessed. The file access time is updated.

File change time (ctime):

```
[alex@example.com ~]$ chmod 0755 script.sh
```

The file permissions are updated (chmod command detailed in a later section); consequently, the inode is altered and the file change time updated.

File modification time (mtime):

```
[alex@example.com ~]$ echo "- a pair of socks" >> shopping.txt
```

The file data is modified; as a result, both *file modification time* and *file change time* are updated.

As you may have noticed, there is no creation time recorded in the inode, so it is impossible to find out when a file was first created. It remains unclear as to why such an important element was left out. Either way if you want to know all the timestamps associated with a file, you may use the `stat` command:

```
[alex@example.com ~]$ stat shopping.txt
```

Important information for SSD (Solid-State Drive) users

It is proven that enabling the access time feature of the filesystem can cause dramatic performance drops on your drive. Every time a file is read, its inode needs to be updated. As a result, frequent write operations are performed and that is obviously a major problem when using this kind of storage device. Be reassured that a simple solution exists for this problem as you have the possibility to completely disable file access time updates. This can be done via one of the options of the `mount` command, `noatime`. The option can be specified in the `/etc/fstab` file if you want to enable it permanently. More documentation can be found online with a simple `noatime ssd` search. Credit goes to Kevin Burton for this important finding.

Symbolic and hard links

Symbolic links in Linux are the equivalent of shortcuts in Microsoft Windows operating systems. There are a number of differences that need to be explained though, the most important one being that read or write accesses to the file performed by applications actually affect the target of the link and not the link itself. However, commands such as `cp` or `rm` affect the link, not its target.

Creating a link is done via the `ln -s` command. Here is an example that will help you understand the particularities of symbolic links:

```
[alex@example.com ~]$ ln -s shoppinglist.txt link_to_list
[alex@example.com ~]$ ls
link_to_list photo.jpg photo2.jpg shoppinglist.txt
[alex@example.com ~]$ cat link_to_list
- toothpaste
- a pair of socks
[alex@example.com ~]$ rm link_to_list
[alex@example.com ~]$ ls
photo.jpg photo2.jpg shoppinglist.txt
```

As you can see, reading the file content can be done via the symbolic link. If you delete the link, the target file is not affected; the same can be said for a copy operation (the link itself would be copied, but not the target file).

Another difference that makes symbolic links stand apart from Microsoft Windows shortcuts is that they can be connected to files using relative paths. This becomes particularly useful for embedding links within archives—deploying a shortcut using an absolute path would make no sense, as users may extract files to any location on the system.

Finally, Microsoft Windows shortcuts have the ability to include additional metadata. This allows the user to select an icon, assign a keyboard shortcut, and more. However, symbolic links are simple connections to the target file path, and as such, they do not offer the same possibilities.

Another type of link that is not available under Windows is hard links. They function a little differently, in the extent that they represent actual connections to file data. Two or more links may connect to the same data on the storage device; when one of those links is deleted, the data itself is unaffected and the other links still point to the data. Only when the last link gets deleted will the data be removed from the storage device.

To illustrate this example, let's create a hard link to that shopping list of ours—same command, but without the -s switch.

```
[alex@example.com ~]$ ln shoppinglist.txt hard_link_to_list
```

If you decide to delete shoppinglist.txt, hard_link_to_list will remain here and the data it points to is still available. Additionally, the newly created link is considered as an actual file by some commands such as ls. If you run ls to calculate the total size occupied by files in this directory, you will notice that link file sizes add up. If the shopping list file itself takes up 5 kilobytes of storage space, the total size reported by ls for the directory will be 10 kilobytes—five for the shopping list file itself, and five for its link. However, some tools such as du (for Disk Usage, evoked further below) are able to dig deeper and report the actual occupied storage.

File manipulation

The next step towards your discovery of the Linux shell is to learn how to manipulate files with a command-line interface. There are many operations that you can perform with simple tools—editing text, compressing files and folders, modifying file attributes, and so on, but let's begin with a more elementary topic—displaying a file.

Reading a file

Before all, you should understand that we are working with a terminal here, in other words, there is no possibility to work with graphical data; only text can be displayed on the screen. In that extent, this section deals with text files only; no binary files such as graphics, videos, or any other form of binary data may be displayed on the screen.

The most used and simplest way to display a text file on the terminal is to use the `cat` command, as you may have noticed in examples from previous sections.

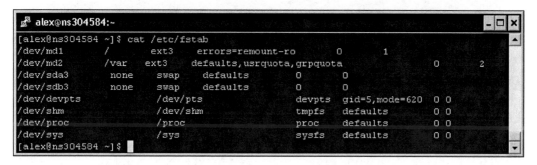

Although the `cat` command can be used to perform more complex operations (such as concatenation from multiple input sources), its simplest form consists of using the syntax—`cat filename`. The content of `filename` will be displayed to the standard output—in other words, the terminal screen.

If you reuse the `grep` mechanism that we approached in the process management section, you can achieve interesting results for filtering the output:

```
[alex@example.com ~]$ cat /etc/fstab | grep sys
/dev/sys      /sys      /sysfs      defaults      0  0
```

As you can see, piping the output to `grep` allows you to specify a text string; all lines that do not contain the specified string will not be displayed.

You can pipe the output to other programs as well, in order to have your text displayed in a different manner. For example, if your file happens to be a large text document, it will probably not fit in the terminal window. The solution to this problem is to pipe the output to `more`:

```
 alex@ns304584:~
[alex@ns304584 ~]$ cat /etc/php.ini | more
[PHP]

;;;;;;;;;;;;;;;;;;;;;;
; About php.ini    ;
;;;;;;;;;;;;;;;;;;;;;;
; This file controls many aspects of PHP's behavior.  In order for PHP to
; read it, it must be named 'php.ini'.  PHP looks for it in the current
--More--
```

More allows you to control the document flow—it displays as many lines of text as your terminal can contain and waits until you push the *Return* key to display more. Pressing *Q* or *Ctrl+C* will let you return to the prompt.

Even better—the `less` command allows you to scroll up and down in the document flow. It is used as a standalone program, no need to pipe its output from `cat`:

[alex@example.com ~]$ less /etc/php.ini

Editing a file

If you are a long time Microsoft Windows or Mac OS user, you might be surprised to learn that there are actually advanced command-line text editors. Several of them come with most Linux distributions—vim, emacs, nano, and so on. The question here is—which one should you use? Since you are reading this, the best choice for you should be `nano`, which has already been mentioned in previous sections.

Nano is a user-friendly text editor that comes with a lot of interesting features such as syntax highlighting, text search and replace, and keyboard shortcuts. Unlike its *competitors* that usually require a lengthy learning process, nano's interface is intuitive.

```
 alex@ns304584:~
  GNU nano 2.0.9              File: /etc/php.ini

[PHP]

;;;;;;;;;;;;;;;;;;;;;;
; About php.ini    ;
;;;;;;;;;;;;;;;;;;;;;;
; This file controls many aspects of PHP's behavior.  In order for PHP to
; read it, it must be named 'php.ini'.  PHP looks for it in the current

^G Get Help  ^O WriteOut  ^R Read File^Y Prev Page^K Cut Text  ^C Cur Pos
^X Exit      ^J Justify   ^U Where Is ^V Next Page^U UnCut Tex^T To Spell
```

Since there is no mouse cursor, the interface is controlled via keyboard shortcuts; available operations are displayed at the bottom in the command bar. Once you finished editing your document, save (*Ctrl+O*) and exit (*Ctrl+X*). Note that the list of available shortcuts is displayed in the bottom bar, the ^ character indicating a *Control* key combination (^*G* stands for *Ctrl+G*, ^*O* stands for *Ctrl+O*, and so on).

There are other ways to write in a file though, using commands that do not require any form of interface at all. One of the possible ways is to use the mechanism of **redirection**. This allows you to specify a location for the input and output streams interacting with a shell command. In other words, by default, the text shows up on the screen; but you do have the option to specify other locations. The most common usage for redirections is writing the output of a command to a file. Here is an example demonstrating the syntax:

```
[alex@example.com ~]$ ls /etc > files_in_etc.txt
```

The command executes normally but does not output any text to the screen; instead, the text is saved to the file you specified. The > character allows you to write the text to the file, and if the specified file already exists on the system, the original is deleted and replaced. In this example, we list the files located in the /etc directory and save the results in a text file. Using >>, you have the possibility to append the output to an eventual existing file (if the file does not exist, it is created):

```
[alex@example.com ~]$ ls /etc/init.d >> files_in_etc.txt
```

The list of files found in /etc/init.d is appended to the text file. There is much more you can do with redirections including replacing standard input, but covering it all would be unnecessary to your understanding of Nginx.

Finally, the touch command allows you to update the access and modification date of a file without having to actually edit its content.

```
[alex@example.com ~]$ touch shopping.txt
```

Compression and archiving

Although the ZIP and RAR formats are popular and wide-spread across the Internet, they are both proprietary software technologies. As a result, they are not mainstream choices in the Linux world; other formats such as Gzip and bzip2 are favored. Of course, solutions exist for both ZIP and RAR under Linux; the point being that most projects and downloadable archives that you will find will come as .tar.gz or .tar.bz2 files.

You read correctly, there are two extensions—*tar*, and *gz* or *bz2*. The first part indicates the method with which files have been gathered together and the second part shows the algorithm used to compress the result. **Tar** (for Tape **ar**chive) is a tool that concatenates multiple files into a single one called *tarball*. It also gives you the option to compress the tarball once it is created, offering various compression alternatives. The tool is available under most distributions, though in some of the most minimal ones, you may have to install it manually with your system package manager (read the section further below).

The syntax for creating a tarball using Gzip and bz2 compressions respectively is as follows:

```
tar czvf archive.tar.gz [file1 file2…]
tar cjvf archive.tar.bz2 [file1 file2…]
```

Conventionally, Linux users do not archive multiple files together; instead they first gather files into a unique folder and then archive the folder. As a result, when users extract the archive, only a single item is appended to their directory listing. Imagine extracting a ZIP file onto your Windows desktop. Would you rather have all files appearing individually on your desktop, or collected neatly in a single directory? Either way, the syntax remains the same whether you want to archive files or directories.

Tar can, of course, perform the opposite operation—extracting files. However, you need to enter a slightly different command depending on the compression algorithm at use:

```
tar xzvf archive.tar.gz
tar xjvf archive.tar.bz2
```

Note that tar.gz files are also found as **.tgz**, and tar.bz2 files as **.tbz**. Other compression formats handled by tar are: *LZMA* (.tar.lzma) and *compress* (.tar.z), but they are now obsolete and there is a good chance you will never have to use them.

If you stumble upon RAR or ZIP files, you may still extract the files they contain by downloading and installing the *unrar* or *unzip* tools for Linux. The syntax that they offer is rather simple:

```
unrar x file.rar
unzip file.zip
```

System administration tools

Since you are going to be installing and configuring Nginx, we assume that you are the administrator of your server. Setting up such an important component on your system requires good understanding of the administration concepts and tools available with your Linux operating system.

Running a command as Superuser

As we discussed in the Superuser Account section, it is important to respect the principle of *least privilege*. In that extent, you should log in to your system with the root account as rarely as possible. When you do so, you put your system at risk in many ways. Firstly, if your network communications were to be intercepted, the potential damage caused by a computer hacker would be greatly reduced if they intercepted a simple user account. Secondly, everyone makes typos. What if you accidentally type `rm -rf / root/file.x`, thus erasing your entire / directory, instead of `rm -rf /root/file.x`? What if you run an application that could cause damage to your filesystem? Being logged in as a regular user minimizes the risks in all situations.

This raises an obvious question—if you are always logged in as a simple user, how do you perform administrative level tasks or tasks that specifically require root privileges? There are two possible answers to this issue—**su** and **sudo**.

Su command

Su, short for *substitute user*, is a command that allows you to start a session with the specified user account. If no user account is specified, the root account is used. You need to specify the password of the account you want to use (unless you are already logged in as root and want to take over a user account).

```
[alex@example.com ~]$ su - root
Password :
[root@example.com ~]# nano /etc/fstab
```

From that point on, you are logged in as root. You can run commands and administrative tasks. When you are finished, type `exit` to return to your previous session.

```
[root@example.com ~]# exit
exit
[alex@example.com ~]$
```

You may have noticed the use of a hyphen between su and the username — it indicates that you are actually creating a shell session for the user, inheriting all of its personal settings and environment variables. If you omit the hyphen, you will remain in the current directory and will conserve all settings of the user account you were originally logged in with.

Sudo command

Although its name is closely similar to *su*, **sudo** works in a totally different manner. Instead of creating a complete session, it's only used to execute a command with the specified account, by default, the Superuser account. Example syntax:

```
sudo nano /etc/fstab
```

There is a major difference in the way su and sudo function; when executing a command with sudo, you are prompted for your own account password. I can already hear you scream — how come I can gain root privileges without the root password? The answer lies within the /etc/sudoers configuration file. This file specifies the list of users that are allowed to use sudo, and more importantly, the commands that are allowed to be executed. Moreover, all actions are recorded into a log including failed sudo login attempts.

By default, a user does not belong to the sudoers. Consequently, you first have to log in as root (or use sudo) and add the specified user to the /etc/sudoers file. Since this configuration file respects a strict syntax, a tool was specifically designed for it — **visudo**. Deriving from the well-known **vi** text editor, visudo checks the syntax of the file upon saving it, and makes sure that there are no simultaneous edits.

Visudo - and by extension, vi - works in two modes — command mode and insert mode. The insert mode lets you to edit the document directly. Press the *Esc* key to switch to command mode, which allows you to enter a command to control the program itself. When you first start visudo, press *I* to switch to insert mode and then make the necessary changes, for instance, adding a new sudo user at the end of the file:

```
alex ALL=(ALL) ALL
```

This grants the alex user all permissions on the commands defined in the sudoers file. Once you finished editing, press *Esc* to enter command mode. Enter the following commands: :w to save your changes and :q to exit. If you wish to exit without saving, type the :q! command. For more information about vi or visudo, use the man command (or if you are familiar with the jargon RTFM!).

System verification and maintenance

Now that you have all the pre-requisites for administering your server, it's time for you to perform actual administrative tasks. The first set of tasks that we will approach is related to system resources. Before proceeding to system changes such as software package installs (covered in the next section), you should always check that your system is in a coherent state and that you have enough disk and memory space available.

Disk Free

The **df** utility allows you to check the available storage space on your mounted devices.

```
alex@ns304584:~                                                    _ □ ×
[alex@ns304584 ~]$ df -h
Filesystem       Size  Used  Avail.  Use% Mounted on
/dev/md1         9,9G  652M   8,8G    7% /
/dev/md2         449G   31G   395G    8% /var
/dev/shm        1001M     0  1001M    0% /dev/shm
tmpfs           1001M     0  1001M    0% /var/usr/local/psa/handlers/before-local
tmpfs           1001M     0  1001M    0% /var/usr/local/psa/handlers/before-queue
tmpfs           1001M     0  1001M    0% /var/usr/local/psa/handlers/before-remote
tmpfs           1001M     0  1001M    0% /var/usr/local/psa/handlers/info
tmpfs           1001M     0  1001M    0% /var/usr/local/psa/handlers/spool
[alex@ns304584 ~]$
```

The -h option allows you to display sizes in a *human-readable* format. You should often check your available storage space: when you happen to run out of space, random behavior may occur in your applications (that is, unintelligible error messages).

Disk Usage

If you notice that your disk is full and do not understand why, you might find **du** to be particularly useful. It allows you to display the space occupied by each folder in a given directory.

```
alex@ns304584:/usr                                        _ □ ×
[alex@ns304584 usr]$ sudo du -h --max-depth=1
Password :
288M    ./bin
4,0K    ./etc
4,0K    ./games
107M    ./include
1,6M    ./kerberos
935M    ./lib
42M     ./libexec
1,7G    ./local
40K     ./man
37M     ./sbin
1,6G    ./share
56K     ./src
8,0K    ./X11R6
4,6G    .
[alex@ns304584 usr]$
```

Again here, the `-h` switch specifies that the tool should display human-readable size statistics. If the `--max-depth` option is not used, `du` will browse your filesystem recursively from the current folder. You can now easily track the folders that take up too much storage space on your system.

Free memory

The **free** utility displays the current system memory usage. It displays both physical and swap memory statistics as well as buffers used by the system. Use the `-m` switch for displaying numbers in megabytes or `-k` in kilobytes.

Software packages

Basic command-line usage? Check. Users and groups management? Check. Enough memory left on your system and space on your storage device? Check! It looks like you are ready to install new software packages and components. There are basically three ways to proceed, and we will study them from the easiest to the most complex one.

Package managers

A package manager is a tool that facilitates the management of software packages on your system by letting you download and install them, update them, uninstall them, and more. There are many different packaging systems in the Linux world, which are often associated with particular distributions—RPM for Red Hat-based distributions, APT for Debian-like distributions, simple TGZ packages for Slackware, and so on. We will only be covering the first two as they are the most commonly-used ones.

For systems using RPM, yum is by far the most popular package manager. As for APT, the `apt-get` tool comes with most distributions. Although their syntax differs slightly, both programs basically have the same features—given a package name, they will download software online and install it automatically.

The following example shows you how to install PHP on your computer using yum:

```
[root@example.com ~]# yum install php
```

Using apt-get:

```
[root@example.com ~]# apt-get install php
```

All required components such as libraries or other software are downloaded and installed first and then the requested software package is processed. There is nothing else that you have to do except to confirm the operation. You may also use the update or remove operations with either tool.

Downloading and installing packages manually

Be aware that there are only a limited number of software packages that you will find with these manager tools, as they are based on lists called *repositories*. The repositories that come with Linux distributions are often strictly regulated, and software developers cannot always use them to distribute their work. As a result, there are many applications that you will not find on the default repositories (you can use custom repositories though), which implies that you cannot use package managers to install them for you.

When you face such a situation, there are two options remaining—finding a package online or building from source, as covered next. This first solution generally consists of visiting the official website of the software you want to install, then finding the RPM release offered in the download section (or the DEB package for Debian systems).

Once you finished downloading the RPM file, for example, using the **wget** download manager, use the rpm -ivh command to install the package:

```
[alex@example.com ~]$ wget ftp://example2.com/mysqlclient.rpm
(Download successful)
[alex@example.com ~]$ sudo rpm -ivh mysqlclient.rpm
```

Use the dpkg -i command for DEB packages:

```
[alex@example.com ~]$ wget ftp://example2.com/mysqlclient.deb
(Download successful)
[alex@example.com ~]$ sudo dpkg -i mysqlclient.deb
```

Note that this method does not process dependencies. The application might not install correctly because a required library was not found on the system, in which case, you would have to install it yourself.

Building from source

The last method, which is valid regardless of the distribution you are using, is to download the application source code and compile it yourself. This method has its own advantages — you usually have the possibility to configure a great variety of options, and you may even make some edits to the code if you are a developer yourself. On the other hand, it requires many development packages to be installed (compilers, libraries, and so on) and compiling might fail for obscure reasons — missing components, invalid version for one of the required libraries, and so on.

The general process is to download a `.tar.gz` archive containing the source code, extract the files, enter the directory, and run three commands — `configure`, `make`, and `make install`. In the following example, we download the latest version of nano and install it:

```
[alex@example.com ~]$ wget http://www.nano-editor.org/dist/v2.0/nano-
2.0.9.tar.gz
(Download successful)
[alex@example.com ~]$ tar zxvf nano-2.0.9.tar.gz
(Extraction successful)
[alex@example.com ~]$ cd nano-2.0.9
[alex@example.com nano-2.0.9]$ ./configure
(Configuration complete)
[alex@example.com nano-2.0.9]$ make
(Build successful)
[alex@example.com nano-2.0.9]$ sudo make install
(Install successful)
```

Depending on the software install process, the output binaries may be copied to the `/usr/bin` folder (or another folder found in the PATH environment variable), but you will sometimes have to do that by yourself.

Some applications require more specific compilation commands and procedures, which are described in the usually included `readme` file. Under no circumstance should you omit to consult the readme file before building an application.

Files and permissions

Unix-based operating systems use a complex permission mechanism to regulate access to files and directories. You should also know that directories are actually regarded as *special files*; they work in the same way when it comes to permissions.

Understanding file permissions

There are three types of access—reading from a file, writing to a file, and executing a file. Each of these accesses can be defined for the original file owner, the file group, and all other users. Permissions on files can be consulted with the `ls -l` command:

```
[alex@example.com photos]$ ls -l
total 2
drwxrwxrwx 2 alex alex 4096 oct 31 11:35 Holidays in France
-rw-rw-r-- 1 alex alex    8 oct 31 09:21 photo2.jpg
```

The first column provides a character representation of the file permissions. It is composed of ten characters:

- First character: File type (-: file, d: directory, l: link; other types exist)
- Second to fourth characters: **Read, write, and execute** permissions for the owner
- Fifth to seventh characters: **Read, write, and execute** permissions for the group
- Eighth to tenth characters: **Read, write, and execute** permissions for other users

Directory permissions

On top of that, directories have specific attributes—*sticky bit* and *set group ID*. The first one ensures that files placed in that directory can only be deleted by their owner (and the root user, naturally). The second one makes it so that new files created in that directory conserve the group ID of the directory.

Permissions on a directory differ from regular file permissions:

- The *x* bit specifies whether or not the folder can be entered (such as using `cd`)
- The *r* bit allows the directory content to be listed (such as using `ls`)
- The *w* bit specifies whether or not new files can be written in the folder (and existing files moved to the folder)

Octal representation

Surely you have already read it somewhere: instructions telling you to change a folder's permission to 0755 or even 777. The given number is actually an octal representation of the file or directory permissions. This format is composed of three or four digits from 0 to 7, where 0 means no permissions and 7 all permissions.

The first digit is optional and indicates special attributes (such as sticky bit); often unspecified or set to 0

The second digit indicates permissions for the file owner

The third digit indicates permissions for the file group

The fourth digit indicates permissions for other users

Digit values from 0 to 7 are calculated using the following method: each attribute has a *weight*; all attribute weights added up together forming the total value. The weights are: 0 for no attribute, 1 for "r", 2 for "w", and 4 for "x". Consequently, each attribute variation has its own octal representation:

Permissions (r, x, w)			Weight	Octal representation
-	-	-	0 + 0 + 0	0
r	-	-	1 + 0 + 0	1
-	w	-	0 + 2 + 0	2
r	w	-	1 + 2 + 0	3
-	-	x	0 + 0 + 4	4
r	-	x	1 + 0 + 4	5
-	w	x	0 + 2 + 4	6
r	w	x	1 + 2 + 4	7

Full permissions for everyone (file owner, file group, and other users) thus translate to rwxrwxrwx, 777 with the octal representation.

Changing permissions

Users may change permissions on their own files only, except for the almighty Superuser. The process is done using a well-known tool — **chmod**. There are two main syntax variations — you may either specify an octal value for a complete reset of the permissions or request a change on a specific attribute.

Using an octal value:

```
[alex@example.com ~]$ chmod 777 photo2.jpg
```

The first argument is the octal value, followed by the file or directory name.

The second syntax is more complex:

```
chmod who+/-what filename
```

The first argument (*who, +/-, or what*) is composed of three elements:

- **Who**: A combination of "u" (user/owner), "g" (group), "o" (others), and "a" (all). If this part is omitted, the new attributes will be applied to all.
- **+ / -**: Use "+" if you want to grant those permissions or "- " to take them away.
- **What**: A combination of "r" (read), "w" (write), and "x" (execute).

Here are a couple of possible examples for this syntax:

`chmod +x script.sh`: Renders a script executable.

`chmod go-rwx photo.jpg`: Nobody is allowed to access the photo other than the owner.

`chmod a-w shopping.txt`: Nobody can edit the text file, not even the owner.

Note that the -R switch applies permission changes recursively on a folder:

`chmod -R g+rx photos`: The "photos" folder can be accessed by all users in the group; all its photos can be viewed.

Changing ownership and group

The **chown** and **chgrp** commands allow you to respectively change a file's owner and group. While the first one can only be executed by the Superuser for obvious security reasons, any user may change a file's group, provided they are the owner.

The chown tool can be used with the following syntax:

```
chown user filename
```

In this case, user is the new owner of the specified file. As for chgrp:

```
chgrp group filename
```

Again here, group is the name of the new group for the specified file. Alternatively, chown supports the following syntax:

```
chown user:group filename
```

Similar to chmod, these commands accept the -R switch allowing you to apply changes recursively. Here are some possible uses for either tool:

chown alex photo.jpg: Executed as root; the new owner of "photo.jpg" is the user "alex".

chown -R root photos: Executed as root; the "photos" directory and all the files it contains now belong to the root user.

chown alex: Students shopping.txt: changes both the file user and group.

chgrp guests shopping.txt: The group for the "shopping.txt" file is changed to "guests".

chgrp -R applications /etc/apps: The "applications" group now owns the /etc/apps folder.

Summary

This last section on file permissions marks the end of this introductory chapter, summarizing commands and tasks that a web server administrator executes on a regular basis. Using the shell is mostly about remembering command names and arguments. It becomes a lot more efficient as you get used to it. After a while, as you get back to Windows, you will even sometimes find yourself opening up a command-line terminal to perform simple tasks!

Anyway, you have all the ingredients you need to start with the next step—downloading and installing the Nginx web server application. By the end of next chapter, you will have a working setup and should be able to load the default page of your server.

2
Downloading and Installing Nginx

In this chapter, we will proceed with the necessary steps towards establishing a functional setup of Nginx. This moment is crucial for the smooth functioning of your web server—there are some required libraries and tools for installing the web server, some parameters that you will have to decide upon when compiling the binaries, and some extra configuration to do on your system.

This chapter covers:

- Downloading and installing the prerequisites for compiling the Nginx binaries
- Downloading a suitable version of the Nginx source code
- Configuring Nginx compile time options
- Controlling the application with an init script
- Configuring the system to launch Nginx automatically on startup

Setting up the prerequisites

As you can see, we have chosen to download the source code of the application and compile it manually, as opposed to installing it using a package manager such as Yum, Aptitude, or Yast. There are two reasons behind this choice—first, the package may not be available in the enabled repositories of your Linux distribution. On top of that, the rare repositories that offer to download and install Nginx automatically mostly contain outdated versions. More importantly, there is the fact that we need to configure a variety of significant compile time options. As a result of this choice, your system will require some tools and libraries for the compilation process.

Depending on the optional modules that you select at compile time, you will perhaps need different prerequisites. We will guide you through the process of installing the most common one such as GCC, PCRE, zlib, and OpenSSL.

GCC — GNU Compiler Collection

Nginx is a program written in C, so you will first need to install a compiler tool such as the GNU Compiler Collection (**GCC**) on your system. GCC usually comes with most distributions, but if, for some reason, you do not already have it, this step will be required.

 GCC is a collection of free open source compilers for various languages — C, C++, Java, Ada, FORTRAN, and so on. It is the most commonly-used compiler suite in Linux world, and Windows versions are also available. A vast amount of processors are supported such as x86, AMD64, PowerPC, ARM, MIPS, and more.

First, make sure it isn't already installed on your system:

```
[alex@example.com ~]$ gcc
```

If you get the following output, GCC is correctly installed on your system and you can skip to the next section:

```
gcc: no input files
```

If you receive the following message, you will have to proceed with the installation of the compiler:

```
~bash: gcc: command not found
```

GCC can be installed using the default repositories of your package manager. Depending on your distribution, the package manager will vary — yum for Red Hat-based distribution, apt for Debian and Ubuntu, yast for SuSE Linux, and so on. Here is the typical way to proceed with the download and installation of the GCC package:

```
[root@example.com ~]# yum install gcc
```

If you use apt-get:

```
[root@example.com ~]# apt-get install gcc
```

If you use another package manager with a different syntax, you will probably find the documentation with the man utility. Either way, your package manager should be able to download and install GCC correctly, after having solved the dependencies automatically.

PCRE library

The Perl Compatible Regular Expression (**PCRE**) library is required for compiling Nginx. The Rewrite and HTTP Core modules of Nginx use PCRE for the syntax of their regular expressions, as we will discover in later chapters. You will need to install two packages—`pcre` and `pcre-devel`. The first one provides the compiled version of the library, whereas the second one provides development headers and source for compiling projects, which are required in our case.

Here are example commands that you can run in order to install both the packages.

Using `yum`:

```
[root@example.com ~]# yum install pcre pcre-devel
```

Or install all PCRE-related packages:

```
[root@example.com ~]# yum install pcre*
```

If you use `apt-get`:

```
[root@example.com ~]# apt-get install libpcre3 libpcre3-dev
```

If these packages are already installed on your system, you will receive a message saying something like **Nothing to do**, in other words, the package manager did not install or update any component.

```
[root@ns304584 ~]# yum install pcre pcre-devel
Loading "fastestmirror" plugin
Loading mirror speeds from cached hostfile
 * rpmfusion-free-updates: download1.rpmfusion.org
 * adobe-linux-i386: linuxdownload.adobe.com
 * updates: mirror.ovh.net
 * base: mirror.ovh.net
 * addons: mirror.ovh.net
Excluding Packages in global exclude list
Finished
Setting up Install Process
Parsing package install arguments
Package pcre - 6.6-2.el5_1.7.i386 is already installed.
Package pcre-devel - 6.6-2.el5_1.7.i386 is already installed.
Nothing to do
[root@ns304584 ~]#
```

zlib library

The `zlib` library provides developers with compression algorithms. It is required for the use of `gzip` compression in various modules of Nginx. Again, you can use your package manager to install this component as it is part of the default repositories. Similar to PCRE, you will need both the library and its source — `zlib` and `zlib-devel`.

Using `yum`:

```
[root@example.com ~]# yum install zlib zlib-devel
```

Using `apt-get`:

```
[root@example.com ~]# apt-get install zlib1g zlib1g-dev
```

These packages install quickly and have no known dependency issues.

OpenSSL

> *The OpenSSL project is a collaborative effort to develop a robust, commercial-grade, full-featured, and open source toolkit implementing the Secure Sockets Layer (SSL v2/v3) and Transport Layer Security (TLS v1) protocols as well as a full-strength general purpose cryptography library. The project is managed by a worldwide community of volunteers that use the Internet to communicate, plan, and develop the OpenSSL toolkit and its related documentation* — `http://www.openssl.org`

The OpenSSL library will be used by Nginx to serve secure web pages. We thus need to install the library and its development package. The process remains the same here — you install `openssl` and `openssl-devel`:

```
[root@example.com ~]# yum install openssl openssl-devel
```

Using `apt-get`:

```
[root@example.com ~]# apt-get install openssl openssl-dev
```

 Please be aware of the laws and regulations in your own country. Some countries do not allow usage of strong cryptography. The author, publisher, and developers of the OpenSSL and Nginx projects will not be held liable for any violations or law infringements on your part.

Now that you have installed all the prerequisites, you are ready to download and compile the Nginx source code.

Downloading Nginx

This approach of the download process will lead us to discover the various resources at the disposal of server administrators—websites, communities, and wikis all relating to Nginx. We will also quickly discuss the different version branches available to you, and eventually select the most appropriate one for your setup.

Websites and resources

Although Nginx is a relatively new and growing project, there are already a good number of resources available on the World Wide Web (WWW) and an active community of administrators and developers.

The official website, which is at `www.nginx.net`, is rather simple and does not provide much information or documentation, other than links for downloading the latest versions. On the contrary, you will find a lot of interesting documentation and examples on the official wiki—`wiki.nginx.org`.

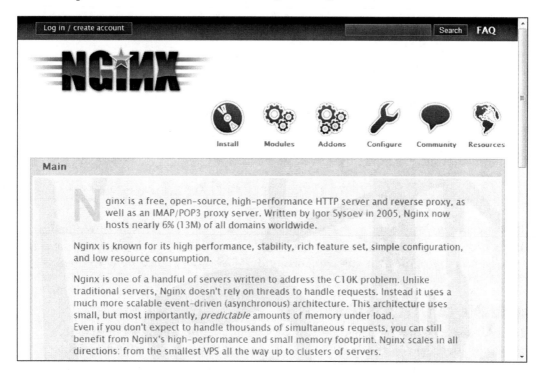

The wiki provides a large variety of documentation and configuration examples—it may prove very useful to you in many situations. If you have specific questions though, you might as well use the forums—forum.nginx.org. An active community of users will answer your questions in no time. Additionally, the Nginx mailing list, which is relayed on the Nginx forum, will also prove to be an excellent resource for any question you may have. And if you need direct assistance, there is always a bunch of regulars helping each other out on the IRC channel #Nginx on Freenode.

Another interesting source of information—the *blogosphere*. A simple query on your favorite search engine should return a good amount of blog articles documenting Nginx, its configuration, and modules.

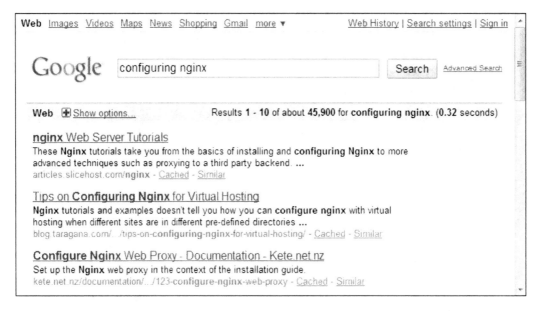

It's now time to head over to the official website and get started with downloading the source code for compiling and installing Nginx. Before you do so, let us have a quick summary of the available versions and the features that come with them.

Version branches

Igor Sysoev, a talented Russian developer and server administrator, initiated this open source project early in 2002. Between the first release in 2004 and the current version, which now serves over 6.55 percent of websites on the Internet, steady progress was made. The features are plenty and render the application both powerful and flexible at the same time.

There are currently three version branches on the project:

- **Stable** version: This version is usually recommended, as it is approved by both developers and users, but is usually a little behind the development version above. The current latest stable version is 0.7.66, released on June 07, 2010.

- **Development** version: This is the the latest version available for download. Although it is generally solid enough to be installed on production servers, you may run into the occasional bug. As such, the stable version is recommended, even though you do not get to use the latest features. The current latest development version is 0.8.40, released on June 07, 2010.

- **Legacy** version: If for some reason you are interested in looking at the older versions, you will find two of them. There's a legacy version and a legacy stable version, respectively coming as 0.5.38 and 0.6.39 releases.

A recurrent question regarding development versions is "are they stable enough to be used on production servers?" Cliff Wells, founder and maintainer of the nginx.org wiki website and community, believes so—"I generally use and recommend the latest development version. It's only bit me once!". Early adopters rarely report critical problems. It is up to you to select the version you will be using on your server, knowing that the instructions given in this book should be valid regardless of the release as the Nginx developers have decided to maintain backwards compatibility in new versions. You can find more information on version changes, new additions, and bug fixes in the dedicated change log page on the official website.

Features

As of the stable version 0.7.66, Nginx offers an impressive variety of features, which, contrary to what you may think, are not all related to serving HTTP content. Here is a list of the main features of the web branch, quoted from the official website nginx.net:

- Handling of static files, index files, and autoindexing; open file descriptor cache.

- Accelerated reverse proxying with caching; simple load balancing and fault tolerance.

- Accelerated support with caching of remote FastCGI servers; simple load balancing and fault tolerance.

- Modular architecture. Filters include Gzipping, byte ranges, chunked responses, XSLT, SSI, and image resizing filter. Multiple SSI inclusions within a single page can be processed in parallel if they are handled by FastCGI or proxied servers.
- SSL and TLS SNI support (TLS with Server Name Indication (SNI), required for using TLS on a server doing virtual hosting).

Nginx can also be used as a mail proxy server, although this aspect is not closely documented in the book:

- User redirection to IMAP/POP3 backend using an external HTTP authentication server
- User authentication using an external HTTP authentication server and connection redirection to an internal SMTP backend
- Authentication methods:
    - POP3: USER/PASS, APOP, AUTH LOGIN/PLAIN/ CRAM-MD5
    - IMAP: LOGIN, AUTH LOGIN/PLAIN/CRAM-MD5
    - SMTP: AUTH LOGIN/PLAIN/CRAM-MD5
- SSL support
- STARTTLS and STLS support

Nginx is compatible with many computer architectures and operating systems like Windows, Linux, Mac OS, FreeBSD, and Solaris. The application runs fine on 32 and 64 bit architectures.

Downloading and extracting

Once you have made your choice as to which version you will be using, head over to nginx.net and find the URL of the file you wish to download. Position yourself in your home directory, which will contain the source code to be compiled, and download the file using wget.

```
[alex@example.com ~]$ mkdir src && cd src
```

```
[alex@example.com src]$ wget
http://nginx.org/download/nginx-0.7.66.tar.gz
```

We will be using version 0.7.66, the latest stable version as of June 07, 2010. Once downloaded, extract the archive contents in the current folder:

```
[alex@example.com src]$ tar zxf nginx-0.7.66.tar.gz
```

You have successfully downloaded and extracted Nginx. Now, the next step will be to configure the compilation process in order to obtain a binary that perfectly fits your operating system.

Configure options

There are usually three steps when building an application from source—the configuration, the compilation, and the installation. The configuration step allows you to select a number of options that will not be *editable* after the program is built, as it has a direct impact on the project binaries. Consequently, it is a very important stage that you need to follow carefully if you want to avoid surprises later, such as the lack of a specific module or files being located in a random folder.

The process consists of appending certain switches to the `configure` script that come with the source code. We will discover the three types of switches that you can activate; but let us first study the easiest way to proceed.

The easy way

If, for some reason, you do not want to bother with the configuration step, such as, for testing purposes or simply because you will be recompiling the application in the future, you may simply use the `configure` command with no switches. Execute the following three commands to build and install a working version of Nginx:

```
[alex@example.com nginx-0.7.66]# ./configure
```

Running this command should initiate a long procedure of verifications to ensure that your system contains all the necessary components. If the configuration process fails, please make sure to check the prerequisites section again, as it is the most common cause of errors. For information about why the command failed, you may also refer to the `objs/autoconf.err` file, which provides a more detailed report.

```
[alex@example.com nginx-0.7.66]# make
```

The `make` command will compile the application; this step should not cause any errors as long as the configuration went fine.

```
[root@example.com nginx-0.7.66]# make install
```

This last step will copy the compiled files as well as other resources to the `installation` directory, by default, `/usr/local/nginx`. You may need to be logged in as root to perform this operation depending on permissions granted to the `/usr/local` directory.

Again, if you build the application without configuring it, you take the risk to miss out on a lot of features, such as the optional modules and others that we are about to discover.

Path options

When running the `configure` command, you have the possibility to enable some switches that let you specify directory or file paths for a variety of elements. Please note that the options offered by the configuration switches may change according to the version you downloaded. The options listed below are valid with the stable version, `release 0.7.66`. If you use another version, run the `configure --help` command to list the available switches for your setup.

Using a switch typically consists of appending some text to the command line. For instance, using the `--conf-path` switch:

```
[alex@example.com nginx-0.7.66]# ./configure --conf-path=/etc/nginx/
nginx.conf
```

Here is an exhaustive list of the configuration switches for configuring paths:

Switch	Usage	Default Value
`--prefix=...`	The base folder in which Nginx will be installed.	`/usr/local/nginx.` Note: If you configure other switches using relative paths, they will connect to the base folder. For example: Specifying `--conf-path=conf/nginx.conf` will result in your configuration file being found at `/usr/local/nginx/conf/nginx.conf`.
`--sbin-path=...`	The path where the nginx binary file should be installed.	`<prefix>/sbin/nginx.`
`--conf-path=...`	The path of the main configuration file.	`<prefix>/conf/nginx.conf.`
`--error-log-path=...`	The location of your error log. Error logs can be configured very accurately in the configuration files. This path only applies in case you do not specify any error logging directive in your configuration.	`<prefix>/logs/error.log.`

Switch	Usage	Default Value
`--pid-path=...`	The path of the Nginx pid file. You can specify the pid file path in the configuration file; if it's not the case, the value you specify for this switch will be used.	`<prefix>/logs/nginx.pid`. Note: The pid file is a simple text file containing the process identifier. It is placed in a well-defined location so that other applications can easily find the pid of a running program.
`--lock-path=...`	The location of the lock file. Again, it can be specified in the configuration file, but if it isn't, this value will be used.	`<prefix>/logs/nginx.lock`. Note: The lock file allows other applications to determine whether or not the program is running. In the case of Nginx, it is used to make sure that the process is not started twice.
`--with-perl_ modules_path=...`	Defines the path to the Perl modules. This switch must be defined if you want to include additional Perl modules.	
`--with-perl=...`	Path to the Perl binary file; used for executing Perl scripts. This path must be set if you want to allow execution of Perl scripts.	
`--http-log- path=...`	Defines the location of the access logs. This path is used only if the access log directive is unspecified in the configuration files.	`<prefix>/logs/access.log`.
`--http-client- body-temp- path=...`	Directory used for storing temporary files generated by client requests.	`<prefix>/client_body_temp`.
`--http-proxy- temp-path=...`	Location of the temporary files used by the proxy.	`<prefix>/proxy_temp`.
`--http-fastcgi- temp-path=...`	Location of the temporary files used by the HTTP FastCGI module.	`<prefix>/fastcgi_temp`.
`--builddir=...`	Location of the application build.	

Prerequisites options

Prerequisites come in the form of libraries and binaries. You should by now have them all installed on your system. Yet, even though they are present on your system, there may be occasions where the configuration script cannot locate them. The reasons might be diverse, for example, if they were installed in nonstandard directories. In order to fix this problem, you are given the option to specify the path of prerequisites using the following switches. Miscellaneous prerequisite-related options are grouped together.

Compiler options	
`--with-cc=...`	Specifies an alternate location for the C compiler.
`--with-cpp=...`	Specifies an alternate location for the C preprocessor.
`--with-cc-opt=...`	Defines additional options to be passed to the C compiler command line.
`--with-ld-opt=...`	Defines additional options to be passed to the C linker command line.
`--with-cpu-opt=...`	Specifies a different target processor architecture, among the following values: `pentium`, `pentiumpro`, `pentium3`, `pentium4`, `athlon`, `opteron`, `sparc32`, `sparc64`, and `ppc64`.
PCRE options	
`--without-pcre`	Disables usage of the PCRE library. This setting is not recommended, as it will remove support for regular expressions, consequently disabling the Rewrite module.
`--with-pcre`	Forces usage of the PCRE library.
`--with-pcre=...`	Allows you to specify the path of the PCRE library source code.
`--with-pcre-opt=...`	Additional options for building the PCRE library.
MD5 options	
`--with-md5=...`	Specifies the path to the MD5 library sources.
`--with-md5-opt=...`	Additional options for building the MD5 library.
`--with-md5-asm`	Uses assembler sources for the MD5 library.
SHA1 options	
`--with-sha1=...`	Specifies the path to the SHA1 library sources.
`--with-sha1-opt=...`	Additional options for building the SHA1 library.
`--with-sha1-asm`	Uses assembler sources for the SHA1 library.

zlib options

`--with-zlib=...`	Specifies the path to the zlib library sources.
`--with-zlib-opt=...`	Additional options for building the zlib library.
`--with-zlib-asm=...`	Uses assembler optimizations for the following target architectures: `pentium`, `pentiumpro`.

OpenSSL options

`--with-openssl=...`	Specifies the path of the OpenSSL library sources.
`--with-openssl-opt=...`	Additional options for building the OpenSSL library.

Module options

Modules, which will be discussed in Chapter 4 and further, need to be selected before compiling the application. Some are enabled by default and some need to be enabled manually, as you will see in the table below.

Modules enabled by default

The following switches allow you to disable modules that are enabled by default.

Modules enabled by default	Description
`--without-http_charset_module`	Disables the Charset module for re-encoding web pages.
`--without-http_gzip_module`	Disables the Gzip compression module.
`--without-http_ssi_module`	Disables the Server Side Include module.
`--without-http_userid_module`	Disables the User ID module providing user identification via cookies.
`--without-http_access_module`	Disables the Access module allowing access configuration for IP address ranges.
`--without-http_auth_basic_module`	Disables the Basic Authentication module.
`--without-http_autoindex_module`	Disables the Automatic Index module.
`--without-http_geo_module`	Disables the Geo module allowing you to define variables depending on IP address ranges.
`--without-http_map_module`	Disables the Map module that allows you to declare `map` blocks.
`--without-http_referer_module`	Disables the Referer control module.
`--without-http_rewrite_module`	Disables the Rewrite module.
`--without-http_proxy_module`	Disables the Proxy module for transferring requests to other servers.

Modules enabled by default	Description
`--without-http_fastcgi_module`	Disables the FastCGI module for interacting with a FastCGI process.
`--without-http_memcached_module`	Disables the Memcached module for interacting with the *memcache daemon*.
`--without-http_limit_zone_module`	Disables the Limit Zone module for restricting resource usage according to defined zones.
`--without-http_limit_req_module`	Disables the Limit Requests module allowing you to limit the amount of requests per user.
`--without-http_empty_gif_module`	Disables the Empty Gif module for serving a blank GIF image from memory.
`--without-http_browser_module`	Disables the Browser module for interpreting the User Agent string.
`--without-http_upstream_ip_hash_ module`	Disables the Upstream module for configuring load-balanced architectures.

Modules disabled by default

The following switches allow you to enable modules that are disabled by default.

Modules disabled by default	Description
`--with-http_ssl_module`	Enables the SSL module for serving pages using HTTPS.
`--with-http_realip_module`	Enables the Real IP module for reading the real IP address from the request header data.
`--with-http_addition_module`	Enables the Addition module which lets you append or prepend data to the response body.
`--with-http_xslt_module`	Enables the XSLT module for applying XSL transformations to XML documents.
	Note: You will need to install the `libxml2` and `libxslt` libraries on your system if you wish to compile these modules.
`--with-http_image_filter_ module`	Enables the Image Filter module that lets you apply modification to images.
	Note: You will need to install the `libgd` library on your system if you wish to compile this module.

Modules disabled by default	Description
`--with-http_geoip_module`	Enables the GeoIP module for achieving geographic localization using MaxMind's GeoIP binary database. Note: You will need to install the `libgeoip` library on your system if you wish to compile this module.
`--with-http_sub_module`	Enables the Substitution module for replacing text in web pages.
`--with-http_dav_module`	Enables the WebDAV module (Distributed Authoring and Versioning via Web).
`--with-http_flv_module`	Enables the FLV module for special handling of .flv (flash video) files.
`--with-http_gzip_static_ module`	Enables the Gzip Static module for sending pre-compressed files.
`--with-http_random_index_ module`	Enables the Random Index module for picking a random file as the directory index.
`--with-http_secure_link_ module`	Enables the Secure Link module to check the presence of a keyword in the URL.
`--with-http_stub_status_ module`	Enables the Stub Status module, which generates a server statistics and information page.
`--with-google_perftools_ module`	Enables the Google Performance Tools module.

Miscellaneous options

Other options are available in the configuration script, for example, regarding the mail server proxy feature or event management.

Mail server proxy options	
`--with-mail`	Enables mail server proxy module. Supports POP3, IMAP4, SMTP. It is disabled by default.
`--with-mail_ssl_module`	Enables SSL support for the mail server proxy. It is disabled by default.
`--without-mail_pop3_module`	Disables the POP3 module for the mail server proxy. It is enabled by default when the mail server proxy module is enabled.
`--without-mail_imap_module`	Disables the IMAP4 module for the mail server proxy. It is enabled by default when the mail server proxy module is enabled.
`--without-mail_smtp_module`	Disables the SMTP module for the mail server proxy. It is enabled by default when the mail server proxy module is enabled.

Event management:

Allows you to select the event notification system for the Nginx sequencer. For advanced users only.

`--with-rtsig_module`	Enables the rtsig module to use rtsig as event notification mechanism.
`--with-select_module`	Enables the select module to use select as event notification mechanism. By default, this module is enabled unless a better method is found on the system—kqueue, epoll, rtsig, or poll.
`--without-select_module`	Disables the select module.
`--with-poll_module`	Enables the poll module to use poll as event notification mechanism. By default, this module is enabled if available, unless a better method is found on the system—kqueue, epoll, or rtsig.
`--without-poll_module`	Disables the poll module.

User and group options

`--user=...`	Default user account for starting the Nginx worker processes. This setting is used only if you omit to specify the `user` directive in the configuration file.
`--group=...`	Default user group for starting the Nginx worker processes. This setting is used only if you omit to specify the `group` directive in the configuration file.

Other options

`--with-ipv6`	Enables IPv6 support.
`--without-http`	Disables the HTTP server.
`--without-http-cache`	Disables HTTP caching features.
`--add-module=PATH`	Adds a third-party module to the compile process by specifying its path. This switch can be repeated indefinitely if you wish to compile multiple modules.
`--with-debug`	Enables additional debugging information to be logged.

Configuration examples

Here are a few examples of configuration commands that may be used for various cases. In these examples, the path switches were omitted as they are specific to each system and leaving the default values may simply function correctly.

Be aware that these configurations do not include additional third-party modules. Please refer to Chapter 5 for more information about installing add-ons.

About the prefix switch

During the configuration, you should take particular care over the --prefix switch. Many of the future configuration directives (we will approach in further chapters) will be based on the path you selected at this point. While it is not a definitive problem since absolute paths can still be employed, you should know that the prefix cannot be changed once the binaries have been compiled.

There is also another issue that you may run into if you plan to keep up with the times and update Nginx as new versions are released. The default prefix (if you do not override the setting by using the `--prefix` switch) is `/usr/local/nginx`—a path that does not include the version number. Consequently, when you upgrade Nginx, if you do not specify a different prefix, the new install files will override the previous ones, which among other problems, could potentially erase your configuration files and running binaries.

It is thus recommended to use a different prefix for each version you will be using:

```
./configure --prefix=/usr/local/nginx-0.7.66
```

Additionally, to make future changes simpler, you may create a symbolic link `/usr/local/nginx` pointing to `/usr/local/nginx-0.7.66`. Once you upgrade, you can update the link to make it point to `/usr/local/nginx-newer.version`. This will (for example) allow the `init` script to always make use of the latest installed version of Nginx.

Regular HTTP and HTTPS servers

The first example describes a situation where the most important features and modules for serving HTTP and HTTPS content are enabled, and the mail-related options are disabled.

```
./configure --user=www-data --group=www-data --with-http_ssl_module --with-http_realip_module
```

As you can see, the command is rather simple and most switches were left out. The reason being: the default configuration is rather efficient and most of the important modules are enabled. You will only need to include the `http_ssl` module for serving HTTPS content, and optionally, the "real IP" module for retrieving your visitors' IP addresses in case you are running Nginx as backend server.

All modules enabled

The next situation: the whole package. All modules are enabled and it is up to you whether you want to use them or not at runtime.

```
./configure --user=www-data --group=www-data --with-http_ssl_module --
with-http_realip_module --with-http_addition_module --with-http_xslt_
module --with-http_image_filter_module --with-http_geoip_module --with-
http_sub_module --with-http_dav_module --with-http_flv_module --with-
http_gzip_static_module --with-http_random_index_module --with-http_
secure_link_module --with-http_stub_status_module
```

This configuration opens up a wide range of possible configuration options. Chapters 4 to 7 provide more detailed information on module configuration.

With this setup, all optional modules are enabled, thus requiring additional libraries to be installed — libgeoip for the Geo IP module, libgd for the Image Filter module, libxml2, and libxslt for the XSLT module. You may install those prerequisites using your system package manager such as running yum install libxml2 or apt-get install libxml2.

Mail server proxy

This last build configuration is somewhat special as it is dedicated to enabling mail server proxy features — a darker side of Nginx. The related features and modules are all enabled.

```
./configure --user=www-data --group=www-data --with-mail --with-mail_ssl_
module
```

If you wish to completely disable the HTTP serving features and only dedicate Nginx to mail proxying, you can add the --without-http switch.

Note that in the commands listed above, the user and group used for running the Nginx worker processes will be www-data which implies that this user and group must exist on your system. Please refer to Chapter 1 for more information on adding users and groups to your system.

Build configuration issues

In some cases, the `configure` command may fail—after a long list of checks, you may receive a few error messages on your terminal. In most (if not all) cases, these errors are related to missing prerequisites or unspecified paths.

In such cases, proceed with the following verifications carefully to make sure you have all it takes to compile the application, and optionally consult the `objs/autoconf.err` file for more details about the compilation problem. This file is generated during the configure process and will tell you exactly where the process failed.

Make sure you installed the prerequisites

There are basically four main prerequisites: GCC, PCRE, zlib, and OpenSSL. The last three are libraries that must be installed in two packages: the library itself and its development sources. Make sure you have installed both for each of them. Please refer to the prerequisites section at the beginning of this chapter. Note that other prerequisites such as LibXML2 or LibXSLT might be required for enabling extra modules, for example, in the case of the HTTP XSLT module.

If you are positive that all prerequisites were installed correctly, perhaps the issue comes from the fact that the configure script is unable to locate the prerequisite files. In that case, make sure that you include the switches related to file paths, as described earlier.

For example, the following switch allows you to specify the location of the OpenSSL library files:

```
./configure [...] --with-openssl=/usr/lib64
```

The OpenSSL library file will be looked for in the specified folder.

Directories exist and are writable

Always remember to check the obvious; everyone makes even the simplest of mistakes sooner or later. Make sure the directory you placed the Nginx files in has *read and write* permissions for the user running the configuration and compilation scripts. Also ensure that all paths specified in the configure script switches are existing, valid paths.

Eventually, when all your issues are solved, you should be seeing a configuration summary more or less similar to the image below:

```
alex@extremejeux:~/src/nginx-0.7.66
Configuration summary
  + using system PCRE library
  + using system OpenSSL library
  + md5: using OpenSSL library
  + sha1 library is not used
  + using system zlib library

  nginx path prefix: "/usr/local/nginx"
  nginx binary file: "/usr/local/nginx/sbin/nginx"
  nginx configuration prefix: "/usr/local/nginx/conf"
  nginx configuration file: "/usr/local/nginx/conf/nginx.conf"
  nginx pid file: "/usr/local/nginx/logs/nginx.pid"
  nginx error log file: "/usr/local/nginx/logs/error.log"
  nginx http access log file: "/usr/local/nginx/logs/access.log"
  nginx http client request body temporary files: "client_body_temp"
  nginx http proxy temporary files: "proxy_temp"
  nginx http fastcgi temporary files: "fastcgi_temp"
[alex@extremejeux nginx-0.7.66]$
```

Compiling and installing

The configuration process is of utmost importance—it generates a `makefile` for the application depending on the selected switches and performs a long list of requirement checks on your system. Once the configure script is successfully executed, you can proceed with compiling Nginx.

Compiling the project equates to executing the `make` command in the project source directory:

[alex@example.com nginx-0.7.66]$ make

A successful build should result in a final message appearing: `make[1]: leaving directory` followed by the project source path.

Again, problems might occur at compile time. Most of these problems can originate in missing prerequisites or invalid paths specified. If this occurs, run the configure script again and triple-check the switches and all the prerequisite options. It may also occur that you downloaded a too recent version of the prerequisites that might not be backwards compatible. In such cases, the best option is to visit the official website of the missing component and download an older version.

If the compilation process was successful, you are ready for the next step: installing the application.

```
[alex@example.com nginx-0.7.66]$ make install
```

The `make install` command executes the `install` section of the `makefile`. In other words, it performs a few simple operations such as copying binaries and configuration files to the specified install folder. It also creates directories for storing log and HTML files if these do not already exist. The `make install` step is not generally a source of problems, unless your system encounters some exceptional error such as a lack of storage space or memory.

 You might require root privileges for installing the application in the `/usr/local/` folder, depending on the folder permissions.

Controlling the Nginx service

At this stage, you should have successfully built and installed Nginx. The default location for the output files is `/usr/local/nginx`, so we will be basing future examples on this.

Daemons and services

The next step is obviously to execute Nginx. However, before doing so, it's important to understand the nature of this application. There are two types of computer applications — those that require immediate user input thus running on the *foreground* and those that do not, thus running in the *background*. Nginx is of the latter type, often referred to as **daemon**. Daemon names usually come with a trailing 'd' and a couple of examples can be mentioned here — `httpd` the HTTP server daemon, `named` the name server daemon, or `crond` the task scheduler — although, as you will notice, it is not the case for Nginx. When started from the command line, a daemon immediately returns the prompt, and in most cases, does not even bother outputting data to the terminal.

Consequently, when starting Nginx you will not see any text appear on the screen and the prompt will return immediately. While this might seem startling, it is on the contrary a good sign; it means the daemon was started correctly and the configuration did not contain any errors.

User and group

It is of utmost importance to understand the process architecture of Nginx and particularly the user and groups its various processes run under. A very common source of troubles when setting up Nginx is invalid file access permissions—due to a user or group misconfiguration, you often end up getting **403 Forbidden** HTTP errors because Nginx cannot access the requested files.

There are two levels of processes with possibly different permission sets:

1. The **Nginx master process**, which should be started as root. In most Unix-like systems, processes started with the root account are allowed to open TCP sockets on any port, whereas other users can only open listening sockets on a port above 1024. If you do not start Nginx as root, standard ports such as 80 or 443 will not be accessible. Additionally, the `user` directive that allows you to specify a different user and group for the worker processes will not be taken into consideration.

2. The **Nginx worker processes**, which are started under the account you specified in the configuration file with the `user` directive (detailed in Chapter 3). The configuration setting takes precedence over the configure switch you may have entered at compile time. If you did not specify any of those, the worker processes will be started as user `nobody`, and group `nobody` (or `nogroup` depending on your OS).

Nginx command-line switches

The Nginx binary accepts command-line arguments for performing various operations, among which is controlling the background processes. To get the full list of commands, you may invoke the help screen using the following commands:

```
[alex@example.com ~]$ cd /usr/local/nginx/sbin
[alex@example.com sbin]$ ./nginx -h
```

```
alex@example:/usr/local/nginx/sbin                          _ □ ×
[alex@example sbin]$ ./nginx -?
nginx version: nginx/0.7.66
Usage: nginx [-?hvVt] [-s signal] [-c filename] [-p prefix] [-g directives]

Options:
  -?,-h          : this help
  -v             : show version and exit
  -V             : show version and configure options then exit
  -t             : test configuration and exit
  -s signal      : send signal to a master process: stop, quit, reopen, reload
  -p prefix      : set prefix path (default: /usr/local/nginx/)
  -c filename    : set configuration file (default: conf/nginx.conf)
  -g directives  : set global directives out of configuration file

[alex@example sbin]$
```

The next few sections will describe the purpose of these switches. Some allow you to control the daemon, some let you perform various operations on the application configuration.

Starting and stopping the daemon

You can start Nginx by running the Nginx binary without any switches. If the daemon is already running, a message will show up indicating that a socket is already listening on the specified port:

```
[emerg]: bind() to 0.0.0.0:80 failed (98: Address already in use) [...]
[emerg]: still could not bind().
```

Beyond this point, you may control the daemon by stopping it, restarting it, or simply reloading its configuration. Controlling is done by sending signals to the process using the `nginx -s` command.

Command	Description
nginx -s stop	Stops the daemon immediately (using the TERM signal)
nginx -s quit	Stops the daemon gracefully (using the QUIT signal)
nginx -s reopen	Reopens the log files
nginx -s reload	Reloads the configuration

Note that when starting the daemon, stopping it, or performing any of the above operations, the configuration file is first *parsed* and verified. If the configuration is invalid, whatever command you have submitted will fail, even when trying to stop the daemon. In other words, you cannot even stop Nginx if the configuration file is invalid.

An alternate way to terminate the process, in desperate cases only, is to use the `kill` or `killall` commands:

```
[alex@example.com ~]$ killall nginx
```

Testing the configuration

As you can imagine, this tiny bit of detail might become an important issue if you constantly tweak your configuration. The slightest mistake in any of the configuration files can result in a loss of control over the service—you are then unable to stop it using a regular method, and obviously, it will refuse to start again.

In consequence, the following command will be useful to you in many occasions. It allows you to check the syntax, validity, and integrity of your configuration.

```
[alex@example.com ~]$ /usr/local/nginx/sbin/nginx -t
```

The -t switch stands for *test configuration*. Nginx will parse the configuration anew and let you know whether or not it is valid. The screenshot below shows an invalid configuration, and as a result, a failed test.

```
alex@example:~
[alex@example ~]$ /usr/local/nginx/sbin/nginx -t
[emerg]: unknown directive "Testfail" in /usr/local/nginx/conf/
nginx.conf:4
configuration file /usr/local/nginx/conf/nginx.conf test failed
[alex@example ~]$
```

A valid configuration file does not necessarily mean Nginx will start though as there might be additional problems such as socket issues, invalid paths, or incorrect access permissions.

Obviously, manipulating your configuration files while your server is in production is a dangerous thing to do and should be avoided at all costs. The best practice, in this case, is to place your new configuration into a separate temporary file and run the test on that file. Nginx makes it possible by offering the -c switch:

```
[alex@example.com sbin]$ ./nginx -t -c /home/alex/test.conf
```

This command will parse /home/alex/test.conf and make sure it is a valid Nginx configuration file. When you are done, after making sure that your new file is valid, proceed to replacing your current configuration file and reload the server configuration.

```
[alex@example.com sbin]$ cp /home/alex/test.conf /usr/local/nginx/conf/
nginx.conf
cp: erase 'nginx.conf' ? yes
[alex@example.com sbin]$ ./nginx -s reload
```

Other switches

Another switch that might come in handy in many situations is -v. Not only does it tell you the current Nginx build version, but more importantly it also reminds you about the arguments that you used during the configuration step—in other words, the command switches that you passed to the configure script before compilation.

```
alex@localhost:~                                    _ □ ✕
[alex@localhost ~]$ /usr/local/nginx/sbin/nginx -V
nginx version: nginx/0.7.66
built by gcc 4.1.2 20080704 (Red Hat 4.1.2-44)
TLS SNI support disabled
configure arguments: --with-http_ssl_module
[alex@localhost ~]$
```

In this case, Nginx was configured with the `--with-http_ssl_module` switch only.

Why is this so important? Well if you ever try to use a module that was not included with the `configure` script during the pre-compilation process, the directive enabling the module will result in a configuration error. Your first reaction will be to wonder where the syntax error comes from. Your second reaction will be to wonder if you even built the module in the first place! Running `nginx -V` will answer this question.

Additionally, the `-g` option lets you specify additional configuration directives in case they were not included in the configuration file:

```
[alex@example.com sbin]$ ./nginx -g "timer_resolution 200ms";
```

Adding Nginx as a system service

In this section, we will create a script that will transform the Nginx daemon into an actual system service. This will result in mainly two outcomes—the daemon will be controllable using standard commands, and more importantly, it will automatically be launched on system startup.

System V scripts

Most Linux-based operating systems to date use a System-V style *init daemon*. In other words, their startup process is managed by a daemon called `init`, which functions in a way that is inherited from the old **System V** Unix-based operating system.

This daemon functions on the principle of *runlevels*, which represent the state of the computer. Here is a table representing the various runlevels and their signification:

Runlevel	State
0	System is halted
1	Single-user mode (rescue mode)
2	Multiuser mode, without NFS support
3	Full multiuser mode

Runlevel	State
4	Not used
5	Graphical interface mode
6	System reboot

You can manually initiate a runlevel transition: use the `telinit 0` command to shut down your computer or `telinit 6` to reboot it.

For each runlevel transition, a set of services are executed. This is the key concept to understand here: when your computer is stopped, its runlevel is 0; when you turn it on, there will be a transition from runlevel 0 to the default computer startup runlevel. The default startup runlevel is defined by your own system configuration (in the `/etc/inittab` file) and the default value depends on the distribution you are using: Debian and Ubuntu use runlevel 2, Red Hat and Fedora use runlevel 3 or 5, CentOS and Gentoo use runlevel 3, and so on, as the list is long.

So let us summarize. When you start your computer running CentOS, it operates a transition from runlevel 0 to runlevel 3. That transition consists of starting all services that are scheduled for runlevel 3. The question is—how to schedule a service to be started at a specific runlevel? For each runlevel, there is a directory containing scripts to be executed.

Name	Ext	Size	Changed	Rights	Owner
..			12/29/2009 4:36:09 PM	rwxr-xr-x	root
init.d			10/18/2009 3:31:43 PM	rwxr-xr-x	root
rc0.d			1/1/2010 6:55:49 PM	rwxr-xr-x	root
rc1.d			1/1/2010 6:55:49 PM	rwxr-xr-x	root
rc2.d			1/1/2010 6:55:49 PM	rwxr-xr-x	root
rc3.d			1/1/2010 6:55:49 PM	rwxr-xr-x	root
rc4.d			1/1/2010 6:55:49 PM	rwxr-xr-x	root
rc5.d			1/1/2010 6:55:49 PM	rwxr-xr-x	root
rc6.d			1/1/2010 6:55:49 PM	rwxr-xr-x	root

If you enter these directories (`rc0.d`, `rc1.d`, to `rc6.d`) you will not find actual files, but rather symbolic links referring to scripts located in the `init.d` directory. Service startup scripts will indeed be placed in `init.d`, and links will be created by tools placing them in the proper directories.

What is an init script?

An init script, also known as service startup script or even *sysv script* is a shell script respecting a certain standard. The script will control a daemon application by responding to some commands such as start, stop, and others, which are triggered at two levels. Firstly, when the computer starts, if the service is scheduled to be started for the system runlevel, the init daemon will run the script with the start argument. The other possibility for you is to manually execute the script by calling it from the shell. That possibility has already been covered in *Chapter 1, Preparing your Work Environment*, the *Programs and processes* section:

```
[root@example.com ~]# service httpd start
```

Or if your system does not come with the service command:

```
[root@example.com ~]# /etc/init.d/httpd start
```

The script must accept at least the start and stop commands as they will be used by the system to respectively start up and shut down the service. However, for enlarging your field of action as a system administrator, it is often interesting to provide further options such as a reload argument to reload the service configuration or a restart argument to stop and start the service again.

Note that since service httpd start and /etc/init.d/httpd start essentially do the same thing, with the exception that the second command will work on all operating systems, we will make no further mention of the service command and will exclusively use the /etc/init.d/ method.

Creating an init script for Nginx

We will thus create a shell script for starting and stopping our Nginx daemon and also restarting and reloading it. The purpose here is not to discuss Linux shell script programming, so we will merely provide the source code of an existing init script, along with some comments to help you understand it.

First, create a file called nginx with the text editor of your choice, and save it in the /etc/init.d/ directory (on some systems, /etc/init.d/ is actually a symbolic link to /etc/rc.d/init.d/). In the file you just created, copy the following script carefully. Make sure that you change the paths to make them correspond to your actual setup.

You will need root permissions to save the script into the `init.d` directory.

```sh
#! /bin/sh
# Author: Ryan Norbauer http://norbauerinc.com
# Modified: Geoffrey Grosenbach http://topfunky.com
# Modified: Clement NEDELCU
# Reproduced with express authorization from its contributors
set -e
PATH=/usr/local/sbin:/usr/local/bin:/sbin:/bin:/usr/sbin:/usr/bin
DESC="nginx daemon"
NAME=nginx
DAEMON=/usr/local/nginx/sbin/$NAME
SCRIPTNAME=/etc/init.d/$NAME

# If the daemon file is not found, terminate the script.
test -x $DAEMON || exit 0

d_start() {
  $DAEMON || echo -n " already running"
}

d_stop() {
  $DAEMON -s quit || echo -n " not running"
}

d_reload() {
  $DAEMON -s reload || echo -n " could not reload"
}

case "$1" in
  start)
    echo -n "Starting $DESC: $NAME"
    d_start
    echo "."
  ;;
  stop)
    echo -n "Stopping $DESC: $NAME"
    d_stop
    echo "."
  ;;
  reload)
    echo -n "Reloading $DESC configuration..."
    d_reload
    echo "reloaded."
```

```
      ;;
      restart)
      echo -n "Restarting $DESC: $NAME"
      d_stop
# Sleep for two seconds before starting again, this should give the
# Nginx daemon some time to perform a graceful stop.
      sleep 2
      d_start
      echo "."
  ;;
  *)
      echo "Usage: $SCRIPTNAME {start|stop|restart|reload}" >&2
      exit 3
  ;;
esac

exit 0
```

Installing the script

Placing the file in the init.d directory does not complete our work. There are additional steps that will be required for enabling the service. First of all, you need to make the script executable. So far, it is only a piece of text that the system refuses to run. Granting executable permissions on the script is done with the chmod command:

[root@example.com ~]# chmod +x /etc/init.d/nginx

Note that if you created the file as the root user, you will need to be logged in as root to change the file permissions.

At this point, you should already be able to start the service using service nginx start or /etc/init.d/nginx start, as well as stopping, restarting, or reloading the service.

The last step here will be to make it so the script is automatically started at the proper runlevels. Unfortunately, doing this entirely depends on what operating system you are using. We will cover the two most popular families—Debian/Ubuntu/other Debian-based distributions and Red Hat/Fedora/CentOS/other Red Hat-derived systems.

Debian-based distributions

For the first one, a simple command will enable the init script for the system runlevel:

```
[root@example.com ~]# update-rc.d -f nginx defaults
```

This command will create links in the default system `runlevel` folders: for the reboot and shutdown runlevels, the script will be executed with the `stop` argument; for all other runlevels, the script will be executed with `start`. You can now restart your system and see your Nginx service being launched during the boot sequence.

Red Hat-based distributions

For the Red Hat-based systems family, the command differs, but you get an additional tool for managing system startup. Adding the service can be done via the following command:

```
[root@example.com ~]# chkconfig --add nginx
```

Once that is done, you can then verify the runlevels for the service:

```
[root@example.com ~]# chkconfig --list nginx
Nginx   0:off   1:off   2:on    3:off   4:on    5:on    6:off
```

Another tool will be useful to you for managing system services, namely, `ntsysv`. It lists all services scheduled to be executed on system startup and allows you to enable or disable them at will.

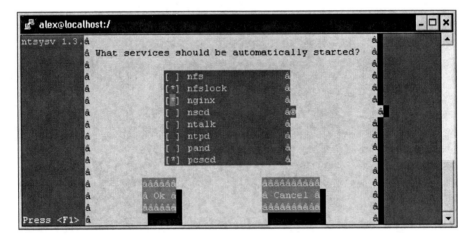

Note that you must first run the `chkconfig --add nginx` command, otherwise **nginx** will not appear in the list of services.

Summary

This chapter covered a number of important points. It first made sure that you have everything Nginx requires for compiling. Then this chapter helped us select the proper version branch for our usage — will you be using the stable version or a more advanced yet potentially unstable one? We then downloaded the source and configured the compilation process by enabling or disabling features and modules such as SSL, GeoIP, and more. Following this step, the source was compiled and the application installed on the system in the directory of your choice. We created an *init script* and modified the system boot sequence to schedule for the service to be started.

From this point on, Nginx is installed on your server and automatically started with the system. Your web server is functional, though it does not yet answer the most basic functionality — serving a website. The first step towards hosting a website will be to establish a configuration file. The next chapter will cover the basic configuration of Nginx and will teach you how to optimize performance based on expected audience and system resources.

Basic Nginx Configuration

3

In this chapter, we will begin to establish an appropriate configuration for the web server. For this purpose, we first need to approach the topic of syntax in use in the configuration files. Then we need to understand the various directives that will let you optimize your server for different traffic patterns and hardware setups. Finally, create some test pages to make sure that everything has been done correctly and that the configuration is valid. We will only approach the basic configuration directives here; the next chapters will detail more advanced topics such as HTTP module configuration and usage, creating virtual hosts, and more.

This chapter covers:

- Presentation of the configuration syntax
- Basic configuration directives
- Establishing an appropriate configuration for your profile
- Serving a test website
- Testing and maintaining your server

Configuration file syntax

A configuration file is generally a text file that is edited by the administrator and parsed by a program. By specifying a set of values, you define the behavior of the program. In Linux-based operating systems, a large share of applications rely on vast, complex configuration files, which often turn out to be a nightmare to manage. Apache, PHP, MySQL, Qmail, and Bind—all these names bring up bad memories. The fact is that all these applications use their own configuration file with different syntaxes and styles. PHP works with a Windows-style `.ini` file, *sendmail* uses the *M4 macro-processor* to compile configuration files, *Zabbix* pulls its configuration from a MySQL database, and so on. There is, unfortunately, no well-established standard. The same applies to Nginx—you will be required to study a new syntax with its own particularities, its own vocabulary.

On the other hand (and this is one of its advantages), configuring Nginx turns out to be rather simple — at least in comparison to Apache or other mainstream web servers. There are only a few mechanisms that need to be mastered — directives, blocks, and the overall logical structure. Most of the actual configuration process will consist of writing values for directives.

Configuration Directives

The Nginx configuration file can be described as a list of directives organized in a logical structure. The entire behavior of the application is defined by the values that you give to those directives.

By default, Nginx makes use of one main configuration file. The path of this file was defined in the steps described in *Chapter 2, Downloading and Installing Nginx* under the *Build configuration* section. If you did not edit the configuration file path and prefix options, it should be located at `/usr/local/nginx/conf/nginx.conf`. Now let's take a quick peek at the first few lines of this initial setup.

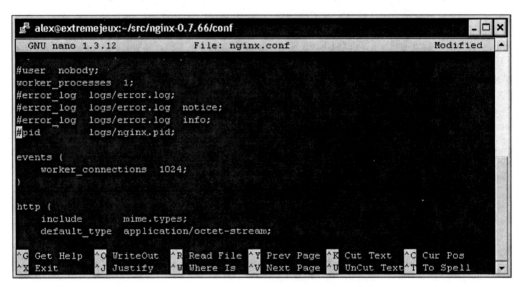

A closer look at the first two lines:

```
#user nobody;
worker_processes 1;
```

As you can probably make out from the # character, the first line is a **comment**. In other words, a piece of text that is not interpreted and has no value whatsoever; its sole purpose is to be read by whoever opens the file. You may use the # character at the beginning of a line or following a directive.

The second line is an actual statement—a **directive**. The first bit (`worker_processes`) represents a setting key to which you append one or more values. In this case, the value is `1`, indicating that Nginx should function with a single worker process (more information about this particular directive is given in further sections).

 Directives always end with a semicolon ('**;**').

Each directive has a special meaning and defines a particular feature of the application. It may also have a particular syntax. For example, the `worker_process` directive only accepts one numeric value, whereas the `user` directive lets you specify up to two character strings—one for the *user account* (the Nginx worker processes should run as) and a second one for the *user group*.

Nginx works in a modular way, and as such, each module comes with a specific set of directives. The most fundamental directives are part of the Nginx *Core module* and will be detailed in this chapter. As for other directives brought in by other modules, they will be explored in later chapters.

Organization and inclusions

In the preceding screenshot, you may have noticed a particular directive—**include**.

```
include mime.types;
```

As the name suggests, this directive will perform an inclusion of the specified file. In other words, the contents of the file will be inserted at this exact location. Here is a practical example that will help you understand.

`nginx.conf`:

```
user nginx nginx;
worker_processes 4;
include other_settings.conf;
```

`other_settings.conf`:

```
error_log logs/error.log;
pid logs/nginx.pid;
```

Final result, as interpreted by Nginx, is as follows:

```
user nginx nginx;
worker_processes 4;
error_log logs/error.log;
pid logs/nginx.pid;
```

Inclusions are processed recursively. In this case, you have the possibility to use the `include` directive again in the `other_settings.conf` file in order to include yet another file.

In the initial configuration setup, there are two files at use — `nginx.conf` and `mime.types`. However, in the case of a more advanced configuration, there may be five or more files, as described in the table below.

Standard name	Description
nginx.conf	Base configuration of the application
mime.types	A list of file extensions and their associated MIME types
fastcgi.conf	FastCGI-related configuration
proxy.conf	Proxy-related configuration
sites.conf	Configuration of the websites served by Nginx, also known as virtual hosts. It's recommended to create separate files for each domain.

These filenames were defined conventionally; nothing actually prevents you from regrouping your FastCGI and proxy settings into a common file named `proxy_and_fastcgi_config.conf`.

Note that the `include` directive supports *filename globbing*, in other words, filenames with the * wildcard, where * may match zero, one, or more consecutive characters:

```
include sites/*.conf;
```

This will include all files with a name that ends with `.conf` in the `sites` folder. This mechanism allows you to create a separate file for each of your websites and include them all at once.

Be careful when including a file — if the specified file does not exist, the configuration checks will fail and Nginx will not start:

```
[alex@example sbin]# ./nginx -t
[emerg]: open() "/usr/local/nginx/conf/dummyfile.conf" failed (2: No
such file or directory) in /usr/local/nginx/conf/nginx.conf:48
```

The previous statement is not true for inclusions with wildcards. Moreover, if you insert `include dummy*.conf` in your configuration and test it (whether there is any file matching this pattern on your system or not), here is what should happen:

```
[alex@example sbin]# ./nginx -t
the configuration file /usr/local/nginx/conf/nginx.conf syntax is ok
configuration file /usr/local/nginx/conf/nginx.conf test is successful
```

Directive blocks

Directives are brought in by modules—if you activate a new module, a specific set of directives becomes available. Modules may also enable **directive blocks**, which allow for a logical construction of the configuration.

```
events {
    worker_connections 1024;
}
```

The `events` block that you can find in the default configuration file is brought in by the *Events module*. The directives that the module enables can only be used within that block—in the `preceding` example, `worker_connections` will only make sense in the context of the `events` block. There is one important exception though—some directives may be placed at the root of the configuration file because they have a global effect on the server. The root of the configuration file is also known as the **main** block.

 This chapter will detail blocks and directives available in the Core modules—modules that are necessary for the smooth functioning of the server. Optional modules (whether they are enabled by default or not) are discussed in later chapters.

Note that in some cases, blocks can be nested into each other, following a specific logic:

```
http {
    server {
        listen 80;
        server_name example.com;
        access_log /var/log/nginx/example.com.log;
        location ^~ /admin/ {
            index index.php;
        }
    }
}
```

This example shows how to configure Nginx to serve a website, as you can tell from the `http` block (as opposed to, say, *imap*, if you want to make use of the mail server proxy features).

Within the `http` block, you may declare one or more server blocks. A `server` block allows you to configure a virtual host. The `server` block, in this example, contains some configuration that applies to all requests with a `Host` HTTP header exactly matching `example.com`.

Within this `server` block, you may insert one or more `location` blocks. These allow you to enable settings only when the requested URI matches the specified path. More information is provided in *Chapter 4, HTTP Configuration* the *Location Block* section.

Last but not least, configuration is inherited within children blocks. The `access_log` directive (defined at the `server` block level in this example) specifies that all HTTP requests for this server should be logged into a text file. This is still true within the `location` child block, although you have the possibility to disable it by reusing the `access_log` directive:

```
[...]
    location ^~ /admin/ {
        index index.php;
        access_log off;
    }
[...]
```

In this case, logging will be enabled everywhere on the website, except for the `/admin/` location path. The value set for the `access_log` directive at the `server` block level is overridden by the one at the `location` block level.

Advanced language rules

There are a number of important observations regarding the Nginx configuration file syntax. These will help you understand certain syntax rules that may seem confusing if you have never worked with Nginx before.

Directives accept specific syntaxes

You may indeed stumble upon complex syntaxes that can be confusing at first sight.

```
rewrite ^/(.*)\.(png|jpg|gif)$ /image.php? file=$1&format=$2 last;
```

Syntaxes are directive-specific. While the listen directive may only accept a port number to open a listening socket, the location block or the rewrite directive support complex expressions in order to match particular patterns. Syntaxes will be explained along with directives in their respective chapters.

Later on, we will approach a module (*the Rewrite module*) that allows for a much more advanced logical structure through the `if`, `set`, `break`, and `return` directives and the use of variables. With all these new elements, configuration files will begin to look like programming scripts. Anyhow, the more modules we discover, the richer the syntax becomes.

Diminutives in directive values

Finally, you may use the following diminutives for specifying a file size in the context of a directive value:

- k or K: Kilobytes
- m or M: Megabytes

As a result, the following two syntaxes are correct and equal:

```
client_max_body_size 2M;
client_max_body_size 2048k;
```

Additionally, when specifying a time value, you may use the following shortcuts:

- ms: Milliseconds
- s: Seconds
- m: Minutes
- h: Hours
- d: Days
- w: Weeks
- M: Months (30 days)
- y: Years (365 days)

This becomes especially useful in the case of directives accepting a period of time as a value:

```
client_body_timeout 3m;
client_body_timeout 180s;
client_body_timeout 180;
```

Note that the default time unit is seconds; the last two lines above thus result in an identical behavior.

Variables

Modules also provide variables that can be used in the definition of directive values. For example, the Nginx HTTP Core module defines the `$nginx_version` variable. When setting the `log_format` directive, you may include all kinds of variables in the format string:

```
[...]
location ^~ /admin/ {
    access_log logs/main.log;
    log_format main '$pid - $nginx_version - $remote_addr';
}
[...]
```

Note that some directives do not allow you to use variables:

```
error_log logs/error-$nginx_version.log;
```

This is a valid configuration directive. However, it simply generates a file named `error-$nginx_version.log`, without parsing the variable.

String values

Character strings that you use as directive values can be written in three forms. First, you may enter the value without quotes:

```
root /home/example.com/www;
```

However, if you want to use a particular character, such as a blank space (" "), a semicolon (`;`), or curly brace (`{` and `}`), you will need to enclose the value in single or double quotes:

```
root '/home/example.com/my web pages';
```

Nginx makes no difference whether you use single or double quotes.

Base module directives

In this section, we will take a closer look at the base modules. We are particularly interested in answering two questions—what are base modules and what directives are made available.

What are base modules?

The base modules offer directives that allow you to define parameters of the basic functionality of Nginx. They cannot be disabled at compile time; as a result, the directives and blocks they offer are always available. Three base modules are distinguished:

- **Core module**: Essential features and directives such as process management and security

- **Events module**: It lets you configure the inner mechanisms of the networking capabilities

- **Configuration module**: Enables the inclusion mechanism

These modules offer a large range of directives; we will be detailing them individually with their syntaxes and default values.

Nginx process architecture

Before we start detailing the basic configuration directives, it's necessary to understand the process architecture, that is, how Nginx works behind the scenes. Although the application comes as a simple binary file, (apparently lightweight background process) the way it functions at runtime is rather intricate.

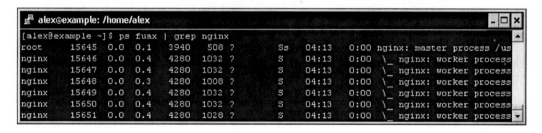

At the very moment of starting Nginx, one unique process exists in memory—the **Master Process**. It is launched with the current user and group permissions—usually root/root if the service is launched at boot time by an init script. The master process itself does not process any client request; instead, it spawns processes that do—the **Worker Process**es, which are affected to a customizable user and group. From the configuration file, you are able to define the amount of worker processes, the maximum connections per worker process, and more.

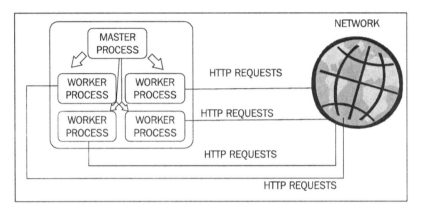

Core module directives

Below is the list of directives made available by the Core module. Most of these directives must be placed at the root of the configuration file and can only be used once. However, some of them are valid in multiple contexts. If that is the case, the list of valid contexts is mentioned below the directive name. root of the configuration file and can only be used once.

Name and context	Syntax and description
daemon	Accepted values: on or off
	Syntax:
	daemon on;
	Default value: on
	Enables or disables daemon mode. If you disable it, the program will not be started in the background; it will stay in the foreground when launched from the shell.

Name and context	Syntax and description
`debug_points`	Accepted values: `stop` or `abort` Syntax: `debug_points stop;` Default value: None. Activates debug points in Nginx. Use `stop` to interrupt the application when a debug point comes about in order to attach a debugger. Use `abort` to abort the debug point and create a core dump file. To disable this option, simply do not use the directive.

`env`	Syntax:
	
	`env MY_VARIABLE;`
	
	`env MY_VARIABLE=my_value;`
	
	Lets you (re)define environment variables.

`error_log`
 	
Context: `main,`
`http, server,`
`and location`
	Syntax:
	
	`error_log /file/path level;`
	
	Default value: `logs/error.log error.`
	
	Where level is one of the following values: `debug`, `info`, `notice`, `warn`, `error`, and `crit` (from most to least detailed: debug provides frequent log entries, crit only reports critical errors).
	
	Enables error logging at different levels: Application, HTTP server, virtual host, and virtual host directory.
	
	By redirecting the log output to `/dev/null`, you can disable error logging. Use the following directive at the root of the configuration file:
	
	`error_log /dev/null crit;`

`lock_file`	Syntax: File path `lock_file logs/nginx.lock;` Default value: Defined at compile time Use a lock file for mutual exclusion. Disabled by default, unless you enabled it at compile time.

`log_not_found`
 	
Context: `main,`
`http, server,` and
`location`
	Accepted values: `on` or `off`
	
	`log_not_found on;`
	
	Default value: `on`
	
	Enables or disables logging of **404 not found** HTTP errors. If your logs get filled with 404 errors due to missing `favicon.ico` or `robots.txt` files, you might want to turn this `off`.

Name and context	Syntax and description
`master_process`	Accepted values: `on` or `off` `master_process on;` Default value: `on` If enabled, Nginx will start multiple processes: A main process (the master process) and worker processes. If disabled, Nginx works with a unique process. This directive should be used for testing purposes only as it disables the master process — clients thus cannot connect to your server.
`pid`	Syntax: File path `pid logs/nginx.pid;` Default value: Defined at compile time. Path of the pid file for the Nginx daemon. The default value can be configured at compile time.
`ssl_engine`	Syntax: Character string `ssl_engine enginename;` Default value: None Where `enginename` is the name of an available hardware SSL accelerator on your system. To check for available hardware SSL accelerators, run this command from the shell: **openssl engine -t**
`thread_stack_size`	Syntax: Numeric (size) `thread_stack_size 1m;` Default value: None Defines the size of thread stack; please refer to the `worker_threads` directive below
`timer_resolution`	Syntax: Numeric (time) `timer_resolution 100ms;` Default value: None Controls the interval between system calls to `gettimeofday()` to synchronize the internal clock. If this value is not specified, the clock is refreshed after each kernel event notification.

Name and context	Syntax and description

`user`	Syntax:
	
	`user username groupname;`
	
	`user username;`
	
	Default value: Defined at compile time. If still undefined, the user and group of the Nginx master process are used.
	
	Lets you define the user account and optionally the user group used for starting the Nginx worker processes.

`worker_threads`	Syntax: Numeric `worker_threads 8;` Default value: None Defines the amount of threads per worker process. Warning! Threads are disabled by default. The author stated that "the code is currently broken".

`worker_cpu_ affinity`	Syntax:
	
	`worker_cpu_affinity 1000 0100 0010 0001;`
	
	`worker_cpu_affinity 10 10 01 01;`
	
	`worker_cpu_affinity;`
	
	Default value: None
	
	This directive works in conjunction with `worker_processes`. It lets you affect worker processes to CPU cores.
	
	There are as many series of digit blocks as worker processes; there are as many digits in a block as your CPU has cores.
	
	If you configure Nginx to use three worker processes, there are three blocks of digits. For a dual-core CPU, each block has two digits.
	
	`worker_cpu_affinity 01 01 10;`
	
	The first block (01) indicates that the first worker process should be affected to the second core.
	
	The second block (01) indicates that the second worker process should be affected to the second core.
	
	The third block (10) indicates that the third worker process should be affected to the first core.
	
	Note that affinity is only recommended for multi-core CPUs, not for processors with hyper-treading or similar technologies.

Name and context	Syntax and description
worker_priority	Syntax: Numeric worker_priority 0; Default value: 0 Defines the priority of the worker processes, from -20 (highest) to 19 (lowest). The default value is 0. Note that kernel processes run at priority level -5, so it's not recommended that you set the priority to -5 or less.
worker_processes	Syntax: Numeric worker_processes 4; Default value: 1 Defines the amount of worker processes. Nginx offers to separate the treatment of requests into multiple processes. The default value is 1, but it's recommended to increase this value if your CPU has more than one core. Besides, if a process gets blocked due to slow I/O operations, incoming requests can be delegated to the other worker processes.
worker_rlimit_core	Syntax: Numeric (size) worker_rlimit_core 100m; Default value: None Defines the size of core files per worker process.
worker_rlimit_nofile	Syntax: Numeric worker_rlimit_nofile 10000; Default value: None Defines the amount of files a worker process may use simultaneously.
worker_rlimit_sigpending	Syntax: Numeric worker_rlimit_sigpending 10000; Default value: None Defines the amount of signals that can be queued per user (user ID of the calling process). If the queue is full, signals are ignored past this limit.
working_directory	Syntax: Directory path working_directory /usr/local/nginx/; Default value: The prefix switch defined at compile time. Working directory used for worker processes; only used to define the location of core files. The worker process user account (user directive) must have write permissions on this folder in order to be able to write core files.

Events module

The Events module comes with directives that allow you to configure network mechanisms. Some of the parameters have an important impact on the application's performance.

All of the directives listed below must be placed in the `events` block, which is located at the root of the configuration file:

```
user nginx nginx;
master_process on;
worker_processes 4;
events {
  worker_connections 1024;
  use epoll;
}
[...]
```

These directives cannot be placed elsewhere (if you do so, the configuration test will fail).

Directive name	Syntax and description
accept_mutex	Accepted values: on or off `accept_mutex on;` Default value: on Enables or disables the use of an accept mutex (mutual exclusion) to open listening sockets.
accept_mutex_ delay	Syntax: Numeric (time) `accept_mutex_delay 500ms;` Default value: 500 milliseconds Defines the amount of time a worker process should wait before trying to acquire the resource again. This value is not used if the accept_mutex directive is set to off.
connections	Replaced by worker_connections. This directive is now deprecated.

Directive name	Syntax and description
debug_connection	Syntax: IP address or CIDR block. ``` debug_connection 172.63.155.21; debug_connection 172.63.155.0/24; ``` Default value: None. Writes detailed logs for clients matching this IP address or address block. The debug information is stored in the file specified with the error_log directive, enabled with the debug level. Note: Nginx must be compiled with the --debug switch in order to enable this feature.
multi_accept	Syntax: on or off ``` multi_accept off; ``` Default value: off Defines whether or not Nginx should accept all incoming connections from the listening queue at once.
use	Accepted values: /dev/poll, epoll, eventport, kqueue, rtsig, or select ``` use kqueue; ``` Default value: Defined at compile time Selects the event model among the available ones (the ones that you enabled at compile time), though Nginx automatically selects the most appropriate one. The supported models are: • select: The default and standard module, it is used if the OS does not support a more efficient one (it's the only available method under Windows) • poll: It is automatically preferred over select, but not available on all systems • kqueue: An efficient method for FreeBSD 4.1+, OpenBSD 2.9+, NetBSD 2.0, and MacOS X operating systems • epoll: An efficient method for Linux 2.6+ based operating systems • rtsig: Real time signals, available as of Linux 2.2.19, but unsuited for high-traffic profiles as default system settings only allow 1,024 queued signals • /dev/poll: An efficient method for Solaris 7 11/99+, HP/UX 11.22+, IRIX 6.5.15+, and Tru64 UNIX 5.1A+ operating systems • eventport: An efficient method for Solaris 10, though a security patch is required

Directive name	Syntax and description
worker_ connections	Syntax: Numeric
	`worker_connections 1024;`
	Default value: None
	Defines the amount of connections that a worker process may treat simultaneously.

Configuration module

The Nginx Configuration module is a simple module enabling file inclusions with the include directive, as previously described in the *Organization and inclusions* section. The directive can be inserted anywhere in the configuration file and accepts a single parameter — the file's path.

```
include /file/path.conf;
include sites/*.conf;
```

Note that if you do not specify an absolute path, the file path is relative to the configuration directory. By default, `include sites/example.conf` will include the following file:

```
/usr/local/nginx/conf/sites/example.conf.
```

A configuration for your profile

Following this long list of directives from the base modules, we can begin to envision a first configuration adapted to your profile in terms of targeted traffic and, more importantly, to your hardware. In this section, we will first take a closer look at the default configuration file to understand the implications of each setting.

Understanding the default configuration

There is a reason why Nginx stands apart from other web servers — it's extremely lightweight, optimized, and to put it simply, fast. As such, the default configuration is efficient, and in many cases, you will not need to apply radical changes to the initial setup.

We will study the default configuration by opening up the main configuration file `nginx.conf`, although you will find this file to be almost empty. The reason lies in the fact that when a directive does not appear in the configuration file, the default value is employed. We will thus consider the default values here as well as the directives found in the original setup.

```
user root root;
worker_processes 1;
worker_priority 0;
error_log logs/error.log error;
log_not_found on;
events {
  accept_mutex on;
  accept_mutex_delay 500ms;
  multi_accept off;
  worker_connections 1024;
}
```

While this configuration may work out of the box, there are some issues you need to address right away.

Necessary adjustments

We will review some of the configuration directives that need immediate changing and the possible values you may set:

- `user root root;`

  This directive specifies that the worker processes will be started as root. It is dangerous for security as it grants full permissions over the filesystem. You need to create a new user account on your system and make use of it here. Refer to *Chapter 1, Preparing your Work Environment*, the *User and group management* section for more information on creating users and groups. Recommended value (granted that you created an `nginx` user account and group on the system beforehand): `user nginx nginx;`

- `worker_processes 1;`

  With this setting, only one worker process will be started, which implies that all requests will be processed by a unique execution flow (the current version of Nginx is not multi-threaded, by choice). This also implies that the execution is delegated to only one core of your CPU. It is highly recommended to increase this value; you should have at least one process per CPU core. Recommended value (granted your server is powered by a quad-core CPU): `worker_processes 4;`

- `worker_priority 0;`

  By default, the worker processes are started with a regular priority. If your system performs other tasks simultaneously, you might want to grant a higher priority to the Nginx worker processes. In this case, you should decrease the value—the smaller the value, the higher the priority. Values range from `-20` (highest priority) to `19` (lowest priority). There is no recommended value here as it totally depends on your situation. However, you should not set it under `-5` as it is the default priority for kernel processes.

- `log_not_found on;`

  This directive specifies whether Nginx should log `404 errors` or not. While these errors may, of course, provide useful information about missing resources, most of them are generated by web browsers trying to reach the *favicon* (the conventional `/favicon.ico` of a website) or robots trying to access the indexing instructions (`robots.txt`). It is recommended that you disable `log_not_found` in the case of conventional files that may clutter your log files. However, do not disable this at the server level. Note that this directive is part of the HTTP Core module. Refer to the next chapter for more information.

- `worker_connections 1024;`

  This setting, combined with the amount of worker processes, allows you to define the total quantity of connections accepted by the server simultaneously. If you enable four worker processes, each accepting 1,024 connections, your server will treat a total of 4,096 simultaneous connections. You need to adjust this setting to match your hardware: the more RAM and CPU power your server relies on, the more connections you can accept concurrently.

Adapting to your hardware

We will now establish three different setups—a standard one to be used by a regular website with decent hardware, a low-traffic setup intended to optimize performance on modest hardware, and finally an adequate setup for production servers in high-traffic situations.

It's always difficult to classify computer power. Firstly, because each situation has its own resources. If you work in a large company, talking about a *powerful computer* will not have the same meaning as in the case of standalone website administrators who need to resort to third-party web hosting providers. Secondly, because computers get more powerful every year: faster CPUs, cheaper RAM, and the rise of new technologies (SSDs). Consequently, the specifications given below are here for reference and need to be adjusted to your own situation and to your era. The recommended values for the directives are directly based on the specifications—one worker process per CPU core, maximum connections depending on the RAM, and so on.

Low-traffic setup	Standard setup	High-traffic setup
CPU: Dual-core	CPU: Quad-core	CPU: 8-core
RAM: 2 GB	RAM: 4 GB	RAM: 12 GB
Requests: ~ 1/s	Requests: ~ 50/s	Requests: ~1000/s
Recommended values		
| ```
worker_processes 2;
worker_rlimit_
nofile 1024;
worker_priority -5;
worker_cpu_affinity
01 10;
events {
   multi_accept on;
   work
er_connections 128;
}
``` | ```
worker_processes 4;
worker_rlimit_
nofile 8192;
worker_priority 0;
worker_cpu_affinity

0001 0010 0100
1000;
events {
   multi_accept off;
   work
er_connections
1024;
}
``` | ```
worker_
processes 8;
worker_
priority
0;events {
   multi_accept
off;
   work
er_connections
8192;
}
``` |

There are two adjustments that have a critical effect on the performance, namely, the amount of worker processes and the connection limit. The first one, if set improperly, may clutter particular cores of your CPU and leave other ones unused or underused. Make sure the `worker_processes` match the quantity of cores in your CPU.

The second one, if set too low, could result in connections being refused; if set too high, could overflow the RAM and cause a system-wide crash. Unfortunately, there is no simple equation to calculate the value of the `worker_connections` directive; you will need to base it on expected traffic estimations.
```

Testing your server

The base configuration of your server is now established. In the following chapters, we will advance to the http modules and how to create virtual hosts. But for now, let's make sure that our setup is correct and suitable for production.

Creating a test server

In order to perform simple tests, such as connecting to the server with a web browser, we need to set up a website for Nginx to serve. A test page comes with the default package in the html folder (/usr/local/nginx/html/index.html) and the original nginx.conf is configured to serve this page. Here is the section that we are interested in for now:

```
http {
    include       mime.types;
    default_type  application/octet-stream;
    sendfile        on;
    keepalive_timeout  65;
    server {
        listen        80;
        server_name  localhost;
        location / {
            root    html;
            index   index.html index.htm;
        }
        error_page   500 502 503 504   /50x.html;
        location = /50x.html {
            root    html;
        }
    }
}
```

As you can already tell, this segment configures Nginx to serve a website:

- By opening a listening socket on port 80
- Accessible at the address: http://localhost/
- The index page is index.html

For more details about these directives, please refer to *Chapter 4, HTTP Configuration* and go to the *HTTP module configuration* section. Anyhow, fire up your favorite web browser and visit http://localhost/:

You should be greeted with a welcome message; if you aren't, then check the configuration again and make sure you reloaded Nginx in order to apply the changes.

Performance tests

Having configured the basic functioning and the architecture of your Nginx setup, you may already want to proceed with running some tests. The methodology here is experimental — run the tests, edit the configuration, reload the server, run the tests again, edit the configuration again, and so on. Ideally, you should avoid running the testing tool on the same computer that is used to run Nginx as it may cause the results to be biased.

> One could question the pertinence of running performance tests at this stage. On one hand, virtual hosts and modules are not fully configured yet and your website might use FastCGI applications (PHP, Python, and so on). On the other hand, we are testing the raw performance of the server without additional components, for example, to make sure that it fully makes use of all CPU cores. Besides, it's always better to come up with a polished configuration before the server is put into production.

We have retained three tools to evaluate the server performance here. All three applications were specifically designed for load tests on web servers and have different approaches due to their origin:

- httperf: A relatively well-known open source utility developed by HP, for Linux operating systems only
- Autobench: Perl wrapper for httperf improving the testing mechanisms and generating detailed reports
- OpenWebLoad: Smaller scale open source load testing application; supports both Windows and Linux platforms

The principle behind each of these tools is to generate a massive amount of HTTP requests in order to clutter the server and study the results.

Httperf

Httperf is a simple command-line tool that can be downloaded from its official website: `http://www.hpl.hp.com/research/linux/httperf/`. The source comes as a `tar.gz` archive and needs to be compiled using the standard method: `./configure`, `make` and `make install`. Once installed, you may execute the following command:

```
[alex@example ~]$ httperf --server 192.168.1.10 --port 80 --uri /
index.html --rate 300 --num-conn 30000 --num-call 1 --timeout 5
```

Replace the values in the command above with your own:

- `--server`: The website hostname you wish to test
- `--uri`: The path of the file that will be downloaded
- `--rate`: How many requests should be sent every second
- `--num-conn`: The total amount of connections
- `--num-call`: How many requests should be sent per connection
- `--timeout`: Quantity of seconds elapsed before a request is considered lost

In this example, `httperf` will download `http://192.168.1.10/index.html` repeatedly, 300 times per second, resulting in a total of 30,000 requests.

```
alex@example: /home/alex                                              - □ ×
Maximum connect burst length: 6298

Total: connections 21767 requests 21710 replies 21710 test-duration 14.692 s

Connection rate: 1481.6 conn/s (0.7 ms/conn, <=1022 concurrent connections)
Connection time [ms]: min 1.4 avg 563.4 max 3922.6 median 197.5 stddev 988.4
Connection time [ms]: connect 397.6
Connection length [replies/conn]: 1.000

Request rate: 1477.7 req/s (0.7 ms/req)
Request size [B]: 72.0

Reply rate [replies/s]: min 1942.8 avg 2077.3 max 2211.8 stddev 190.2 (2 samples)
Reply time [ms]: response 165.7 transfer 0.0
Reply size [B]: header 215.0 content 151.0 footer 0.0 (total 366.0)
Reply status: 1xx=0 2xx=21702 3xx=0 4xx=0 5xx=8

CPU time [s]: user 0.22 system 8.88 (user 1.5% system 60.5% total 62.0%)
Net I/O: 633.5 KB/s (5.2*10^6 bps)

Errors: total 78290 client-timo 57 socket-timo 0 connrefused 0 connreset 0
Errors: fd-unavail 78233 addrunavail 0 ftab-full 0 other 0
```

The results indicate the response times and the amount of successful requests. If the success ratio is 100 percent or the response time near 0 ms, increase the request rate and run the test again until the server shows signs of weakness. Once the results begin to look a little less perfect, tweak the appropriate configuration directives and run the test again.

Autobench

Autobench is a Perl script that makes use of `httperf` more efficiently — it runs continuous tests and automatically increases request rates until your server gets saturated. One of the interesting features of Autobench is that it generates a `.tsv` report that you can open with various applications to generate graphs. You may download the source code from the author's personal website: `http://www.xenoclast.org/autobench/`. Once again, extract the files from the archive, run `make` then `make install`.

Although it supports testing of multiple hosts at once, we will only be using the single host test for more simplicity. The command we will execute resembles the `httperf` one:

```
[alex@example ~]$ autobench --single_host --host1 192.168.1.10 --uri1 /
index.html --quiet --low_rate 20 --high_rate 200 --rate_step 20 --num_
call 10 --num_conn 5000 --timeout 5 --file results.tsv
```

The switches can be configured as follows:

- `--host1`: The website host name you wish to test.
- `--uri1`: The path of the file that will be downloaded.
- `--quiet`: Does not display httperf information on the screen.
- `--low_rate`: Connections per second at the beginning of the test.
- `--high_rate`: Connections per second at the end of the test.
- `--rate_step`: The number of connections to increase the rate by after each test.
- `--num_call`: How many requests should be sent per connection.
- `--num_conn`: Total amount of connections.
- `--timeout`: The number of seconds elapsed before a request is considered lost.
- `--file`: Export results as specified (.tsv file).

Once the test terminates, you end up with a `.tsv` file that you can import in applications such as Microsoft Excel. Here is a graph generated from results on a test server (note that the report file contains up to 10 series of statistics):

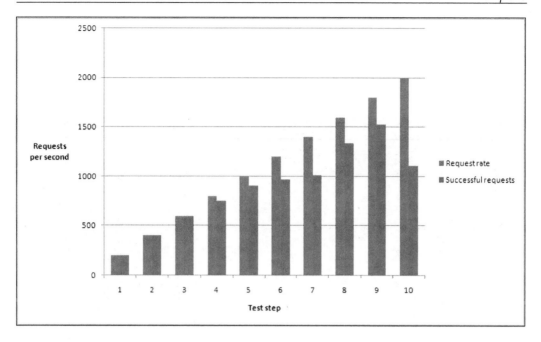

As you can tell from the graph, this test server supports up to 600 requests per second without a loss. Past this limit, some connections get dropped as Nginx cannot handle the load. It stills gets up to over 1,500 successful requests per second at step 9.

 Warning: These tests were carried out on a virtual machine and do not reflect the actual capabilities of Nginx running on a production server.

OpenWebLoad

OpenWebLoad is a free open source application. It is available for both Linux and Windows platforms and was developed in the early 2000s, back in the days of *Web 1.0*. A different approach is offered here—instead of throwing loads of requests at the server and seeing how many are handled correctly, it will simply send as many requests as possible using a variable amount of connections and report to you every second.

You may download it from its official website: `http://openwebload.` `sourceforge.net`. Extract the source from the `.tar.gz` archive, run `./configure`, `make` and `make install`.

Its usage is simpler than the previous two utilities:

```
[alex@example ~]$ openload example.com/index.html 10
```

The first argument is the URL of the website you want to test. The second one is the amount of connections that should be opened.

```
C:\WINDOWS\system32\cmd.exe                                              _ □ ✕

C:\>openload.exe example.com/index.html 10
URL: http://example.com:80/index.html
Clients: 10
MaTps 210.37, Tps 210.37, Resp Time  0.046, Err   0%, Count    211
MaTps 211.51, Tps 221.78, Resp Time  0.045, Err   0%, Count    433
MaTps 212.69, Tps 223.33, Resp Time  0.045, Err   0%, Count    657
MaTps 213.38, Tps 219.56, Resp Time  0.046, Err   0%, Count    877
MaTps 214.63, Tps 225.87, Resp Time  0.044, Err   0%, Count   1104
MaTps 215.20, Tps 220.34, Resp Time  0.045, Err   0%, Count   1325
Total TPS: 216.40
Avg. Response time:   0.045 sec.
Max Response time:    0.097 sec
Total Requests:       1325
Total Errors:         0

C:\>
```

A new result line is produced every second. Requests are sent continuously until you press the *Enter* key, following which, a result summary is displayed. Here is how to decipher the output:

- **Tps** (transactions per second): A transaction corresponds to a completed request (back and forth)
- **MaTps**: Average Tps over the last 20 seconds
- **Resp Time**: Average response time for the elapsed second
- **Err** (error rate): Errors occur when the server returns a response that is not the expected HTTP 200 OK
- **Count**: Total transaction count

You can fiddle with the amount of simultaneous connections and see how your server performs in order to establish a balanced configuration for your setup. Three tests were run here with a different amount of connections. The results speak for themselves:

	Test 1	Test 2	Test 3
Simultaneous connections	1	20	1000
Transactions per second (Tps)	67.54	205.87	185.07
Average response time	14 ms	91 ms	596 ms

Too few connections result in a low Tps rate; however, the response times are optimal. Too many connections produce a relatively high Tps, but the response times are critically high. You thus need to find a happy medium.

Upgrading Nginx gracefully

There are many situations where you need to replace the Nginx binary, for example, when you compile a new version and wish to put it in production or simply after having enabled new modules and rebuilt the application. What most administrators would do in this situation is stop the server, copy the new binary over the old one, and start Nginx again. While this is not considered to be a problem for most websites, there may be some cases where uptime is critical and connection losses should be avoided at all costs. Fortunately, Nginx embeds a mechanism allowing you to switch binaries with uninterrupted uptime—zero percent request loss is guaranteed if you follow these steps carefully:

1. Replace the old Nginx binary (by default, `/usr/local/nginx/sbin/nginx`) with the new one.

2. Find the pid of the Nginx master process, for example, with `ps x | grep nginx | grep master` or by looking at the value found in the pid file.

3. Send a `USR2` (12) signal to the master process—`kill -USR2 ***`, replacing `***` with the pid found in step 2. This will initiate the upgrade by renaming the old `.pid` file and running the new binary.

4. Send a `WINCH` (28) signal to the old master process—`kill -WINCH ***`, replacing `***` with the pid found in step 2. This will engage a graceful shutdown of the old worker processes.

5. Make sure that all the old worker processes are terminated, and then send a `QUIT` signal to the old master process—`kill -QUIT ***`, replacing `***` with the pid found in step 2.

Congratulations! You have successfully upgraded Nginx and have not lost a single connection.

Summary

This chapter provided a first approach of the configuration architecture by studying the syntax and the core module directives that have an impact on the overall server performance. We then went through a series of adjustments in order to fit your own profile, followed by performance tests that have probably led you to fine-tune some more.

This is just the beginning though—practically everything that we will be doing from now on is to establish configuration sections. The next chapter will detail more advanced directives by further exploring the module system and the exciting possibilities that are offered to you.

4
HTTP Configuration

At this stage, we have a working Nginx setup—not only is it installed on the system and launched automatically on startup, but it's also organized and optimized with the help of basic directives. It's now time to go one step further into the configuration by discovering the HTTP Core module. This module constitutes the essential component of the HTTP configuration—it allows you to set up websites to be served, also known as *virtual hosts*.

This chapter will cover:

- An introduction to the HTTP Core module
- The `http` / `server` / `location` structure
- HTTP Core module directives, thematically
- HTTP Core module variables
- The in-depths of the `location` block

HTTP Core module

The HTTP Core module is the component that contains all the fundamental blocks, directives, and variables of the HTTP server. It's enabled by default when you configure the build (as described in Chapter 2); but as it turns out, it's actually optional—you can decide not to include it in your custom build. Doing so will completely disable all HTTP functionalities, and all the other HTTP modules will not be compiled. Though obviously if you purchased this book, it's highly likely that you are interested in the web serving capacities of Nginx, so you will have this enabled.

This module is the largest of all Nginx modules—it provides an impressive amount of directives and variables. In order to understand all these new elements and how they come into play, we first need to understand the logical organization introduced by the three main blocks—*http*, *server*, and *location*.

Structure blocks

In the previous chapter, we discovered the Core module by studying the default Nginx configuration file—a sequence of directives and values, with no organization whatsoever. Then came the Events module, which introduced the first block (`events`). This block would be the only placeholder for all the directives brought in by the Events module.

As it turns out, the HTTP module introduces three new logical blocks:

- `http`: This block is inserted at the root of the configuration file. It allows you to start defining directives and blocks from all modules related to the HTTP facet of Nginx. Although there is no real purpose in doing so, the block can be inserted multiple times—in which case the directive values inserted in the last block will override the previous ones.

- `server`: This block allows you to *declare a website*. In other words, make it so that a specific website (identified by a hostname, for example, `www.mywebsite.com`) becomes acknowledged by Nginx and let it have its own configuration. This block can only be used within the `http` block.

- `location`: Lets you define a group of settings to be applied to a particular location on a website. The next part of this section provides more details about the location block. This block can be used within a `server` block or nested within another `location` block.

The following diagram summarizes the final structure by providing a couple of basic examples corresponding to actual situations:

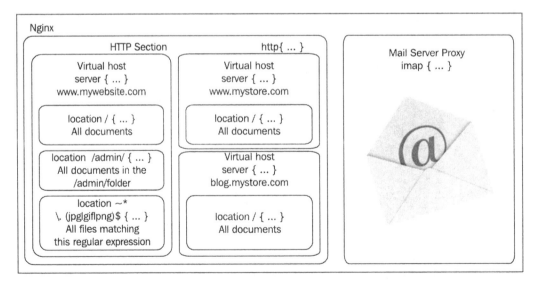

The HTTP section, defined by the **http** block, encompasses the entire web-related configuration. It may contain one or more **server** blocks, defining the domains and sub-domains that you are hosting. For each of these websites, you have the possibility to define **location** blocks that let you apply additional settings to a particular request URI or request URIs matching a pattern.

Remember that the principle of setting inheritance applies here. If you define a setting at the http block level (for example, `gzip on` to enable gzip compression), the setting will preserve its value in the potentially incorporated server and location blocks:

```
http {
    # Enable gzip compression at the http block level
    gzip on;

    server {
        server_name localhost;
         listen 80;

        # At this stage, gzip still set to on

        location /downloads/ {
            gzip off;
    #       This directive only applies to documents found
    #       in /downloads/
        }
    }
}
```

Module directives

At each of the three levels, directives can be inserted in order to affect the behavior of the web server. The following is the list of all directives that are introduced by the main HTTP module, grouped by thematic. For each directive, an indication regarding the context is given — some cannot be used at certain levels, for instance, it would make no sense to insert a `server_name` directive inside a `location` block. In that extent, the table indicates the possible levels where each directive is allowed — the `http` block, the `server` block, the `location` block, and additionally the `if` block, later introduced by the *Rewrite module*.

 Note that this documentation is valid as of stable version 0.7.66. Future updates may alter the syntax of some directives or provide new features that are not discussed here.

Socket and host configuration

This set of directives will allow you to configure your virtual hosts. In practice, this materializes by creating server blocks that you identify either by a host name or by an IP address and port combination. In addition, some directives will let you fine-tune your network settings by configuring TCP socket options.

Directive	Description

`listen`
 	
Context: `server`
	Specifies the IP address and/or the port to be used by the listening socket that will serve the website. Sites are generally served on port `80` (the default value).
	
	Syntax: `listen [address] [:port] [additional options];`
	
	Additional options:
	
	• `default`: Specifies that this server block is to be used as the default website for any request received at the specified IP address and port
	
	• `ssl`: Specifies that the website should be served using SSL
	
	• Other options are related to the *bind* and *listen* system calls: `backlog=num`, `rcvbuf=size`, `sndbuf=size`, `accept_filter=filter`, `deferred`, and `bind`
	
	Examples:
	`listen 192.168.1.1:80;`
	`listen 127.0.0.1;`
	`listen 80 default;`
	`listen [:::a8c9:1234]:80; # IPv6 ad dresses can be put between square brackets`
	`listen 443 ssl;`

Directive	Description

`server_name`
 	
Context: `server`
	Assigns one or more hostnames to the server block. When Nginx receives an HTTP request, it matches the `Host` header of the request against all the server blocks. The first server block to match this hostname is selected.
	
	Plan B: If no `server` block matches the desired host, Nginx selects the first `server` block that matches the parameters of the `listen` directive (such as `listen *:80` would be a catch-all for all requests received on port 80), giving priority to the first block that has the `default` option enabled on the `listen` directive.
	
	Note that this directive accepts wildcards as well as regular expressions (in which case, the hostname should start with the ~ character).
	
	Syntax: `server_name hostname1 [hostname2...];`
	
	Examples:
	<pre>server_name www.website.com;
	server_name www.website.com web
	site.com;
	server_name *.website.com;
	server_name .website.com; # combines
	both *.website.com and website.com
	server_name *.website.*;
	server_name ~^\.example\.com$;</pre>**Note**: You may use an empty string as the directive value in order to catch all requests that do not come with a `Host` header, but only after at least one regular name (or "_" for a dummy host name):
	<pre>server_name website.com "";
	server_name _ "";</pre>

`server_name_in_ redirect` Context: `http, server, location`	This directive applies the case of internal redirects (for more information about internal redirects, check the *Rewrite Module* section below). If set to `on`, Nginx will use the first hostname specified in the `server_name` directive. If set to `off`, Nginx will use the value of the `Host` header from the HTTP request. Syntax: `on` or `off` Default value: `on` <pre>server_name_in_redirect on;</pre>

Directive	Description
server_names_ hash_max_size Context: http	Nginx uses hash tables for various data collections in order to speed up the processing of requests. This directive defines the maximum size of the server names hash table. If your server uses a total of more than 512 hostnames, you will have to increase this value. Syntax: Numeric value Default value: 512 `server_names_hash_max_size 512;`
server_names_ hash_bucket_size Context: http	Defines the maximum length of an entry in the server names hash table. If one of your hostnames is longer than 32 characters, you will have to increase this value. Syntax: Numeric value Default value: 32 (or 64, or 128, depending on your processor cache specifications). `server_names_hash_bucket_size 32;`
port_in_redirect Context: http, server, location	In the case of a redirect, this directive defines whether or not Nginx should append the port number to the redirection URL. Syntax: on or off Default value: on `port_in_redirect on;`
tcp_nodelay Context: http, server, location	Enables or disables the TCP_NODELAY socket option for keep-alive connections only. Quoting the Linux documentation on sockets programming: *TCP_NODELAY is for a specific purpose; to disable the Nagle buffering algorithm. It should only be set for applications that send frequent small bursts of information without getting an immediate response, where timely delivery of data is required (the canonical example is mouse movements).* Syntax: on or off Default value: on `tcp_nodelay on;`

Directive	Description
`tcp_nopush` Context: `http, server, location`	Enables or disables the `TCP_NOPUSH` (FreeBSD) or `TCP_CORK` (Linux) socket option. Note that this option only applies if the `sendfile` directive is enabled. If `tcp_nopush` is set to `on`, Nginx will attempt to transmit the entire HTTP response headers in a single TCP packet. Syntax: `on` or `off` Default value: `off` `tcp_nopush off;`
`sendfile` Context: `http, server, location`	If this directive is enabled, Nginx will use the `sendfile` kernel call to handle file transmission. If disabled, Nginx will handle the file transfer by itself. Depending on the physical location of the file being transmitted (such as NFS) this option may affect the server performance. Syntax: `on` or `off` Default value: `off` `sendfile off;`
`sendfile_max_chunk` Context: `http, server`	This directive defines a maximum size of data to be used for each call to `sendfile` (read above). Syntax: Numeric value (size) Default value: `0`
`send_lowat` Context: `http, server`	An option allowing you to make use of the `SO_SNDLOWAT` flag for TCP sockets under FreeBSD only. This value defines the minimum number of bytes in the buffer for output operations. Syntax: Numeric value (size) Default value: `0`
`reset_timedout_connection` Context: `http, server, location`	When a client connection times out, its associated information may remain in memory depending on the state it was on. Enabling this directive will erase all memory associated to the connection after it times out. Syntax: `on` or `off` Default value: `off` `reset_timedout_connection off;`

Paths and documents

This section describes directives that configure the documents that should be served for each website such as the document root, the site index, error pages, and so on.

Directive	Description

`root`
 	
Context: `http`,
`server`,
`location`, `if`
 	
Variables accepted
	Defines the document root, containing the files you wish to serve to your visitors.
	
	Syntax: Directory path
	
	Default value: `html`
	
	    `root /home/website.com/public_html;`
| `alias`<br><br>Context:<br>`location`<br><br>Variables accepted | `alias` is a directive that you place in a `location` block only. It assigns a different path for Nginx to retrieve documents for a specific request.<br><br>As an example, consider this configuration:<br><br>```
http {
    server {
        server_name localhost;
        root /var/www/website.com/html;
         location /admin/ {
         alias /var/www/locked/;
        }
    }
}
```<br><br>When a request for `http://localhost/` is received, files are served from the `/var/www/website.com/html/` folder. However, if Nginx receives a request for `http://localhost/admin/`, the path used to retrieve the files is `/home/website.com/locked/`. Moreover, the value of the document root directive (`root`) is not altered; this procedure is invisible in the eyes of dynamic scripts.<br><br>Syntax: Directory (do not forget the trailing /) or file path |
```

Directive	Description
error_page Context: http, server, location, if	Allows you to affect URIs to HTTP response code and optionally to substitute the code with another. Syntax: `error_page code1 [code2...] [=replacement code] [=@block | URI]`

Variables accepted	Examples :
	
	`error_page 404 /not_found.html;`
	`error_page 500 501 502 503 504 /server_error.html;`
	`error_page 403 http://website.com/;`
	`error_page 404 @notfound; # jump to a named`
	`# location block`
	`error_page 404 =200 /index.html; # in case of`
	`# 404 error, redirect to index.html with a 200`
	`# OK response code`

if_modified_since Context: http, server, location	Defines how Nginx handles the `If-Modified-Since` HTTP header. This header is mostly used by search engine spiders (such as Google web crawling bots). The robot indicates the date and time of the last pass; if the requested file was not modified since, the server simply returns a `304 Not Modified` response code with no body. This directive accepts three values: • `off`: Ignores the `If-Modified-Since` header. • `exact`: Returns `304 Not Modified` if the date and time specified in the HTTP header are an exact match with the actual requested file modification date. If the file modification date is anterior or ulterior, the file is served normally (`200 OK` response). • `before`: Returns `304 Not Modified` if the date and time specified in the HTTP header is anterior or equal to the requested file modification date. Syntax: `if_modified_since off | exact | before` Default value: `exact` `if_modified_since exact;`

Directive	Description

index
 	
Context: http, server, location
 	
Variables accepted
	Defines the default page that Nginx will serve if no filename is specified in the request (in other words, the index page). You may specify multiple filenames; the first file to be found will be served. If none of the specified files are found, Nginx will either attempt to generate an automatic index of the files, if the autoindex directive is enabled (check the HTTP Autoindex module) or return a 403 Forbidden error page.
	
	Optionally, you may insert an absolute filename (such as /page.html, based from the document root directory) but only as the last argument of the directive.
	
	Syntax: index file1 [file2...] [absolute_file];
	
	Default value: index.html
	
	`index index.php index.html index.htm;`
	`index index.php index2.php /catchall.php;`

recursive_ error_pages Context: http, server, location	Sometimes an error page itself served by the error_page directive may trigger an error, in which case, the error_page directive is used again (recursively). This directive enables or disables recursive error pages. Syntax: on or off Default value: off `recursive_error_pages off;`

try_files
 	
Context: location
	Attempts to serve the specified files (arguments 1 to N-1), if none of these files exist, jumps to the respective named location block (last argument) or serves the specified URI.
	
	Syntax: Multiple file paths, followed by a named location block or a URI
	
	Example:
	
	`location / {`
	`    try_files $uri $uri.html $uri.php $uri.xml @proxy;`
	`}`
	`# the following is a "named location block"`
	`location @proxy {`
	`    proxy_pass 127.0.0.1:8080;`
	`}`
	
	In this example, Nginx tries to serve files normally. If the request URI does not correspond to any existing file, Nginx appends .html to the URI and tries to serve the file again. If it still fails, it tries with .php, then .xml. Eventually if all these possibilities fail, another location block (@proxy) handles the request.

Client requests

This section documents the way that Nginx will handle client requests. Among other things, you are allowed to configure the keep-alive mechanism behavior and possibly logging client requests into files.

Directive	Description
`keepalive_requests` Context: `http`, `server`, `location`	Maximum amount of requests served over a single keep-alive connection. Syntax: Numeric value Default value: 100 `keepalive_requests 100;`

`keepalive_timeout`
 	
Context: `http`, `server`, `location`
	This directive defines the amount of seconds the server will wait before closing a keep-alive connection.
	
	The second (optional) parameter is transmitted as the value of the `Keep-Alive: timeout=` HTTP response header; the intended effect is to let the client browser close the connection itself after this period has elapsed. Note that some browsers ignore this setting; Internet Explorer for instance automatically closes the connection after 60-ish seconds.
	
	Syntax: `keepalive_timeout time1 [time2];`
	
	Default value: 75
	    `keepalive_timeout 75;`
	    `keepalive_timeout 75 60;`

`send_timeout` Context: `http`, `server`, `location`	The amount of time after which Nginx closes an inactive connection. A connection becomes inactive the moment a client stops transmitting data. Syntax: Time value (seconds) Default value: 60 `send_timeout 60;`

Directive	Description
client_body_in_file_ only Context: http, server, location	If this directive is enabled, the body of incoming HTTP requests will be stored into actual files on the disk. The *client body* corresponds to the client HTTP request raw data, minus the headers (in other words, the content transmitted in POST requests). Files are stored as plain text documents. This directive accepts three values: • off: Do not store the request body in a file • clean: Store the request body in a file and remove the file after a request is processed • on: Store the request body in a file, but do not remove the file after the request is processed (not recommended unless for debugging purposes) Syntax: client_body_in_file_only on | clean | off Default value: off client_body_file_only off;
client_body_in_single_ buffer Context: http, server, location	Defines whether or not Nginx should store the request body in a single buffer in memory Syntax: on or off Default value: off client_body_in_single_buffer off;
client_body_buffer_size Context: http, server, location	Specifies the size of the buffer holding the body of client requests. If this size is exceeded, the body (or at least part of it) will be written to the disk. Note that if the client_body_in_file_only directive is enabled, request bodies are always stored to a file on the disk, regardless of their size (whether they fit in the buffer or not). Syntax: Size value Default value: 8 k or 16 k (2 memory pages) depending on your architecture client_body_buffer_size 8k;

Directive	Description

`client_body_temp_path`
 	
Context: `http, server, location`
	Allows you to define the path of the directory that will store the client request body files.
	
	An additional option lets you separate those files into a folder hierarchy over up to three levels.
	
	Syntax: `client_body_temp_path path [level1] [level2] [level3]`
	
	Default value: `client_body_temp`
	
	`client_body_temp_path /tmp/nginx_rbf;`
	`client_body_temp_path temp 2; # Nginx will create 2-digit folders to hold re quest body files`
	`client_body_temp_path temp 1 2 4; # Nginx will create 3 levels of folders (first level: 1 digit, second level: 2 digits, third level: 4 digits)`

`client_body_timeout` Context: `http, server, location`	Defines the inactivity timeout while reading a client request body. A connection becomes inactive the moment the client stops transmitting data. If the delay is reached, Nginx returns a `408 Request timeout` HTTP error. Syntax: Time value (seconds) Default value: 60 `send_timeout 60;`
`client_header_buffer_ size` Context: `http, server, location`	This directive allows you to define the size of the buffer that Nginx allocates to request headers. Usually 1 k is enough. However, in some cases, the headers contain large chunks of cookie data or the request URI is lengthy. If that is the case, then Nginx allocates one or more larger buffers (the size of larger buffers is defined by the `large_client_header_buffers` directive). Syntax: Size value Default value: 1 k `client_header_buffer_size 1k;`
`client_header_timeout` Context: `http, server, location`	Defines the inactivity timeout while reading a client request header. A connection becomes inactive the moment the client stops transmitting data. If the delay is reached, Nginx returns a `408 Request timeout` HTTP error. Syntax: Time value (seconds) Default value: 60 `send_timeout 60;`

Directive	Description
client_max_body_size Context: http, server, location	It is the maximum size of a client request body. If this size is exceeded, Nginx returns a 413 Request entity too large HTTP error. This setting is particularly important if you are going to allow users to upload files to your server over HTTP. Syntax: Size value Default value: 1 m; client_max_body_size 1m;
large_client_header_ buffers Context: http, server, location	Defines the amount and size of larger buffers to be used for storing client requests, in case the default buffer (client_header_buffer_size) was insufficient. Each line of the header must fit in the size of a single buffer. If the request URI line is greater than the size of a single buffer, Nginx returns the 414 Request URI too large error. If another header line exceeds the size of a single buffer, Nginx returns a 400 Bad request error. Syntax: large_client_header_buffers amount size Default value: 4 buffers of 4 or 8 kilobytes (1 memory page, the size of a page depends on your architecture) large_client_header_buffers 4 4k;
lingering_time Context: http, server, location	This directive applies to client requests with a request body. As soon as the amount of uploaded data exceeds max_client_body_size, Nginx immediately sends a 413 Request entity too large HTTP error response. However, most browsers continue uploading data regardless of that notification. This directive defines the amount of time Nginx should wait after sending this error response before closing the connection. Syntax: Numeric value (time) Default value: 30 seconds

Directive	Description
`lingering_timeout` Context: `http, server, location`	This directive defines the amount of time that Nginx should wait between two read operations before closing the client connection. Syntax: Numeric value (time) Default value: 5 seconds
`ignore_invalid_headers` Context: `http, server`	If this directive is disabled, Nginx returns a `400 Bad Request` HTTP error in case request headers are misformed. Syntax: `on` or `off` Default value: `on`

MIME Types

Nginx offers two particular directives that will help you configure MIME types: `types` and `default_type`, which defines the default MIME types for documents. This will affect the *Content-Type* HTTP header sent within responses. Read on.

Directive	Description

`types`
 	
Context: `http, server, location`
	This directive allows you to establish correlations between MIME types and file extensions. It's actually a block accepting a particular syntax:
	
	```\ntypes {\n mimetype1 extension1;\n mimetype2 extension2 [extension3…];\n […]\n}\n```
	
	When Nginx serves a file, it checks the file extension in order to determine the MIME type. The MIME type is then sent as the value of the Content-Type HTTP header in the response. This header usually affects the way browsers handle files. For example, if the MIME type is application/octet-stream, the browser downloads the file to the disk instead of displaying it. If the MIME type is text/plain, the file will be displayed as plain text in the browser without HTML rendering.
	
	Nginx includes a basic set of MIME types as a standalone file (mime.types) to be included with the include directive:
	
	```\ninclude mime.types;\n```

Directive	Description
	This file already covers the most important file extensions so you will probably not need to edit it. If the extension of the served file is not found within the listed types, the default type is used, as defined by the default_type directive (read below).
	Note that you may override the list of types by re-declaring the types block. A useful example would be to force all files in a folder to be downloaded instead of being displayed:

```
http {
    include mime.types;
    [...]
    location /downloads/ {
        # removes all MIME types
        types { }
        default_type application/octet-stream;
    }
    [...]
}
```

| | Note that some browsers ignore MIME types and may still display files if their filename ends with a known extension such as .html or .txt. |
| | Default values, if the mime.types file is not included, are: |

```
types {
    text/html html;
    image/gif gif;
    image/jpeg jpg;
}
```

Directive	Description

default_type
 	
Context: http, server, location
	Defines the default MIME type. When Nginx serves a file, the file extension is matched against the known types declared within the types block in order to return the proper MIME type as value of the Content-Type HTTP response header. If the extension doesn't match any of the known MIME types, the value of the default_type directive is used.
	
	`Syntax: MIME type.`
	`Default value: text/plain.`
	`default_type text/plain;`

types_hash_max_size Context: http, server, location	Defines the maximum size of an entry in the MIME types hash table. Syntax: Numeric value. Default value: 4 k or 8 k (1 line of CPU cache)

Limits and restrictions

This set of directives will allow you to add restrictions that apply when a client attempts to access a particular location or document on your server. Note that you will find additional directives for restricting access in the next chapter.

Directive	Description

`limit_except`
 	
Context:
`location`
	This directive allows you to prevent the use of all HTTP methods, except the ones that you explicitly allow.
	
	Within a `location` block, you may want to restrict the use of some HTTP methods, such as forbid clients from sending POST requests. You need to define two elements—firstly, the methods that are not forbidden (the allowed methods; all others will be forbidden). Secondly, the audience that is affected by the restriction.
	
	```\nlocation /admin/ {\n limit_except GET {\n allow 192.168.1.0/24;\n deny all;\n }\n}\n```
	
	This example applies a restriction to the `/admin/` location—all visitors are only allowed to use the GET method. Visitors that have a local IP address, as specified with the `allow` directive (detailed in the HTTP Access module), are not affected by this restriction. If a visitor uses a forbidden method, Nginx will return in a `403 Forbidden` HTTP error. Note that the GET method implies the HEAD method (if you allow GET, both GET and HEAD are allowed).
	
	The syntax is particular:
	
	``\nlimit_except METHOD1 [METHOD2...] {\n allow
		deny	auth_basic	auth_basic_user_file\n	proxy_pass	perl;\n}\n```
						
						The directives that you are allowed to insert within the block are documented in their respective module section.

`limit_rate`
 	
Context: `http,`
`server,`
`location, if`
	Allows you to limit the transfer rate of individual client connections. The rate is expressed in bytes per second:
	
	```\nlimit_rate 500k;\n```
	
	This will limit connection transfer rates to 500 kilobytes per second. If a client opens two connections, the client will be allowed 2 * 500 kilobytes.
	
	Syntax: Size value
	
	Default value: No limit

Directive	Description
limit_rate_ after Context: http, server, location, if	Defines the amount of data transferred before the limit_rate directive takes effect. `limit_rate 10m;` Nginx will send the first 10 megabytes at maximum speed. Past this size, the transfer rate is limited by the value specified with the limit_rate directive (see above). Similar to the limit_rate directive, this setting only applies to a single connection. Syntax: Size value Default: None

satisfy
 	
Context:
location
	The satisfy directive defines whether clients require all access conditions to be valid (satisfy all) or at least one (satisfy any).
	
	``
	location /admin/ {
	    allow 192.168.1.0/24;
	    deny all;
	    auth_basic "Authentication required";
	    auth_basic_user_file conf/htpasswd;
	}
	``
	
	In the previous example, there are two conditions for clients to be able to access the resource:
	
	• Through the allow and deny directives (HTTP Access module), we only allow clients that have a local IP address; other clients are denied access
	• Through the auth_basic and auth_basic_user_file directives (HTTP Auth_basic module), we only allow clients that provide a valid username and password
	
	With satisfy all, the client must satisfy both conditions in order to gain access to the resource. With satisfy any, if the client satisfies either condition, they are granted access.
	
	Syntax: satisfy any | all
	
	Default value: all
	
	    `satisfy all;`

Directive	Description
internal Context: location	This directive specifies that the location block is internal; in other words, the specified resource cannot be accessed by external requests. ```\nserver {\n [...]\n server_name .website.com;\n location /admin/ {\n internal;\n }\n}\n``` With the previous configuration, clients will not be able to browse http://website.com/admin/. Such requests will be met with 404 Not found errors. The only way to access the resource is via internal redirects (check the *Rewrite module* section for more information on internal redirects).

File processing and caching

It's important for your website to be built upon solid foundations. File access and caching is a critical aspect of web serving. In this perspective, Nginx lets you perform precise tweaking with the use of the following directives:

Directive	Description
direction Context: http, server, location	If this directive is enabled, files with a size greater than the specified value will be read with the **Direct I/O** system mechanism. This allows Nginx to read data from the storage device and place it directly in memory with no intermediary caching process involved. Enabling this directive will automatically disable the sendfile directive as they cannot be used together. Syntax: Size value, or off Default value: off ```\ndirectio 5m;\n```

Directive	Description
open_file_cache Context: http, server, location	This directive allows you to enable the cache which stores information about open files. It does not actually store file contents itself but only information such as: • File descriptors (file size, modification time, and so on). • The existence of files and directories. • File errors, such as Permission denied, File not found, and so on. Note that this can be disabled with the open_file_cache_errors directive. This directive accepts two arguments: • max=X, where X is the amount of entries that the cache can store. If this amount is reached, older entries will be deleted in order to leave room for newer entries. • Optionally inactive=Y, where Y is the amount of seconds that a cache entry should be stored. By default, Nginx will wait 60 seconds before clearing a cache entry. If the cache entry is accessed, the timer is reset. If the cache entry is accessed more than the value defined by open_file_cache_min_uses, the cache entry will not be cleared (until Nginx runs out of space and decides to clear out older entries). Syntax: open_file_cache max=X [inactive=Y] | off Default value: off `open_file_cache max=5000 inactive=180;`
open_file_cache_errors Context: http, server, location	Enables or disables the caching of file errors with the open_file_cache directive (read above). Syntax: on or off Default value: off `open_file_cache_errors on;`

Directive	Description
open_file_cache_min_uses Context: http, server, location	By default, entries in the open_file_cache are cleared after a period of inactivity (60 seconds, by default). If there is activity though, you can prevent Nginx from removing the cache entry. This directive defines the amount of time an entry must be accessed in order to be eligible for protection. open_file_cache_min_uses 3; If the cache entry is accessed more than three times, it becomes permanently active and is not removed until Nginx decides to clear out older entries to free up some space. Syntax: Numeric value Default value: 1
open_file_cache_valid Context: http, server, location	The open file cache mechanism is important, but cached information quickly becomes obsolete especially in the case of a fast-moving filesystem. In that perspective, information needs to be re-verified after a short period of time. This directive specifies the amount of seconds that Nginx will wait before revalidating a cache entry. Syntax: Time value (in seconds) Default value: 60 open_file_cache_valid 60;

Other directives

The following directives relate to various aspects of the web server—logging, URI composition, DNS, and so on.

Directive	Description
log_not_found Context: http, server, location	Enables or disables logging of 404 Not found HTTP errors. If your logs get filled with 404 errors due to missing favicon.ico or robots.txt files, you might want to turn this off. Syntax: on or off Default value: on log_not_found on;
log_subrequest Context: http, server, location	Enables or disables logging of sub-requests triggered by internal redirects (see the *Rewrite module* section) or SSI requests (see the *Server Side Includes module* section). Syntax: on or off Default value: off log_subrequest off;

Directive	Description
| `merge_slashes`<br><br>Context: `http, server, location` | Enabling this directive will have the effect to merge multiple consecutive slashes in a URI. It turns out to be particularly useful in situations resembling the following:<br><br>```
server {
    [...]
    server_name website.com;
    location /documents/ {
        type { }
        default_type text/plain;
    }
}
```<br><br>By default, if the client attempts to access `http://website.com//documents/` (note the `//` in the middle of the URI), Nginx will return a `404 Not found` HTTP error. If you enable this directive, the two slashes will be merged into one and the location pattern will be matched.<br><br>Syntax: `on` or `off`<br><br>Default value: `off`<br><br>```
merge_slashes off;
``` |
| `msie_padding`<br><br>Context: `http, server, location` | This directive was specifically designed for the Microsoft Internet Explorer browser family. In the case of error pages (with error code 400 or higher), if the length of the response body is less than 512 bytes, these browsers will display their own error page, sometimes at the expense of a more informative page provided by the server.<br><br>If you enable this option, the body of responses with a status code of 400 or higher will be padded to 512 bytes.<br><br>Syntax: `on` or `off`<br><br>Default value: `off`<br><br>```
msie_padding off;
``` |
| `msie_refresh`<br><br>Context: `http, server, location` | It is another MSIE-specific directive that will take effect in the case of HTTP response codes `301 Moved permanently` and `302 Moved temporarily`. When enabled, Nginx sends clients running an MSIE browser a response body containing a *refresh* meta tag (`<meta http-equiv="Refresh"...>`) in order to redirect the browser to the new location of the requested resource.<br><br>Syntax: `on` or `off`<br><br>Default value: `off`<br><br>```
msie_refresh off;
``` |

Directive	Description
`resolver` Context: `http, server, location`	Specifies the name server that should be employed by Nginx to resolve hostnames to IP addresses and vice-versa. Syntax: IP address Default value: None (system default) `resolver 127.0.0.1; # use local DNS`
`resolver_timeout` Context: `http, server, location`	Timeout for a hostname resolution query. Syntax: Time value (in seconds) Default value: 30 `resolver_timeout 30s;`
`server_tokens` Context: `http, server, location`	This directive allows you to define whether or not Nginx should inform the clients of the running version number. There are two situations where Nginx indicates its version number: • In the `server` header of HTTP responses (such as `nginx/0.7.66`). If you set `server_tokens` to off, the `server` header will only indicate Nginx. • On error pages, Nginx indicates the version number in the footer. If you set `server_tokens` to `off`, the footer of error pages will only indicate *nginx*. If you are running an older version of Nginx and do not plan to update it, it might be a good idea to hide your version number. Syntax: on or `off` Default value: `on` `server_tokens on;`
`underscores_in_ headers` Context: `http, server`	Allows or disallows underscores in custom HTTP header names. If this directive is set to `on`, the following example header is considered valid by Nginx: `test_header: value`. Syntax: on or `off` Default value: `off` `underscores_in_headers off;`
`variables_hash_ max_size` Context: `http`	This directive defines the maximum size of the variables' hash table. If your server configuration uses a total of more than 512 variables, you will have to increase this value. Syntax: Numeric value Default value: 512

Directive	Description
`variables_hash_bucket_size` Context: `http`	Defines the maximum length of a variable in the variables hash table. If one of your variables is longer than 64 characters, you will have to increase this value. Syntax: Numeric value Default value: 64 (or 32, or 128, depending on your processor cache specifications)

`post_action`
 	
Context: `http`, `server`, `location`, `if`
	Defines a *post-completion action*, a URI that will be called by Nginx after the request has been completed.
	
	Syntax: URI or named `location` block.
	
	Example:
	`location /payment/ {`
	    `post_action /scripts/done.php;`
	`}`

Module variables

The HTTP Core module introduces a large set of variables that you can use within the value of directives. Be careful though, as only a handful of directives accept variables in the definition of their value. If you insert a variable in the value of a directive that does not accept variables, no error is reported; instead the variable name appears as raw text.

There are three different kinds of variables that you will come across. The first set represents the values transmitted in the headers of the client request. The second set corresponds to the headers of the response sent to the client, and finally, the third set comprises variables that are completely generated by Nginx.

Request headers

Nginx lets you access the client request headers under the form of variables that you will be able to employ later on in the configuration:

Variable	Description
`$http_host`	Value of the *Host* HTTP header, a string indicating the hostname that the client is trying to reach.
`$http_user_agent`	Value of the *User-Agent* HTTP header, a string indicating the web browser of the client.
`$http_referer`	Value of the *Referer* HTTP header, a string indicating the URL of the previous page from which the client comes.

Variable	Description
`$http_via`	Value of the *Via* HTTP header, which informs us about possible proxies used by the client.
`$http_x_forwarded_for`	Value of the *X-Forwarded-For* HTTP header, which shows the actual IP address of the client if the client is behind a proxy.
`$http_cookie`	Value of the *Cookie* HTTP header, which contains the cookie data sent by the client.
`$http_...`	Additional headers sent by the client can be retrieved using `$http_` followed by the header name in lowercase and with dashes (-) replaced by underscores (_).

Response headers

In a similar fashion, you are allowed to access the HTTP headers of the response that was sent to the client. These variables are not available at all times—they will only carry a value after the response is sent, for instance, at the time of writing messages in the logs.

Variable	Description
`$sent_http_content_type`	Value of the *Content-Type* HTTP header, indicating the MIME type of the resource being transmitted.
`$sent_http_content_length`	Value of the *Content-Length* HTTP header informing the client of the response body length.
`$sent_http_location`	Value of the *Location* HTTP header, which indicates that the location of the desired resource is different than the one specified in the original request.
`$sent_http_last_modified`	Value of the *Last-Modified* HTTP header corresponding to the modification date of the requested resource.
`$sent_http_connection`	Value of the *Connection* HTTP header, defining whether the connection will be kept alive or closed.
`$sent_http_keep_alive`	Value of the *Keep-Alive* HTTP header that defines the amount of time a connection will be kept alive.
`$sent_http_transfer_encoding`	Value of the *Transfer-Encoding* HTTP header, giving information about the response body encoding method (such as compress, gzip).
`$sent_http_cache_control`	Value of the *Cache-Control* HTTP header, telling us whether the client browser should cache the resource or not.
`$sent_http_...`	Additional headers sent to the client can be retrieved using `$sent_http_` followed by the header name, in lowercase and with dashes (-) replaced by underscores (_).

Nginx generated

Apart from the HTTP headers, Nginx provides a large amount of variables concerning the request, the way it was and will be handled, as well as settings in use with the current configuration.

Variable	Description
`$arg_XXX`	Allows you to access the query string (GET parameters), where XXX is the name of the parameter you want to utilize.
`$args`	All the arguments of the query string combined together.
`$binary_remote_addr`	IP address of the client as binary data (4 bytes).
`$body_bytes_sent`	Amount of bytes sent in the body of the response.
`$content_length`	Equates to the *Content-Length* HTTP header.
`$content_type`	Equates to the *Content-Type* HTTP header.
`$cookie_XXX`	Allows you to access cookie data where XXX is the name of the parameter you want to utilize.
`$document_root`	Returns the value of the `root` directive for the current request.
`$document_uri`	Returns the current URI of the request. It may differ from the original request URI if internal redirects were performed. It is identical to the `$uri` variable.
`$host`	This variable equates to the *Host* HTTP header of the request. Nginx itself gives this variable a value for cases where the *Host* header is not provided in the original request.
`$hostname`	Returns the system hostname of the server computer
`$is_args`	If the `$args` variable is defined, `$is_args` equates to ?. If `$args` is empty, `$is_args` is empty as well.
`$limit_rate`	Returns the per-connection transfer rate limit, as defined by the `limit_rate` directive. You are allowed to edit this variable by using `set` (directive from the Rewrite module): `    set $limit_rate 128k;`
`$nginx_version`	Returns the version of Nginx you are running.
`$pid`	Returns the Nginx process identifier.
`$query_string`	Identical to `$args`.
`$remote_addr`	Returns the IP address of the client.
`$remote_port`	Returns the port of the client socket.
`$remote_user`	Returns the client username if they used authentication.
`$realpath_root`	Returns the document root in the client request, with symbolic links resolved into the actual path.
`$request_body`	Returns the body of the client request, or - if the body is empty.

Variable	Description
$request_body_file	If the request body was saved (see the client_body_in_file_only directive) this variable indicates the path of the temporary file
$request_completion	Returns OK if the request is completed, an empty string otherwise
$request_filename	Returns the full file name served in the current request.
$request_method	Indicates the HTTP method used in the request, such as GET or POST
$request_uri	Corresponds to the original URI of the request, remains unmodified all along the process (unlike $document_uri/$uri)
$scheme	Returns either http or https, depending on the request
$server_addr	Returns the IP address of the server. Be aware as each use of the variable requires a system call, which could potentially affect overall performance in the case of high-traffic setups.
$server_name	Indicates the value of the server_name directive that was used while processing the request
$server_port	Indicates the port of the server socket that received the request data
$server_protocol	Returns the protocol and version, usually HTTP/1.0 or HTTP/1.1
$uri	Identical to $document_uri

The Location block

We have established that Nginx offers you the possibility to fine-tune your configuration down to three levels — at the *protocol* level (http block), at the server level (server block), and at the requested URI level (location block). Let us now detail the latter.

Location modifier

Nginx allows you to define location blocks by specifying a pattern that will be matched against the requested URI.

```
server {
    server_name website.com;
    location /admin/ {
    # The configuration you place here only applies to
    # http://website.com/admin/
    }
}
```

Instead of a simple folder name, you can indeed insert complex patterns. The syntax of the `location` block is:

```
location [=|~|~*|^~|@] pattern { ... }
```

The first optional argument is a symbol called **location modifier** that will define the way Nginx matches the pattern and also defines the very nature of the pattern (simple string or regular expression). The following table details the different behaviors:

Modifier	Description
=	The location URI must match the specified pattern exactly. The pattern here is limited to a simple literal string; you cannot use a regular expression.

```
server {
    server_name website.com;
    location = /abcd {
    [...]
    }
}
```

The configuration in the location block:

- Applies to `http://website.com/abcd` (exact match)
- Applies to `http://website.com/ABCD` (case-sensitive if your operating system uses case-sensitive filenames)
- Applies to `http://website.com/abcd?param1&param2` (regardless of query string arguments)
- Does not apply to `http://website.com/abcd/` (trailing slash)
- Does not apply to `http://website.com/abcde` (extra characters after the specified pattern)

Modifier	Description
(None)	The location URI must begin with the specified pattern. You may not use regular expressions.

```
server {
    server_name website.com;
    location /abcd {
    [...]
    }
}
```

The configuration in the `location` block:

- Applies to `http://website.com/abcd` (exact match)
- Applies to `http://website.com/ABCD` (case-sensitive if your operating system uses case-sensitive filenames)
- Applies to `http://website.com/abcd?param1&param2` (regardless of query string arguments)
- Applies to `http://website.com/abcd/` (trailing slash)
- Applies to `http://website.com/abcde` (extra characters after the specified pattern)

| ~ | The requested URI must be a case-sensitive match to the specified regular expression. |

```
server {
    server_name website.com;
    location ~ ^/abcd$ {
    [...]
    }
}
```

The `^/abcd$` regular expression used in this example specifies that the pattern must begin (`^`) with /, be followed by abc, and finish (`$`) with d.

Consequently, the configuration in the location block:

- Applies to `http://website.com/abcd` (exact match)
- Does not apply to `http://website.com/ABCD` (case-sensitive)
- Applies to `http://website.com/abcd?param1&param2` (regardless of query string arguments)
- Does not apply to `http://website.com/abcd/` (trailing slash) due to the specified regular expression
- Does not apply to `http://website.com/abcde` (extra characters) due to the specified regular expression

Note: With operating systems such as Microsoft Windows, ~ and ~* are both case-insensitive, as the OS is case-insensitive itself.

Modifier	Description

~*	The requested URI must be a case-insensitive match to the specified regular expression.
	
	``
	server {
	    server_name website.com;
	    location ~* ^/abcd$ {
	    [...]
	    }
	}
	``
	
	The regular expression used in the example is similar to the previous one. Consequently, the configuration in the location block:
	
	• Applies to `http://website.com/abcd` (exact match)
	
	• Applies to `http://website.com/ABCD` (case-insensitive)
	
	• Applies to `http://website.com/abcd?param1&param2` (regardless of query string arguments)
	
	• Does not apply to `http://website.com/abcd/` (trailing slash) due to the specified regular expression
	
	• Does not apply to `http://website.com/abcde` (extra characters) due to the specified regular expression

^~	Similar to the *no symbol* behavior, the location URI must begin with the specified pattern. The difference is that if the pattern is matched, Nginx stops searching for other patterns (read the section below).
@	Defines a named `location` block. These blocks cannot be accessed by the client but only by internal requests generated by other directives such as `try_files` or `error_page`.

Search order and priority

Since it's possible to define multiple `location` blocks with different patterns, you need to understand that when Nginx receives a request, it searches for the `location` block that best matches the requested URI:

```
server {
    server_name website.com;
    location /files/ {"
    # applies to any request starting with "/files/"
    # for example /files/doc.txt, /files/, /files/temp/
    }
    location = /files/ {
    # applies to the exact request to "/files/"
```

```
# and as such does not apply to /files/doc.txt
# but only /files/
}
}
```

When a client visits `http://website.com/files/doc.txt`, the first location block applies. However, when they visit `http://website.com/files/`, the second block applies (even though the first one matches) because it has priority over the first one (it is an exact match).

The order you established in the configuration file (placing the `/files/` block before the `= /files/` block) is irrelevant. Nginx will search for matching patterns in a specific order:

1. `location` blocks with the `=` modifier: If the specified string exactly matches the requested URI, Nginx retains the `location` block

2. `location` blocks with no modifier: If the specified string exactly matches the requested URI, Nginx retains the `location` block

3. `location` blocks with the `^~` modifier: If the specified string matches the beginning of the requested URI, Nginx retains the `location` block

4. `location` blocks with `~` or `~*` modifier: If the regular expression matches the requested URI, Nginx retains the `location` block

5. `location` blocks with no modifier: If the specified string matches the beginning of the requested URI, Nginx retains the `location` block

In that extent, the `^~` modifier begins to make sense, and we can envision cases where it becomes useful.

Case 1:

```
server {
    server_name website.com;
    location /doc {
    [...] # requests beginning with "/doc"
    }
    location ~* ^/document$ {
    [...] # requests exactly matching "/document"
    }
}
```

One might wonder when a client requests `http://website.com/document`, which `location` block applies? Indeed, both blocks match this request. Again, the answer does not lie in the order the blocks appear in the configuration files. In this case, the second location block will apply as the `~*` modifier has priority over the other.

Case 2:

```
server {
    server_name website.com;
    location /document {
    […] # requests beginning with "/document"
    }
    location ~* ^/document$ {
    […] # requests exactly matching "/document"
    }
}
```

The question remains the same — what happens when a client sends a request to download `http://website.com/document`? There is a trick here. The string specified in the first block now exactly matches the requested URI. As a result, Nginx prefers it over the regular expression.

Case 3:

```
server {
    server_name website.com;
    location ^~ /doc {
    […] # requests beginning with "/doc"
    }
    location ~* ^/document$ {
    […] # requests exactly matching "/document"
    }
}
```

This last case makes use of the `^~` modifier. Which block applies when a client visits `http://website.com/document`? Answer: The first block. The reason being that `^~` has priority over `~*`. As a result, any request with a URI beginning with `/doc` will be affected to the first block, even if the request URI matches the regular expression defined in the second block.

Summary

All along this chapter, we studied key concepts of the Nginx HTTP configuration. First, we learned about creating virtual hosts by declaring `server` blocks. Then we discovered the directives and variables of the HTTP Core module that can be inserted within those blocks and eventually understood the mechanisms governing the `location` block.

The job is done—your server now actually serves websites. We are going to take it one step further by discovering the modules that make up the power of Nginx. The next chapter will deal with advanced topics such as the Rewrite and SSI modules, as well as additional components of the HTTP server.

Module Configuration

5

The true richness of Nginx lies within its modules. The entire application is built on a modular system, and each module can be enabled or disabled at compile time. Some bring up simple functionality such as the *Autoindex* module that generates a listing of the files in a directory. Some will transform your perception of a web server (such as the Rewrite module). Developers are also invited to create their own modules; a quick overview of the third-party module system can be found at the end of the chapter.

This chapter covers:

- The Rewrite module, which does more than just rewriting URIs
- The SSI module, a server-side scripting language
- Additional modules enabled in the default Nginx build
- Optional modules that must be enabled at compile time
- A quick note on third-party modules

Rewrite module

This module, in particular, brings much more functionality to Nginx than a simple set of directives. It defines a whole new level of request processing that will be explained all along this section.

Initially, the purpose of this module (as the name suggests) is to perform *URL rewriting*. This mechanism allows you to get rid of *ugly* URLs containing multiple parameters, for instance, `http://example.com/article.php?id=1234&comment=32` — such URLs being particularly uninformative and meaningless for a regular visitor. Instead, links to your website will contain useful information that indicate the nature of the page you are about to visit. The URL given in the example becomes `http://website.com/article-1234-32-US-economy-strengthens.html`. This solution is more interesting for your visitors, but also for search engines — URL rewriting is a key element to Search Engine Optimization (SEO).

The principle behind this mechanism is simple—it consists of rewriting the URI of the client request after it is received, before serving the file. Once rewritten, the URI is matched against `location` blocks in order to find the configuration that should be applied to the request. The technique is further detailed in the coming sections.

Reminder on regular expressions

First and foremost, this module requires a certain understanding of *regular expressions*. Indeed, URL rewriting is performed by the `rewrite` directive, which accepts a pattern followed by the replacement URI.

It's a vast topic—entire books are dedicated to explaining the ins and outs. However, the simplified approach that we are about to examine should be more than sufficient to make the most of the mechanism.

Purpose

The first question we must answer is: What's the purpose of regular expressions? To put it simply—the main purpose is to verify that a string matches a pattern. The said pattern is written in a particular language that allows defining extremely complex and accurate rules.

String	Pattern	Matches?	Explanation
hello	^hello$	Yes	The string begins by character h (^h), followed by e, l, l, and then finishes by o (o$).
hell	^hello$	No	The string begins by character h (^h), followed by e, l, l but does not finish by o.
Hello	^hello$	Depends	If the engine performing the match is *case-sensitive*, the string doesn't match the pattern.

This concept becomes a lot more interesting when complex patterns are employed, such as one that validates an e-mail address: `^[A-Z0-9._%+-]+@[A-Z0-9.-]+\.[A-Z]{2,4}$`. Validating the well-forming of an e-mail address programmatically would require a great deal of code, while all the work can be done with a single regular expression pattern matching.

PCRE syntax

The syntax that Nginx employs originates from the Perl Compatible Regular Expression (**PCRE**) library, which (if you remember Chapter 2) is a pre-requisite for making your own build (unless you disable modules that make use of it). It's the most commonly-used form of regular expression, and nearly everything you learn here remains valid for other language variations.

In its simplest form, a pattern is composed of one character, for example, x. We can match strings against this pattern. Does `example` match the pattern x? Yes, `example` contains the character x. It can be more than one specific character — the pattern `[a-z]` matches any character between a and z, or even a combination of letters and digits: `[a-z0-9]`. In consequence, the pattern `hell[a-z0-9]` validates the following strings: `hello` and `hell4`, but not `hell` or `hell!`.

You probably noticed that we employed the characters `[` and `]`. These are called metacharacters and have a special effect on the pattern. There are a total of 11 metacharacters, and all play a different role. If you want to actually create a pattern containing one of these characters, you need to escape them with the `\` character.

Metacharacter	Description
^ Beginning	The entity after this character must be found at the beginning.
	Example pattern: `^h`
	Matching strings: `hello, h, hh`
	Non-matching strings: `character, ssh`
$ End	The entity before this character must be found at the end.
	Example pattern: `e$`
	Matching strings: `sample, e, file`
	Non-matching strings: `extra, shell`
. Any	Matches any character.
	Example pattern: `hell.`
	Matching strings: `hello, hellx, hell5, hell!`
	Non-matching strings: `hell, helo`
[] Set	Matches any character within the specified set.
	Syntax: `[a-z]` for a range, `[abcd]` for a set, and `[a-z0-9]` for two ranges
	Example pattern: `hell[a-y123]`
	Matching strings: `hello, hell1, hell2, hell3`
	Non-matching strings: `hellz, hell4, heloo`
[^] Negate set	Matches any character that is not within the specified set.
	Example pattern: `hell[^a-np-z0-9]`
	Matching strings: `hello, hell;`
	Non-matching strings: `hella, hell5`

Metacharacter	Description
| Alternation	Matches the entity placed either before or after the |. Example pattern: `hello|welcome` Matching strings: `hello`, `welcome`, `helloes`, `awelcome` Non-matching strings: `hell`, `ellow`, `owelcom`
( ) Grouping	Groups a set of entities, often to be used in conjunction with |. Example pattern: `^(hello|hi) there$` Matching strings: `hello there`, `hi there`. Non-matching strings: `hey there`, `ahoy there`
\\ Escape	Allows you to escape special characters. Example pattern: `Hello\.` Matching strings: `Hello.`, `Hello. How are you?`, `Hi! Hello...` Non-matching strings: `Hello`, `Hello, how are you?`

Quantifiers

So far, you are able to express simple patterns with a limited number of characters. Quantifiers allow you to extend the amount of accepted entities:

Quantifier	Description
* 0 or more times	The entity preceding * must be found 0 or more times. Example pattern: `he*llo` Matching strings: `hllo`, `hello`, `heeeello` Non-matching strings: `hallo`, `ello`
+ 1 or more times	The entity preceding + must be found 1 or more times. Example pattern: `he+llo` Matching strings: `hello`, `heeeello` Non-matching strings: `hllo`, `helo`
? 0 or 1 time	The entity preceding ? must be found 0 or 1 time. Example pattern: `he?llo` Matching strings: `hello`, `hllo` Non-matching strings: `heello`, `heeeello`
{x} x times	The entity preceding {x} must be found x times. Example pattern: `he{3}llo` Matching strings: `heeello`, `oh heeello there!` Non-matching strings: `hello`, `heello`, `heeeello`

Quantifier	Description
{x, }	The entity preceding {x, } must be found at least x times.
At least x times	Example pattern: he{3}llo
	Matching strings: heeello, heeeeeeello
	Non-matching strings: hllo, hello, heello
{x,y}	The entity preceding {x,y} must be found between x and y times.
x to y times	Example pattern: he{2,4}llo
	Matching strings: heello, heeello, heeeello
	Non-matching strings: hello, heeeeello

As you probably noticed, the { and } characters in the regular expressions conflict with the block delimiter of the Nginx configuration file syntax language. If you want to write a regular expression pattern that includes curly brackets, you need to place the pattern between quotes (single or double quotes):

```
rewrite hel{2,}o /hello.php; # invalid
rewrite "hel{2,}o" /hello.php; # valid
rewrite 'hel{2,}o' /hello.php; # valid
```

Captures

One last feature of the regular expression mechanism is the ability to capture sub-expressions. Whatever text is placed between parentheses ( ) is captured and can be used after the matching process. Here are a couple of examples to illustrate the principle:

Pattern	String	Captured
^(hello|hi) (sir|mister)$	hello sir	$1 = hello
		$2 = sir
^(.*)$	nginx rocks	$1 = nginx rocks
^(.{1,3})([0-9]{1,4})([?!]{1,2})$	abc1234!?	$1 = abc
		$2 = 1234
		$3 = !?

When you use a regular expression in Nginx, for example, in the context of a `location` block, the buffers that you capture can be employed in later directives:

```
server {
    server_name website.com;
    location ~* ^/(downloads|files)/(.*)$ {
        add_header Capture1 $1;
        add_header Capture2 $2;
    }
}
```

In the example above, the `location` block will match the request URI against a regular expression. A couple of URIs that would apply here: `/downloads/file.txt`, `/files/archive.zip`, or even `/files/docs/report.doc`. Two parts are captured: `$1` will contain either `downloads` or `files` and `$2` will contain whatever comes after `/downloads/` or `/files/`. Note: The `add_header` directive (syntax: `add_header header_name header_value`, see the *HTTP headers module* section) is employed here to append arbitrary headers to the client response for the sole purpose of demonstration.

Internal requests

Nginx differentiates external and internal requests. External requests directly originate from the client; the URI is then matched against possible `location` blocks:

```
server {
    server_name website.com;
    location = /document.html {
        deny all; # example directive
    }
}
```

A client request to `http://website.com/document.html` would directly fall into the above `location` block.

Opposite to this, internal requests are triggered by Nginx via specific directives. In default Nginx modules, there are several directives capable of producing internal requests: `error_page`, `index`, `rewrite`, `try_files`, `add_before_body`, `add_after_body` (from the Addition module), the `include` SSI command, and more.

There are two different kinds of internal requests:

- **Internal redirects**: Nginx redirects the client requests internally. The URI is changed, and the request may thus match another location block and become eligible for different settings. The most common case of internal redirects is when using the Rewrite directive, which allows you to rewrite the request URI.

- **Sub-requests**: Additional requests that are triggered internally to generate content that is complementary to the main request. A simple example would be with the Addition module. The `add_after_body` directive allows you to specify a URI that will be processed after the original one, the resulting content being appended to the body of the original request. The SSI module also makes use of sub-requests to insert content with the `include` command.

error_page

Detailed in the module directives of the Nginx HTTP Core module, `error_page` allows you to define the server behavior when a specific error code occurs. The simplest form is to affect a URI to an error code:

```
server {
    server_name website.com;
    error_page 403 /errors/forbidden.html;
    error_page 404 /errors/not_found.html;
}
```

When a client attempts to access a URI that triggers one of these errors, Nginx is supposed to serve the page corresponding to the error code. In fact, it does not just send the client the error page — it actually initiates a completely new request based on the new URI. Consequently, you can end up falling back on a different configuration, like in the example below:

```
server {
    server_name website.com;
    root /var/www/vhosts/website.com/httpdocs/;
    error_page 404 /errors/404.html;
    location /errors/ {
        alias /var/www/common/errors/;
        internal;
    }
}
```

When a client attempts to load a document that does not exist, they will initially receive a 404 error. We employed the error_page directive to specify that 404 errors should create an internal redirect to /errors/404.html. As a result, a new request is generated by Nginx with the URI /errors/404.html. This URI falls under the location /errors/ block so the configuration applies.

A raw, but trimmed, excerpt from the debug log summarizes the mechanism (note that the log level must be set to *debug* for you to be able to see such entries; refer to the error_log directive for more information):

```
->http request line: "GET /page.html HTTP/1.1"
->http uri: "/page.html"
->test location: "/errors/"
->using configuration ""
->http filename: "/var/www/vhosts/website.com/httpdocs/page.html"
-> open() "/var/www/vhosts/website.com/httpdocs/page.html" failed (2:
No such file or directory), client: 127.0.0.1, server: website.com,
request: "GET /page.html HTTP/1.1", host: "website.com"
->http finalize request: 404, "/page.html?" 1
->http special response: 404, "/page.html?"
->internal redirect: "/errors/404.html?"
->test location: "/errors/"
->using configuration "/errors/"
->http filename: "/var/www/common/errors/404.html"
->http finalize request: 0, "/errors/404.html?" 1
```

Note that the use of the internal directive in the location block forbids clients from accessing the /errors/ directory. This location can only be accessed from an internal redirect.

The mechanism is the same for the index directive (detailed further on in the Index module)—if no file path is provided in the client request, Nginx will attempt to serve the specified index page by triggering an internal redirect.

Rewrite

While the previous directive error_page is not part of the Rewrite module, detailing its functioning provides a solid introduction to the way Nginx handles requests.

Similar to how the error_page directive redirects to another location, rewriting the URI with the rewrite directive generates an internal redirect.

```
server {
    server_name website.com;
    root /var/www/vhosts/website.com/httpdocs/;
    location /storage/ {
```

```
        internal;
        alias /var/www/storage/;
    }
    location /documents/ {
        rewrite ^/documents/(.*)$ /storage/$1;
    }
}
```

A client query to `http://website.com/documents/file.txt` initially matches the second `location` block (`location /documents/`). However, the block contains a rewrite instruction that transforms the URI from `/documents/file.txt` to `/storage/file.txt`. The URI transformation reinitializes the process — the new URI is matched against the `location` blocks. This time, the first `location` block (`location /storage/`) matches the URI (`/storage/file.txt`).

Again, a quick peek at the debug log confirms the mechanism:

```
->http request line: "GET /documents/file.txt HTTP/1.1"
->http uri: "/documents/file.txt"
->test location: "/storage/"
->test location: "/documents/"
->using configuration "/documents/"
->http script regex: "^/documents/(.*)$"
->"^/documents/(.*)$" matches "/documents/file.txt", client:
127.0.0.1, server: website.com, request: "GET /documents/file.txt
HTTP/1.1", host: "website.com"
->rewritten data: "/storage/file.txt", args: "", client: 127.0.0.1,
server: website.com, request: "GET /documents/file.txt HTTP/1.1",
host: "website.com"
->test location: "/storage/"
->using configuration "/storage/"
->http filename: "/var/www/storage/file.txt"
->HTTP/1.1 200 OK
->http output filter "/storage/test.txt?"
```

Infinite loops

With all the different syntaxes and directives, you may easily get confused. Worse — you might get Nginx confused. This happens, for instance, when your rewrite rules are redundant and cause internal redirects to loop infinitely.

```
server {
    server_name website.com;
    location /documents/ {
        rewrite ^(.*)$ /documents/$1;
    }
}
```

You thought you were doing well, but this configuration actually triggers internal redirects /documents/anything to /documents//documents/anything. Moreover, since the location patterns are re-evaluated after an internal redirect, /documents// documents/anything becomes /documents//documents//documents/anything.

Here is the corresponding excerpt from the debug log:

```
->test location: "/documents/"
->using configuration "/documents/"
->rewritten data: "/documents//documents/file.txt", [...]
->test location: "/documents/"
->using configuration "/documents/"
->rewritten data: "/documents//documents//documents/file.txt" [...]
->test location: "/documents/"
->using configuration "/documents/"
->rewritten data: -
>"/documents//documents//documents//documents/file.txt" [...]
->[...]
```

You probably wonder if this goes on indefinitely — the answer is no. The amount of cycles is restricted to 10. You are only allowed 10 internal redirects; past this limit, Nginx will produce a 500 Internal Server Error.

Server Side Includes (SSI)

A potential source of sub-requests is the Server Side Include (**SSI**) module. The purpose of SSI is for the server to parse documents before sending the response to the client in a somewhat similar fashion to PHP or other preprocessors.

Within a regular HTML file (for example), you have the possibility to insert tags corresponding to commands interpreted by Nginx:

```
<html>
<head>
  <!--# include file="header.html" -->
</head>
<body>
  <!--# include file="body.html" -->
</body>
</html>
```

Nginx processes these two commands; in this case, it reads the contents of head.html and body.html and inserts them into the document source, which is then sent to the client.

Several commands are at your disposal; they are detailed in the SSI module section in this chapter. The one we are interested in for now is the `include` command — including a file into another file-.

```
<!--# include virtual="/footer.php?id=123" -->
```

The specified file is not just opened and read from a static location. Instead, a whole subrequest is processed by Nginx, and the body of the response is inserted instead of the `include` tag.

Conditional structure

The Rewrite module introduces a new set of directives and blocks, among which is the **if** conditional structure.

```
server {
    if ($request_method = POST) {
        [...]
    }
}
```

This gives you the possibility to apply a configuration according to the specified condition. If the condition is true, the configuration is applied; otherwise it isn't.

The table below describes the different syntaxes accepted when forming a condition:

Operator	Description

None	The condition is true if the specified variable or data is not equal to an empty string or a string starting with character 0.
	
	`if ($string) {`
	`    [...]`
	`}`

=, !=	The condition is true if the argument preceding the = symbol is equal to the argument following it. The example below can be read as "if the `request_method` is equal to POST, then apply the configuration".
	
	`if ($request_method = POST) {`
	`    [...]`
	`}`
	
	The != operator does the opposite: "if the request method is different than GET, then apply the configuration".
	
	`if ($request_method != GET) {`
	`    [...]`
	`}`

Operator	Description
| ~, ~*, !~, !~* | The condition is true if the argument preceding the ~ symbol matches the pattern placed after it.<br><br>```
if ($request_filename ~ "\.txt$") {
    [...]
}
```<br><br>~ is case-sensitive, ~* is case-insensitive. Use the ! symbol to negate the matching:<br><br>```
if ($request_filename !~* "\.php$") {
    [...]
}
```<br><br>Note that you can insert capture buffers in the regular expression:<br><br>```
if ($uri ~ "^/search/(.*)$") {
    set $query $1;
    rewrite ^ http://google.com/search?q=$query;
}
``` |
| -f, !-f | Tests the existence of the specified file:<br><br>```
if (-f $request_filename) {
    [...] # if the file exists
}
```<br><br>Use !-f to test the non-existence of the file:<br><br>```
if (!-f $request_filename) {
    [...] # if the file does not exist
}
``` |
-d, !-d	Similar to the -f operator, for testing the existence of a directory.
-e, !-e	Similar to the -f operator, for testing the existence of a file, directory, or symbolic link.
-x, !-x	Similar to the -f operator, for testing if a file exists and is executable.

As of version 0.7.66, there is no else- or else if-like instruction. However, other directives allowing you to control the flow sequencing are available.

You might wonder: what are the advantages of using a location block over an if block? Indeed, in the example below, both seem to have the same effect:

```
if ($uri ~ /search/) {
    [...]
}
location ~ /search/ {
    [...]
}
```
```

As a matter of fact, the main difference lies within the directives that can be employed within either block—some can be inserted in an `if` block and some can't; on the contrary, almost all directives are authorized within a `location` block, as you probably noticed in the directive listings. In general, it's best to only insert directives from the Rewrite module within an `if` block, as other directives were not originally intended for such usage.

Directives

The Rewrite module provides you with a set of directives that do more than just rewriting a URI. The following table describes these directives along with the context in which they can be employed:

Directive	Description
`rewrite` Context: `server, location, if`	As discussed previously, the `rewrite` directive allows you to rewrite the URI of the current request, thus resetting the treatment of the said request. Syntax: `rewrite regexp replacement [flag];` Where regexp is the regular expression the URI should match in order for the replacement to apply. flag may take one of the following values: • `last`: The current rewrite rule should be the last to be applied. After its application, the new URI is processed by Nginx and a location block is searched for. However, further `rewrite` instructions will be disregarded. • `break`: The current rewrite rule is applied, but Nginx does not initiate a new request for the modified URI (does not restart the search for matching location blocks). All further rewrite directives are ignored. • `redirect`: Returns a `302 Moved temporarily` HTTP response, with the replacement URI set as value of the `location` header. • `permanent`: Returns a `301 Moved permanently` HTTP response, with the replacement URI set as the value of the `location` header. • If you specify a URI beginning with `http://` as the replacement URI, Nginx will automatically use the `redirect` flag.

Directive	Description
	• Note that the request URI processed by the directive is a relative URI: It does not contain the host name and protocol. For a request such as `http://website.com/documents/page.html`, the request URI is `/documents/page.html`.
	• Is decoded: The URI corresponding to a request such as `http://website.com/my%20page.html` would be `/my page.html`.
	• Does not contain arguments: For a request such as `http://website.com/page.php?id=1&p=2`, the URI would be `/page.php`. When rewriting the URI, you don't need to consider including the arguments in the replacement URI—Nginx does it for you. If you wish for Nginx to not include the arguments in the rewritten URI, then insert a ? at the end of the replacement URI: `rewrite ^/search/(.*)$ /search.php?q=$1?`.

	• Examples:
	```rewrite ^/search/(.*)$ /search.php?q=$1;```
	```rewrite ^/search/(.*)$ /search.php?q=$1?;```
	```rewrite ^ http://website.com;```
	```rewrite ^ http://website.com permanent;```

`break`
 	
Context: `server, location, if`
	The `break` directive is used to prevent further rewrite directives. Past this point, the URI is fixed and cannot be altered.
	
	Example:
	```if (-f $uri) {```
	``` break; # break if the file exists```
	```}```
	```if ($uri ~ ^/search/(.*)$) {```
	``` set $query $1;```
	``` rewrite ^ /search.php?q=$query?;```
	```}```
	
	This example rewrites `/search/anything`-like queries to `/search.php?q=anything`. However, if the requested file exists (such as `/search/index.html`), the break instruction prevents Nginx from rewriting the URI.

Directive	Description

`return`
 	
Context: `server,`
`location, if`
	Interrupts the request treatment process and returns the specified HTTP status code.
	
	Syntax: `return code;`
	
	Where code is picked among the following status codes: `204`, `400`, `402` to `406`, `408`, `410`, `411`, `413`, `416`, and `500` to `504`. In addition, you may use Nginx-specific code `444` in order to return a HTTP `200 OK` status code with no further header or body data.
	
	Example:
	`if ($uri ~ ^/admin/) {`
	`    return 403;`
	`    # the instruction below is NOT executed`
	`    # as Nginx already completed the request`
	`    rewrite ^ http://website.com;`
	`}`

`set`
 	
Context: `server,`
`location, if`
	Initializes or redefines a variable. Note that some variables cannot be redefined, for example, you are not allowed to alter `$uri`.
	
	Syntax: `set $variable value;`
	
	Examples:
	`set $var1 "some text";`
	`if ($var1 ~ ^(.*) (.*)$) {`
	`    set $var2 $1$2; #concatenation`
	`    rewrite ^ http://website.com/$var2;`
	`}`

`uninitialized_`
`variable_warn`
 	
Context: `http,`
`server,`
`location, if`
	If set to on, Nginx will issue log messages when the configuration employs a variable that has not yet been initialized.
	
	Syntax: on or off
	`    uninitialized_variable_warn on;`

`rewrite_log`
 	
Context: `http,`
`server,`
`location, if`
	If set to on, Nginx will issue log messages for every operation performed by the rewrite engine at the `notice` error level (see `error_log` directive).
	
	Syntax: on or off
	
	Default value: `off`
	`    rewrite_log off;`

Common rewrite rules

Here is a set of rewrite rules that satisfy basic needs for dynamic websites that wish to beautify their page links thanks to the URL rewriting mechanism. You will obviously need to adjust these rules according to your particular situation as every website is different.

Performing a search

This rewrite rule is intended for search queries. Search keywords are included in the URL.

Input URI	`http://website.com/search/some-search-keywords`
Rewritten URI	`http://website.com/search.php?q=some-search-keywords`
Rewrite rule	`rewrite ^/search/(.*)$ /search.php?q=$1?;`

User profile page

Most dynamic websites that allow visitors to register, offer a profile view page. URLs of this form can be employed, containing both the user ID and the username.

Input URI	`http://website.com/user/31/James`
Rewritten URI	`http://website.com/user.php?id=31&name=James`
Rewrite rule	`rewrite ^/user/([0-9]+)/(.+)$ /user.php?id=$1&name=$2?;`

Multiple parameters

Some websites may use different syntaxes for the argument string, for example, by separating non-named arguments with slashes.

Input URI	`http://website.com/index.php/param1/param2/param3`
Rewritten URI	`http://website.com/index.php?p1=param1&p2=param2&p3=param3`
Rewrite rule	`rewrite ^/index.php/(.*)/(.*)/(.*)$ /index.php?p1=$1&p2=$2&p3=$3?;`

Wikipedia-like

Many websites have now adopted the URL style introduced by Wikipedia: a prefix folder, followed by an article name.

Input URI	http:// website.com/wiki/Some_keyword
Rewritten URI	http://website.com/wiki/index.php?title=Some_keyword
Rewrite rule	rewrite ^/wiki/(.*)$ /wiki/index.php?title=$1?;

News website article

This URL structure is often employed by news websites as URLs contain indications of the articles' contents. It is formed of an article identifier, followed by a slash, then a list of keywords. The keywords can usually be ignored and not included in the rewritten URI.

Input URI	http://website.com/33526/us-economy-strengthens
Rewritten URI	http://website.com/article.php?id=33526
Rewrite rule	rewrite ^/([0-9]+)/.*$ /article.php?id=$1?;

Discussion board

Modern bulletin boards now use *pretty URLs* for the most part. This example shows how to create a *topic view* URL with two parameters—the topic identifier and the starting post. Once again, keywords are ignored.

Input URI	http://website.com/topic-1234-50-some-keywords.html
Rewritten URI	http://website.com/viewtopic.php?topic=1234&start=50
Rewrite rule	rewrite ^/topic-([0-9]+)-([0-9]+)-(.*)\.html$ /viewtopic.php?topic=$1&start=$2?;

SSI module

SSI, for Server Side Includes, is actually a sort of server-side programming language interpreted by Nginx. Its name is based on the fact that the most used functionality of the language is the include command. Back in the 1990s, such languages were employed in order to render web pages dynamic, from simple static .html files with client-side scripts to complex pages with server-processed compositions. Within the HTML source code, webmasters could now insert server-interpreted directives, which would then lead the way to more advanced pre-processors such as PHP or ASP.

The most famous illustration of SSI is the *quote of the day*. In order to insert a new quote every day at the top of each page of their website, webmasters would have to edit out the HTML source of every page, replacing the former quote manually. With Server Side Includes, a single command suffices to simplify the task:

```
<html>
<head><title>My web page</title></head>
<body>
  <h1>Quote of the day: <!--# include file="quote.txt" -->
  </h1>
</body>
</html>
```

All you would have to do to insert a new quote is to edit the contents of the quoted. text file. Automatically, all pages would show the updated quote. As of today, most of the major web servers (Apache, IIS, Lighttpd, and so on) support Server Side Includes.

Module directives and variables

Having directives inserted within the actual content of files that Nginx serves raises one major issue — what files should Nginx parse for SSI commands? It would be a waste of resources to parse binary files such as images (.gif, .jpg, .png) or other kinds of media. You need to make sure to configure Nginx correctly with the directives introduced by this module:

Directive	Description
ssi Context: http, server, location, if	Enables parsing files for SSI commands. Nginx only parses files corresponding to MIME types selected with the ssi_types directive. Syntax: on or off Default value: off ssi on;
ssi_types Context: http, server, location	Defines the MIME file types that should be eligible for SSI parsing. The text/html type is always included. Syntax: ssi_types type1 [type2] [type3...]; Default value: text/html ssi_types text/plain;

Directive	Description
`ssi_silent_errors` Context: `http, server, location`	Some SSI commands may generate errors; when that is the case, Nginx outputs a message at the location of the command—`an error occurred while processing the directive`. Enabling this option silences Nginx and the message does not appear. Syntax: `on` or `off` Default value: `off` `ssi_silent_errors off;`
`ssi_value_length` Context: `http, server, location`	SSI commands have arguments that accept a value (for example, `<!--# include file="value" -->`). This parameter defines the maximum length accepted by Nginx. Syntax: Numeric Default: 256 (characters) `ssi_value_length 256;`
`ssi_ignore_recycled_buffers` Context: `http, server, location`	When set to `on`, this directive prevents Nginx from making use of recycled buffers. Syntax: `on` or `off` Default: `off`
`ssi_min_file_chunk` Context: `http, server, location`	If the size of a buffer is greater than `ssi_min_file_chunk`, data is stored in a file and then sent via `sendfile`. In other cases, it is transmitted directly from the memory. Syntax: Numeric value (size) Default: 1,024

A quick note regarding possible concerns about the SSI engine resource usage—by enabling the SSI module at the `location` or `server` block level, you enable parsing of at least all `text/html` files (pretty much any page to be displayed by the client browser). While the Nginx SSI module is efficiently optimized, you might want to disable parsing for files that do not require it.

Firstly, all your pages containing SSI commands should have the `.shtml` (Server HTML) extension. Then, in your configuration, at the `location` block level, enable the SSI engine under a specific condition. The name of the served file must end with `.shtml`:

```
server {
    server_name website.com;
    location ~* \.shtml$ {
        ssi on;
    }
}
```

On one hand, all HTTP requests submitted to Nginx will go through an additional regular expression pattern matching. On the other hand, static HTML files or files to be processed by other interpreters (`.php` for instance) will not be parsed unnecessarily.

Finally, the SSI module enables two variables:

- `$date_local`: Returns the current time according to the current system time zone.
- `$date_gmt`: Returns the current GMT time, regardless of the server time zone.

SSI Commands

Once you have got the SSI engine enabled for your web pages, you are ready to start writing your first dynamic HTML page. Again, the principle is simple — design the pages of your website using regular HTML code, inside which you will insert SSI commands.

These commands respect a particular syntax — at first sight, they look like regular HTML comments: `<!-- A comment -->`, and that is the good thing about it — if you accidentally disable SSI parsing of your files, the SSI commands do not appear on the client browser; they are only visible in the source code as actual HTML comments. The full syntax is:

```
<!--# command param1="value1" param2="value2" … -->
```

File includes

The main command of the Server Side Include module is obviously the `include` command. It comes in two different fashions.

First, you are allowed to make a simple file include:

```
<!--# include file="header.html" -->
```

This command generates an HTTP sub-request to be processed by Nginx. The body of the response that was generated is inserted instead of the command itself.

The second possibility is to use the `include virtual` command:

```
<!--# include virtual="/sources/header.php?id=123" -->
```

This also performs a sub-request to the server; the difference lies within the way that Nginx fetches the specified file (when using `include file`, the `wait` parameter is automatically enabled). Indeed, two parameters can be inserted within the `include` command tag. By default, all SSI requests are issued simultaneously, in parallel. This can cause slowdowns and timeouts in the case of heavy loads. Alternatively, you can use the `wait="yes"` parameter to specify that Nginx should wait for the completion of the request before moving on to other includes.

```
<!--# include virtual="header.php" wait="yes" -->
```

If the result of your `include` command is empty or triggered an error (`404`, `500`, and so on), Nginx inserts the corresponding error page with its HTML: `<html>`[...]`404 Not Found</body></html>`. The message is displayed at the exact same place where you inserted the `include` command. If you wish to revise this behavior, you have the possibility to create a named block. By linking the block to the `include` command, the contents of the block will show at the location of the `include` command tag, in case an error occurs:

```
<html>
<head><title>SSI Example</title></head>
<body>
<center>
  <!--# block name="error_footer" -->Sorry, the footer file was not
found.<!--# endblock -->
  <h1>Welcome to nginx</h1>
  <!--# include virtual="footer.html" stub="error_footer" -->
</center>
</body>
</html>
```

The result as output in the client browser is shown as follows:

As you can see, the contents of the `error_footer` block were inserted at the location of include command, after the `<h1>` tag.

Working with variables

The Nginx SSI module also offers the possibility to work with variables. Displaying a variable (in other words, inserting the variable value into the final HTML source code) can be done with the echo command:

```
<!--# echo var="variable_name" -->
```

The command accepts three parameters:

- var: The name of the variable you want to display, for example, REMOTE_ADDR to display the IP address of the client.
- default: A string to be displayed in case the variable is empty. If you don't specify this parameter, the output is (none).
- encoding: Encoding method for the string. The accepted values are none (no particular encoding), url (encode text like a URL—a blank space becomes %20, and so on) and entity (uses HTML entities: & becomes &).

You may also affect your own variables with the set command:

```
<!--# set var="my_variable" value="your value here" -->
```

The value parameter is itself parsed by the engine; as a result, you are allowed to make use of existing variables:

```
<!--# echo var="MY_VARIABLE" -->
<!--# set var="MY_VARIABLE" value="hello" -->
<!--# echo var="MY_VARIABLE" -->
<!--# set var="MY_VARIABLE" value="$MY_VARIABLE there" -->
<!--# echo var="MY_VARIABLE" -->
```

Here is the code that Nginx outputs for each of the three echo commands from the example above:

```
(none)
hello
hello there
```

Conditional structure

The following set of commands will allow you to include text or other directives depending on a condition. The conditional structure can be established with the following syntax:

```
<!--# if expr="expression1" -->
[...]
<!--# elif expr="expression2" -->
[...]
<!--# else -->
[...]
<!--# endif -->
```

The expression can be formulated in three different ways:

- Inspecting a variable: `<!--# if expr="$variable" -->`. Similar to the `if` block in the Rewrite module, the condition is true if the variable is not empty.

- Comparing two strings: `<!--# if expr="$variable = hello" -->`. The condition is true if the first string is equal to the second string. Use `!=` instead of `=` to revert the condition (the condition is true if the first string is not equal to the second string).

- Matching a regular expression pattern: `<!--# if expr="$variable = / pattern/" -->`. Note that the pattern must be enclosed with / characters, otherwise it is considered to be a simple string. For example, `<!--# if expr="$MY_VARIABLE = /^/documents//" -->`. Similar to the comparison, use `!=` to negate the condition.

The content that you insert within a condition block can contain regular HTML code or additional SSI directives, with one exception—you cannot nest `if` blocks.

Configuration

Last and probably least (for once) of the SSI commands offered by Nginx is the `config` command. It allows you to configure two simple parameters.

First, the message that appears when the SSI engine faces an error is malformed tags or invalid expressions. By default, Nginx displays `[an error occurred while processing the directive]`. If you want it to display something else, enter the following:

```
<!--# config errmsg="Something terrible happened" -->
```

Additionally, you can configure the format of the dates that are returned by the `$date_local` and `$date_gmt` variables using the `timefmt` parameter:

```
<!--# config timefmt="%A, %d-%b-%Y %H:%M:%S %Z" -->
```

The string you specify here is passed as the format string of the `strftime` C function. For more information about the arguments that can be used in the format string, please refer to the documentation of the `strftime` C language function at `http://www.opengroup.org/onlinepubs/009695399/functions/strftime.html.Additional`.

Additional modules

The first half of this chapter covered two of the most important Nginx modules, namely, the Rewrite module and the SSI module. There are a lot more modules that will greatly enrich the functionality of the web server; they are regrouped here, by thematic.

Among the modules described in this section, some are included in the default Nginx build, but some are not. This implies that unless you specifically configured your Nginx build to include these modules (as described in *Chapter 2*), they will not be available to you.

Website access and logging

The following set of modules allows you to configure how visitors access your website and the way your server logs requests.

Index

The Index module provides a simple directive `index`, which lets you define the page that Nginx will serve by default if no filename is specified in the client request (in other words, defines the website index page). You may specify multiple filenames; the first file to be found will be served. If none of the specified files are found, Nginx will either attempt to generate an automatic index of the files, if the `autoindex` directive is enabled (check the HTTP Autoindex module), or return a `403 Forbidden` error page.

Optionally, you may insert an absolute filename (such as `/page.html`) but only as the last argument of the directive.

Syntax: `index file1 [file2...] [absolute_file];`

Default value: `index.html`.

```
index index.php index.html index.htm;
index index.php index2.php /catchall.php;
```

This directive is valid in the following contexts: `http`, `server`, `location`.

Autoindex

If Nginx cannot provide an index page for the requested directory, the default behavior is to return a `403 Forbidden` HTTP error page. With the following set of directives, you enable an automatic listing of the files that are present in the requested directory.

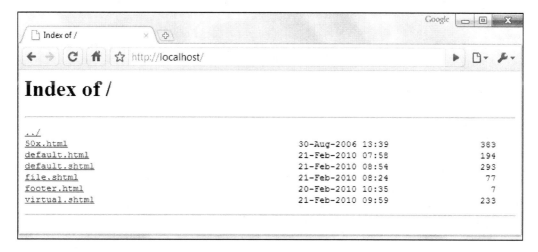

Three columns of information appear for each file — the filename, the file date and time, and the file size in bytes.

Directive	Description
`autoindex` Context: `http`, `server`, `location`	Enables or disables automatic directory listing for directories missing an index page. Syntax: `on` or `off`
`autoindex_exact_size` Context: `http`, `server`, `location`	If set to on, this directive ensures that the listing displays file sizes in bytes. Otherwise another unit is employed, such as KB, MB, or GB. Syntax: `on` or `off` Default value: `on`;

Directive	Description
`autoindex_localtime` Context: `http, server, location`	By default, this directive is set to `off`, so the date and time of files in the listing appears as GMT time. Set it to `on` to make use of the local server time. Syntax: `on` or `off` Default value: `off`

Random index

This module enables a simple directive, `random_index`, which can be used within a `location` block in order for Nginx to return an index page selected randomly among the files of the specified directory.

 This module is not included in the default Nginx build.

Syntax: `on` or `off`

Log

This module controls the behavior of Nginx regarding access logs. It is a key module for system administrators as it allows analyzing the runtime behavior of web applications. It is composed of three essential directives:

Directive	Description
`access_log` Context: `http, server, location`	This parameter defines the access log file path, the format of entries in the access log by selecting a template name, or disables access logging. Syntax: `access_log path [format [buffer=size]] | off;` Some remarks concerning the directive syntax: • Use `access_log off` to disable access logging at the current level • The `format` argument corresponds to a template declared with the `log_format` directive, described below • If the `format` argument is not specified, the default format is employed (`combined`) • You may use variables in the file path

Directive	Description
log_format Context: http, server, location	Defines a template to be utilized by the access_log directive, describing the contents that should be included in an entry of the access log. Syntax: log_format template_name format_string; The default template is called combined and matches the following example: ``` log_format combined '$remote_addr - $remote_ user [$time_local] '"$request" $status $body_bytes_sent '"$http_referer" "$http_user_agent"'; # Other example log_format simple '$remote_addr $request'; ```
open_log_file_cache Context: http, server, location	Configures the cache for log file descriptors. Please refer to the open_file_cache directive of the HTTP Core module for additional information. Syntax: open_log_file_cache max=N [inactive=time] [min_uses=N] [valid=time] | off; The arguments are similar to the open_file_cache and other related directives; the difference being that this applies to access log files only.

The Log module also enables several new variables, though they are only accessible when writing log entries:

- $connection: The connection number
- $pipe: The variable is set to 'p', if the request was pipelined
- $time_local: Local time (at the time of writing the log entry)
- $msec: Local time (at the time of writing the log entry) to the microsecond
- $request_time: Total length of the request processing, in milliseconds
- $status: Response status code
- $bytes_sent: Total number of bytes sent to the client
- $body_bytes_sent: Number of bytes sent to the client for the response body
- $apache_bytes_sent: Similar to $body_bytes, which corresponds to the %B parameter of Apache's mod_log_config
- $request_length: Length of the request body

Limits and restrictions

The following modules allow you to regulate access to the documents of your websites — require users to authenticate, match a set of rules, or simply restrict access to certain visitors.

Auth_basic module

The `auth_basic` module enables the basic authentication functionality. With the two directives that it reveals, you can make it so that a specific location of your website (or your server) is restricted to users that authenticate using a username and password.

```
location /admin/ {
    auth_basic "Admin control panel";
    auth_basic_user_file access/password_file;
}
```

The first directive, `auth_basic`, can be set to either `off` or a text message usually referred to as authentication challenge. This message is displayed by web browsers in a username/password box when a client attempts to access the protected resource.

The second one, `auth_basic_user_file`, defines the path of the password file relative to the directory of the configuration file. A password file is formed of lines respecting the following syntax: `username:password[:comment]`. The password must be encrypted with the `crypt(3)` function, for example, using the `htpasswd` command-line utility from Apache.

Access

Two important directives are brought up by this module: `allow` and `deny`. They let you allow or deny access to a resource for a specific IP address or IP address range.

Both directives have the same syntax: `allow IP | CIDR | all`, where `IP` is an IP address, `CIDR` is an IP address range (CIDR syntax), and `all` specifies that the directive applies to all clients.

```
location {
    allow 127.0.0.1; # allow local IP address
    deny all; # deny all other IP addresses
}
```

Note that rules are processed from top-down — if your first instruction is `deny all`, all possible `allow` exceptions that you place afterwards will have no effect. The opposite is also true — if you start with `allow all`, all possible `deny` directives that you place afterwards will have no effect, as you already allowed all IP addresses.

Limit zone

The mechanism induced by this module is a little more complex than regular ones. It allows you to define the maximum amount of simultaneous connections to the server for a specific *zone*.

The first step is to define the zone using the `limit_zone` directive:

- Define as `limit_zone zone_name $variable memory_max_size;`
- `zone_name` is an arbitrary name given to the zone
- `$variable` is the variable that will be used to differentiate one client from another, typically `$binary_remote_addr` — the IP address of the client in binary format (more efficient than ASCII)
- `memory_max_size` is the maximum size you allocate to the table storing session states

The following example defines zones based on the client IP addresses:

```
limit_zone myzone $binary_remote_addr 10m;
```

Now that you have defined a zone, you can limit connections using `limit_conn`:

```
limit_conn zone_name connection_limit;
```

When applied to the previous example it becomes:

```
location /downloads/ {
    limit_conn myzone 1;
}
```

As a result, requests that share the same `$binary_remote_addr` are subject to the connection limit (one simultaneous connection). If the limit is reached, all additional concurrent requests will be answered with a `503 Service unavailable` HTTP response.

Limit request

In a similar fashion, the *Limit request* module allows you to limit the amount of requests for a defined zone.

Defining the zone is done via the `limit_req_zone` directive; its syntax differs from the *Limit zone* equivalent directive:

```
limit_req_zone $variable zone=name:max_memory_size rate=rate;
```

The directive parameters are identical, except for the trailing `rate`: expressed in requests per second (r/s) or requests per minute (r/m). It defines a request rate that will be applied to clients where the zone is enabled. To apply a zone to a location, use the `limit_req` directive:

```
limit_req zone=name burst=burst [nodelay];
```

The `burst` parameter defines the maximum possible bursts of requests — when the amount of requests received from a client exceeds the limit defined in the zone, the responses are delayed in a manner that respects the rate that you defined. To a certain extent, only a maximum of `burst` requests will be accepted simultaneously. Past this limit, Nginx returns a `503 Service Unavailable` HTTP error response.

```
limit_req_zone $binary_remote_addr zone=myzone:10m rate=2r/s;
[...]
location /downloads/ {
    limit_req zone=myzone burst=10;
}
```

Content and encoding

The following set of modules provides functionalities having an effect on the contents served to the client, either by modifying the way the response is encoded, by affecting the headers, or by generating a response from scratch.

Empty GIF

The purpose of this module is to provide a directive that serves a *1 x 1* transparent GIF image from the memory. Such files are sometimes used by web designers to tweak the appearance of their website. With this directive, you get an empty GIF straight from the memory instead of reading and processing an actual GIF file from the storage space.

To utilize this feature, simply insert the `empty_gif` directive in the location of your choice:

```
location = /empty.gif {
    empty_gif;
}
```

FLV

This module enables a simple functionality that becomes useful when serving Flash Video (FLV) files. It parses a special argument of the request `start`, which indicates the offset of the section the client wishes to download. The FLV file must thus be accessed with the following URI: `video.flv?start=XXX`.

> This module is not included in the default Nginx build.

To utilize this feature, simply insert the FLV directive in the location of your choice:

```
location ~* \.flv {
    flv;
}
```

HTTP headers

Two directives are introduced by this module that will affect the header of the response sent to the client.

First, `add_header Name value` lets you add a new line in the response headers, respecting the following syntax: `Name: value`. The line is added only for responses of the following code: `200`, `204`, `301`, `302`, and `304`. You may insert variables in the `value` argument.

Additionally, the `expires` directive allows you to control the value of the *Expires and Cache-Control HTTP header* sent to the client, affecting requests of the same code, as listed above. It accepts a single value among the following:

- `off`: Does not modify either headers.
- A time value: The expiration date of the file is set to *the current time +, the time you specify*. For example, `expires 24h` will return an expiry date set to 24 hours from now.
- `epoch`: The expiration date of the file is set to January 1, 1970. The Cache-Control header is set to `no-cache`.
- `max`: The expiration date of the file is set to December 31, 2037. The Cache-Control header is set to 10 years.

Addition

The Addition module allows you (through simple directives) to add content before or after the body of the HTTP response.

 This module is not included in the default Nginx build.

The two main directives are:

```
add_before_body file_uri;
add_after_body file_uri;
```

As stated previously, Nginx triggers a sub-request for fetching the specified URI. Additionally, you can define the type of files to which the content is appended in case your `location` block pattern is not specific enough (default: `text/html`):

```
addition_types mime_type1 [mime_type2...];
```

Note: As of version 0.7.64, the preceding directive is misspelled in the source code — use `addtion_types` instead. It has been fixed in version 0.7.65.

Substitution

Along the lines of the previous module, the Substitution module allows you to search and replace text directly from the response body:

```
sub_filter searched_text replacement_text;
```

 This module is not included in the default Nginx build.

Two additional directives provide more flexibility:

- `sub_filter_once` (on or off, default on): Only replaces the text once and stops after the first occurrence.
- `sub_filter_types` (default `text/html`): Affects additional MIME types that will be eligible for the text replacement.

Gzip filter

This module allows you to compress the response body with the Gzip algorithm before sending it to the client. To enable Gzip compression, use the `gzip` directive (`on` or `off`) at the `http`, `server`, `location`, and even the `if` level (though that is not recommended). The following directives will help you further configure the filter options:

Directive	Description
`gzip_buffers` Context: `http`, `server`, `location`	Defines the amount and size of buffers to be used for storing the compressed response. Syntax: `gzip_buffers amount size;` Default: `gzip_buffers 4 4k` (or 8 k depending on the OS).
`gzip_comp_level` Context: `http`, `server`, `location`	Defines the compression level of the algorithm. The specified value ranges from 1 (low compression, faster for the CPU) to 9 (high compression, slower). Syntax: Numeric value. Default: 1
`gzip_disable` Context: `http`, `server`, `location`	Disables Gzip compression for requests where the User-Agent HTTP header matches the specified regular expression. Syntax: Regular expression Default: None
`gzip_http_version` Context: `http`, `server`, `location`	Enables Gzip compression for the specified protocol version. Syntax: `1.0` or `1.1` Default: 1.1
`gzip_min_length` Context: `http`, `server`, `location`	If the response body length is inferior to the specified value, it is not compressed. Syntax: Numeric value (size) Default: 0

Directive	Description

`gzip_proxied`
 	
Context: `http,`
`server, location`
	Enables or disables Gzip compression for the body of responses received from a proxy (see reverse-proxying mechanisms in later chapters).
	
	The directive accepts the following parameters; some can be combined:
	
	• `off`/`any`: Disables or enables compression for all requests
	
	• `expired`: Enables compression if the *Expires* header prevents caching
	
	• `no-cache`/`no-store`/`private`: Enables compression if the *Cache-Control* header is set to `no-cache`, `no-store`, or `private`
	
	• `no_last_modified`: Enables compression in case the *Last-Modified* header is not set
	
	• `no_etag`: Enables compression in case the *ETag* header is not set
	
	• `auth`: Enables compression in case an *Authorization* header is set

`gzip_types`
 	
Context: `http,`
`server, location`
	Enables compression for types other than the `default text/html` MIME type.
	
	Syntax: `gzip_types mime_type1 [mime_type2...]`
	
	Default: `text/html` (cannot be disabled)

`gzip_vary`
 	
Context: `http,`
`server, location`
	Adds the *Vary: Accept-Encoding HTTP* header to the response.
	
	Syntax: `on` or `off`
	
	Default: `off`

`gzip_window`
 	
Context: `http,`
`server, location`
	Sets the size of the window buffer (`windowBits` argument) for Gzipping operations. This directive value is used for calls to functions from the Zlib library.
	
	Syntax: Numeric value (size)
	
	Default: MAX_WBITS constant from the Zlib library

`gzip_hash`
 	
Context: `http,`
`server, location`
	Sets the amount of memory that should be allocated for the internal compression state (`memLevel` argument). This directive value is used for calls to functions from the Zlib library.
	
	Syntax: Numeric value (size)
	
	Default: `MAX_MEM_LEVEL` constant from the Zlib pre-requisite library

Directive	Description
postpone_ gzipping Context: http, server, location	Defines a minimum data threshold to be reached before starting the Gzip compression. Syntax: Size (numeric value) Default: 0
gzip_no_buffer Context: http, server, location	By default, Nginx waits until at least one buffer (defined by gzip_buffers) is filled with data before sending the response to the client. Enabling this directive disables buffering. Syntax: on or off Default: off

Gzip static

This module adds a simple functionality to the Gzip filter mechanism — when its gzip_static directive (on or off) is enabled, Nginx will automatically look for a .gz file corresponding to the requested document before serving it. This allows Nginx to send pre-compressed documents instead of compressing documents on-the-fly at each request.

 This module is not included in the default Nginx build.

If a client requests /documents/page.html, Nginx checks for the existence of a /documents/page.html.gz file. If the .gz file is found, it is served to the client. Note that Nginx does not generate .gz files itself, even after serving the requested files.

Charset filter

With the *Charset filter* module, you can control the character set of the response body more accurately. Not only are you able to specify the value of the charset argument of the Content-Type HTTP header (such as Content-Type: text/html; charset=utf-8), but Nginx can also re-encode data to a specified encoding method automatically.

Directive	Description
charset Context: http, server, location, if	This directive adds the specified encoding to the Content-Type header of the response. If the specified encoding differs from the source_charset one, Nginx re-encodes the document. Syntax: charset encoding | off; Default: off Example: charset utf-8;

Directive	Description
source_charset Context: http, server, location, if	Defines the initial encoding of the response; if the value specified in the charset directive differs, Nginx re-encodes the document. Syntax: source_charset encoding;
override_charset Context: http, server, location, if	When Nginx receives a response from the proxy or FastCGI gateway, this directive defines whether or not the character encoding should be checked and potentially overridden. Syntax: on or off Default: off
charset_types Context: http, server, location	Defines the MIME types that are eligible for re-encoding. Syntax: charset_types mime_type1 [mime_type2...]; Default: text/html, text/xml, text/plain, text/vnd.wap.wml, application/x-javascript, application/rss+xml
charset_map Context: http	Lets you define character re-encoding tables. Each line of the table contains two hexadecimal codes to be exchanged. You will find re-encoding tables for the koi8-r character set in the default Nginx configuration folder (koi-win and koi-utf). Syntax: charset_map src_encoding dest_encoding { ... }

Memcached

Memcached is a daemon application that can be connected to via sockets. Its main purpose, as the name suggests, is to provide an efficient distributed key/value memory caching system. The *Nginx Memcached* module provides directives allowing you to configure access to the Memcached daemon.

Directive	Description
memcached_pass Context: location, if	Defines the hostname and port of the Memcached daemon. Syntax: memcached_pass hostname:port; Example: memcached_pass localhost:11211;
memcached_connect_timeout Context: http, server, location	Defines the connection timeout in milliseconds (default: 60,000). Example: memcached_connect_timeout 5000;
memcached_send_timeout Context: http, server, location	Defines the data writing operations timeout in milliseconds (default: 60,000). Example: memcached_send_timeout 5,000;

Directive	Description
`memcached_read_timeout` Context: `http, server, location`	Defines the data reading operations timeout in milliseconds (default: 60,000). Example: `memcached_read_timeout 5,000;`
`memcached_buffer_size` Context: `http, server, location`	Defines the size of the read and write buffer, in bytes (default: page size). Example: `memcached_buffer_size 8k;`
`memcached_next_upstream` Context: `http, server, location`	When the `memcached_pass` directive is connected to an upstream block (see Upstream module), this directive defines the conditions that should be matched in order to skip to the next upstream server. Syntax: Values selected among `error, timeout, invalid_response, not_found,` or `off` Default: `error timeout` Example: `memcached_next_upstream off;`

Additionally, you will need to define the `$memcached_key` variable that defines the key of the element that you are placing or fetching from the cache. You may, for instance, use `set $memcached_key $uri` or `set $memcached_key $uri?$args`.

Note that the Nginx Memcached module is only able to retrieve data from the cache; it does not store the result of requests. Storing data in the cache should be done by a server-side script. You just need to make sure to employ the same key naming scheme in both your server-side scripts and the Nginx configuration. As an example, we could decide to use memcached to retrieve data from the cache before passing the request to a proxy, if the requested URI is not found (see Chapter 7 for more details about the Proxy module):

```
server {
    server_name example.com;
    [...]
    location / {
        set $memcached_key $uri;
        memcached_pass 127.0.0.1:11211;
        error_page 404 @notcached;
    }
    location @notcached {
        internal;
        # if the file is not found, forward request to proxy
        proxy_pass 127.0.0.1:8080;
    }
}
```

Image filter

This module provides image processing functionalities through the *GD Graphics Library* (also known as *gdlib*).

 This module is not included in the default Nginx build.

Make sure to employ the following directives on a location block that filters image files only, such as `location ~* \.(png|jpg|gif)$ { ... }`.

Directive	Description
`image_filter` Context: `location`	Lets you apply a transformation on the image before sending it to the client. There are four options available: • `test`: Makes sure that the requested document is an image file, returns a `415 Unsupported media type` HTTP error if the test fails. • `size`: Composes a simple JSON response indicating information about the image such as the size and type (for example; `{ "img": { "width":50, "height":50, "type":"png" }}`). If the file is invalid, a simple `{}` is returned. • `resize width height`: Resizes the image to the specified dimensions. • `crop width height`: Selects a portion of the image of the specified dimensions. Example: `image_filter resize 200 100;`
`image_filter_buffer` Context: `http, server, location`	Defines the maximum file size for images to be processed. Default: `image_filter_buffer 1m;`
`image_filter_jpeg_quality` Context: `http, server, location`	Defines the quality of output JPEG images. Default: `image_filter_jpeg_quality 75;`

XSLT

The Nginx XSLT module allows you to apply an XSLT transform on an XML file or response received from a backend server (proxy, FastCGI, and so on) before serving the client.

 This module is not included in the default Nginx build.

Directive	Description
`xml_entities` Context: `http, server, location`	Specifies the DTD file containing symbolic element definitions. Syntax: File path Example: `xml_entities xml/entities.dtd;`
`xslt_stylesheet` Context: `location`	Specifies the XSLT template file path with its parameters. Variables may be inserted in the parameters. Syntax: `xslt_stylesheet template [param1] [param2...];` Example: `xslt_stylesheet xml/sch.xslt param=value;`
`xslt_types` Context: `http, server, location`	Defines additional MIME types to which the transforms may apply, other than `text/xml`. Syntax: MIME type Example: `xslt_types text/xml text/plain;`

About your visitors

The following set of modules provides extra functionality that will help you find out more information about the visitors, such as by parsing client request headers for browser name and version, assigning an identifier to requests presenting similarities, and so on.

Browser

The Browser module parses the User-Agent HTTP header of the client request in order to establish values for variables that can be employed later in the configuration. The three variables produced are:

- `$modern_browser`: If the client browser is identified as being a modern web browser, the variable takes the value defined by the `modern_browser_value` directive.
- `$ancient_browser`: If the client browser is identified as being an old web browser, the variable takes the value defined by `ancient_browser_value`.
- `$msie`: This variable is set to `1` if the client is using a Microsoft IE browser.

To help Nginx recognize web browsers, telling the old from the modern, you need to insert multiple occurrences of the `ancient_browser` and `modern_browser` directives.

```
modern_browser opera 10.0;
```

With this example, if the User-Agent HTTP header contains Opera 10.0, the client browser is considered modern.

Map

Just like the Browser module, the Map module allows you to create maps of values depending on a variable.

```
map $uri $variable {
    /page.html   0;
    /contact.html   1;
    /index.html   2;
    default 0;
}
rewrite ^ /index.php?page=$variable;
```

Note that the `map` directive can only be inserted within the `http` block. Following this example, $variable may have three different values. If $uri was set to /page.html, $variable is now defined to 0; if $uri was set to /contact.html, $variable is now 1; if $uri was set to /index.html, $variable now equals 2. For all other cases (`default`), $variable is set to 0. The last instruction rewrites the URL accordingly. Apart from `default`, the map directive accepts another special keyword: `hostnames`. It allows you to match hostnames using wildcards such as `*.domain.com`.

Two additional directives allow you to tweak the way Nginx manages the mechanism in memory:

- `map_hash_max_size`: Sets the maximum size of the hash table holding a map
- `map_hash_bucket_size`: The maximum size of an entry in the map

Geo

The purpose of this module is to provide a functionality that is quite similar to the `map` directive—affecting a variable based on client data (in this case, the IP address). The syntax is slightly different in the extent that you are allowed to specify address ranges (in CIDR format):

```
geo $variable {
    default unknown;
    127.0.0.1   local;
    123.12.3.0/24   uk;
    92.43.0.0/16   fr;
}
```

GeoIP

Although the name suggests some similarities with the previous one, this optional module provides accurate geographical information about your visitors by making use of the *MaxMind* (www.maxmind.com) GeoIP binary databases. You need to download the database files from the MaxMind website and place them in your Nginx directory.

 This module is not included in the default Nginx build.

All you have to do then is to specify the database path with either directive:

```
geoip_country country.dat; # country information db
geoip_city city.dat; # city information db
```

The first directive enables three variables: $geoip_country_code (two-letter country code), $geoip_country_code3 (three-letter country code), and $geoip_country_name (full country name). The second directive includes the same variables but provides additional information: $geoip_region, $geoip_city, $geoip_postal_code, $geoip_city_continent_code, $geoip_latitude, $geoip_longitude.

UserID filter

This module assigns an identifier to clients by issuing cookies. The identifier can be accessed from variables $uid_got and $uid_set further in the configuration.

Directive	Description
userid Context: http, server, location	Enables or disables issuing and logging of cookies. The directive accepts four possible values: • on: Enables v2 cookies and logs them • v1: Enables v1 cookies and logs them • log: Does not send cookie data but logs incoming cookies • off: Does not send cookie data Default value: userid off;
userid_service Context: http, server, location	Defines the IP address of the server issuing the cookie. Syntax: userid_service ip; Default: IP address of the server

[181]

Directive	Description
userid_name	Defines the name assigned to the cookie.
Context: http, server, location	Syntax: userid_name name;
	Default value: The user identifier.
userid_domain	Defines the domain assigned to the cookie.
Context: http, server, location	Syntax: userid_domain domain;
	Default value: None (the domain part is not sent).
userid_path	Defines the path part of the cookie.
Context: http, server, location	Syntax: userid_path path;
	Default value: /
userid_expires	Defines the cookie expiration date.
Context: http, server, location	Syntax: userid_expires date | max;
	Default value: No expiration date.
userid_p3p	Assigns a value to the P3P header sent with the cookie.
Context: http, server, location	Syntax: userid_p3p data;
	Default value: None

Referer

A simple directive is introduced by this module: valid_referers. Its purpose is to check the Referer HTTP header from the client request and possibly to deny access based on the value. If the referrer is considered invalid, $invalid_referer is set to 1. In the list of valid referrers, you may employ three kinds of values:

- None: The absence of a referrer is considered to be a valid referrer
- Blocked: A masked referrer (such as xxxxx) is also considered valid
- A server name: The specified server name is considered to be a valid referrer

Following the definition of the $invalid_referer variable, you may, for example, return an error code if the referrer was found invalid:

```
valid_referers none blocked *.website.com *.google.com;
  if ($invalid_referer) {
  return 403;
}
```

Be aware that spoofing the Referer HTTP header is a very simple process, so checking the referrer of client requests shouldn't be used as a security measure.

Real IP

This module provides one simple feature — it replaces the client IP address by the one specified in the *X-Real-IP* HTTP header, for clients that visit your website behind a proxy or for retrieving IP addresses from the proper header if Nginx is used as a backend server (it essentially has the same effect as Apache's `mod_rpaf`, see Chapter 7 for more details). To enable this feature, you need to insert the `real_ip_header` directive that defines the HTTP header to be exploited — either `X-Real-IP` or `X-Forwarded-For`. The second step is to define trusted IP addresses, in other words, the clients that are allowed to make use of those headers. This can be done thanks to the `set_real_ip_from` directive, which accepts both IP addresses and CIDR address ranges:

```
real_ip_header X-Forwarded-For;
set_real_ip_from 192.168.0.0/16;
set_real_ip_from 127.0.0.1;
```

 This module is not included in the default Nginx build.

SSL and security

Nginx provides secure HTTP functionalities through the SSL module but also offers an extra module called *Secure Link* that helps you protect your website and visitors in a totally different way.

SSL

The SSL module enables HTTPS support, HTTP over SSL/TLS in particular. It gives you the possibility to serve secure websites by providing a certificate, a certificate key, and other parameters defined with the following directives:

 This module is not included in the default Nginx build.

Directive	Description
ssl Context: http, server	Enables HTTPS for the specified server. This directive is the equivalent of listen 443 ssl or listen port ssl more generally.
	Syntax: on or off
	Default: ssl off;
ssl_certificate Context: http, server	Sets the path of the PEM certificate.
	Syntax: File path
ssl_certificate_key Context: http, server	Sets the path of the PEM secret key file.
	Syntax: File path
ssl_client_certificate Context: http, server	Sets the path of the client PEM certificate.
	Syntax: File path
ssl_dhparam Context: http, server	Sets the path of the *Diffie-Hellman* parameters file.
	Syntax: File path.
ssl_protocols Context: http, server	Specifies the protocol that should be employed.
	Syntax: ssl_protocols [SSLv2] [SSLv3] [TLSv1];
	Default: ssl_protocols SSLv2 SSLv3 TLSv1;
ssl_ciphers Context: http, server	Specifies the ciphers that should be employed. The list of available ciphers can be obtained running the following command from the shell: openssl ciphers.
	Syntax: ssl_ciphers cipher1[:cipher2...];
	Default: ssl_ciphers ALL:!ADH:RC4+RSA:+HIGH:+MEDIUM:+LOW:+SSLv2:+EXP;
ssl_prefer_server_ciphers Context: http, server	Specifies whether server ciphers should be preferred over client ciphers.
	Syntax: on or off
	Default: off
ssl_verify_client Context: http, server	Enables verifying certificates transmitted by the client.
	Syntax: on or off
	Default: off
ssl_verify_depth Context: http, server	Specifies the verification depth of the client certificate chain.
	Syntax: Numeric value
	Default: 1

Directive	Description
ssl_session_cache Context: http, server	Configures the cache for SSL sessions. Syntax: off, none, builtin:size or shared:name:size Default: off (disables SSL sessions)
ssl_session_timeout Context: http, server	When SSL sessions are enabled, this directive defines the timeout for using session data. Syntax: Time value Default: 5 minutes

Additionally, the following variables are made available:

- $ssl_cipher: Indicates the cipher used for the current request
- $ssl_client_serial: Indicates the serial number of the client certificate
- $ssl_client_s_dn and $ssl_client_i_dn: Indicate the value of the Subject and Issuer DN of the client certificate
- $ssl_protocol: Indicates the protocol at use for the current request
- $ssl_client_cert and $ssl_client_raw_cert: Returns client certificate data, which is raw data for the second variable
- $ssl_verify: Set to SUCCESS if the client certificate was successfully verified

Setting up an SSL certificate

Although the SSL module offers a lot of possibilities, in most cases only a couple of directives are actually useful for setting up a secure website. This guide will help you configure Nginx to use an SSL certificate for your website (in the example, your website is identified by secure.website.com). Before doing so, ensure that you already have the following elements at your disposal:

- A .key file generated with the following command: openssl genrsa -out secure.website.com.key 1024 (other encryption levels work too)
- A .csr file generated with the following command: openssl req -new -key secure.website.com.key -out secure.website.com.csr
- Your website certificate file, as issued by the Certificate Authority, for example, secure.website.com.crt. (Note: In order to obtain a certificate from the CA, you will need to provide your .csr file)
- The CA certificate file as issued by the CA, for example, gd_bundle.crt if you purchased your certificate from GoDaddy.com

The first step is to merge your website certificate and the CA certificate together with the following command:

```
cat secure.website.com.crt gd_bundle.crt > combined.crt
```

You are then ready to configure Nginx to serve secure content:

```
server {
    listen 443;
    server_name secure.website.com;
    ssl on;
    ssl_certificate /path/to/combined.crt;
    ssl_certificate_key /path/to/secure.website.com.key;
    [...]
}
```

Secure link

Totally independent from the SSL module, Secure link provides a basic protection by checking the presence of a specific hash in the URL before allowing the user to access a resource:

```
location /downloads/ {
    secure_link_secret "secret";
    if ($secure_link = "") {
      return 403;
    }
    rewrite ^ /downloads/$secure_link break;
}
```

With this configuration, documents in the /downloads/ folder must be accessed from a URL containing a hash of the combination of the requested filename and the secret password. Regular accesses such as http://website.com/downloads/file.zip will result in a 403 error.

 This module is not included in the default Nginx build.

The correct hash that should be included in the URL is an MD5 hash calculated with the following formula: *MD5 (file name + `secure_link_secret` directive value)*. In the previous example, if a client wishes to download /downloads/file.zip, they need to provide a URI containing the MD5 of file.zipsecret. The final URL will be:

```
http://website.com/downloads/63666cbff4e08672ebbb0ed3e7c2f011/
file.zip
```

The $secure_link variable is empty if the URI does not contain the proper hash; otherwise it is set to the requested filename and can be employed in a rewrite rule.

Other miscellaneous modules

The remaining three modules are optional (all need to be enabled at compile time) and provide additional advanced functionality.

Stub status

The stub status module was designed to provide information about the current state of the server, such as the amount of active connections, the total handled requests, and more. To activate it, place the stub_status directive in a location block. All requests matching the location block will produce the status page:

```
location = /nginx_status {
    stub_status on;
    allow 127.0.0.1; # you may want to protect the information
    deny all;
}
```

 This module is not included in the default Nginx build.

An example result produced by Nginx:

```
Active connections: 1
server accepts handled requests
 10 10 23
Reading: 0 Writing: 1 Waiting: 0
```

It's interesting to note that there are several server monitoring solutions such as *Monitorix* that offer Nginx support through the stub status page by calling it at regular intervals and parsing the statistics.

Google-perftools

This module interfaces the Google Performance Tools profiling mechanism for the Nginx worker processes. The tool generates a report based on performance analysis of the executable code. More information can be discovered from the official website of the project: http://code.google.com/p/google-perftools/.

This module is not included in the default Nginx build.

In order to enable this feature, you need to specify the path of the report file that will be generated using the `google_perftools_profiles` directive:

```
google_perftools_profiles logs/profiles;
```

WebDAV

WebDAV is an extension of the well-known HTTP protocol. While HTTP was designed for visitors to download resources from a website, in other words reading data, WebDAV extends the functionality of web servers by adding write operations such as creating files and folders, moving and copying files, and more. The Nginx WebDAV module implements a small subset of the WebDAV protocol:

 This module is not included in the default Nginx build.

Directive	Description
dav_methods	Selects the DAV methods you want to enable.
Context: http, server, location	Syntax: dav_methods [off | [PUT] [DELETE] [MKCOL] [COPY] [MOVE]];
	Default: off
dav_access	Defines access permissions at the current level.
Context: http, server, location	Syntax: dav_access [user:r|w|rw] [group:r|w|rw] [all:r|w|rw];
	Default: dav_access user:rw;
create_full_put_path	This directive defines the behavior when a client requests to create a file in a directory that does not exist. If set to on, the directory path is created. If set to off, the file creation fails.
Context: http, server, location	Syntax: on or off
	Default: off
min_delete_depth	This directive defines a minimum URI depth for deleting files or directories when processing the DELETE command.
Context: http, server, location	Syntax: Numeric value
	Default: 0

Third-party modules

The Nginx community has been growing larger over the past few years and many additional modules were written by third-party developers. These can be downloaded from the official wiki website: `http://wiki.nginx.org/nginx3rdPartyModules`.

The currently available modules offer a wide range of new possibilities, among which are:

- An *Access Key* module to protect your documents in a similar fashion as Secure link, by *Mykola Grechukh*

- A *Fancy Indexes* module that improves the automatic directory listings generated by Nginx, by *Adrian Perez de Castro*

- The *Headers More* module that improves flexibility with HTTP headers, by *Yichun Zhang* (*agentzh*)

- Many more features for various parts of the web server

To integrate a third-party module into your Nginx build, you need to follow these three simple steps:

1. Download the `.tar.gz` archive associated with the module you wish to download

2. Extract the archive with the following command: `tar xzf module.tar.gz`

3. Configure your Nginx build with the following command:

   ```
   ./configure --add-module=/module/source/path [...]
   ```

Once you finished building and installing the application, the module is available just like a regular Nginx module with its directives and variables.

If you are interested in writing Nginx modules yourself, *Evan Miller* published an excellent walkthrough: *Emiller's Guide to Nginx Module Development*. The complete guide may be consulted from his personal website at `http://www.evanmiller.org/`.

Summary

All throughout this chapter, we have been discovering modules that help you improve or fine-tune the configuration of your web server. Nginx fiercely stands up to other concurrent web servers in terms of functionality, and its approach of virtual hosts and the way they are configured will probably convince many administrators to make the switch.

Three additional modules were left out though. Firstly, the FastCGI module will be approached in the next chapter, as it will allow us to configure a gateway to applications such as PHP or Python. Secondly, the proxy module that lets us design complex setups will be described in *Chapter 7, Apache and Nginx Together*. Finally, the Upstream module is tied to both, so it will be detailed in parallel.

6
PHP and Python with Nginx

The 2000s is the decade of server-side technologies. Over the past ten years or so, an overwhelming majority of websites have migrated from simple static HTML content to highly and fully dynamic pages, taking the web to a whole new level in terms of interaction with visitors. Software solutions emerged quickly, including open source ones; some became mature enough to process high-traffic websites. In this chapter, we will study the ability of Nginx to interact with these applications. We have retained two for different reasons. The first one is obviously PHP—according to a survey from Nexen Services, as of October 2008, nearly 33 percent of the World Wide Web was powered by PHP. The second one is Python—the reason being the way it's installed and configured to work with Nginx; the mechanism effortlessly applies to other applications such as Perl or Ruby on Rails.

This chapter covers:

- Discovering the CGI and FastCGI technologies
- The Nginx FastCGI module
- Load balancing via the Upstream module
- Setting up PHP and PHP-FPM
- Setting up Python and Django
- Configuring Nginx to work with PHP and Python

Introduction to FastCGI

Before we begin, you should know that (as the name suggests) FastCGI is actually a variation of CGI. Explaining CGI first is thus in order; the improvements introduced by FastCGI are detailed next.

Understanding the mechanism

The initial purpose of a web server is to answer requests from clients by serving files located on a storage device. The client sends a request to download a file; the server processes the request and sends the appropriate response—200 OK if the file can be served normally, 404 if the file was not found, and other variants.

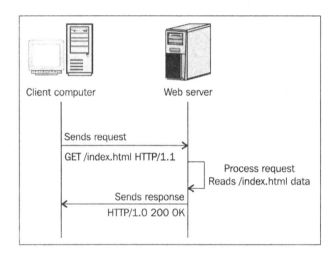

This mechanism has been in use since the beginning of the World Wide Web and it still is. However, as stated before, static websites are being progressively abandoned at the expense of dynamic ones that contain scripts to be processed by applications such as PHP and Python among others. The web serving mechanism thus evolved into the following:

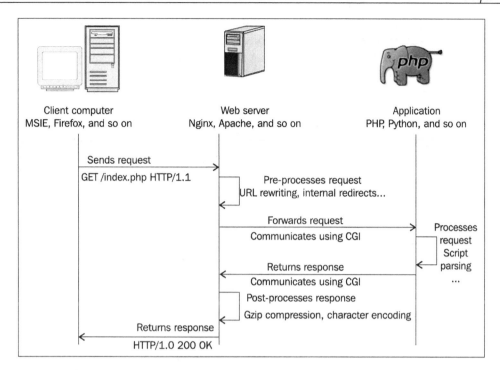

When a client attempts to visit a dynamic page, the web server receives the request and forwards it to a third-party application. The application processes the script independently and returns the produced response to the web server, which then forwards the response back to the client.

In order for the web server to communicate with that application, the CGI protocol was invented early in the 1990s.

Common Gateway Interface (CGI)

As stated in RFC 3875 (CGI protocol v1.1), designed by the Internet Society (ISOC),

> *The Common Gateway Interface (CGI) allows an HTTP server and a CGI script to share responsibility for responding to client requests. [...] The server is responsible for managing connection, data transfer, transport, and network issues related to the client request, whereas the CGI script handles the application issues such as data access and document processing.*

CGI is the protocol that describes the way information is exchanged between the web server (Nginx) and the gateway application (PHP, Python, and so on). In practice, when the web server receives a request that should be forwarded to the gateway application, it simply executes the command corresponding to the desired application, for example, /usr/bin/php. Details about the client request (such as the User Agent and other request information) are passed either as command-line arguments or in environment variables, while actual data from POST or PUT requests is transmitted via the standard input. The invoked application then writes the processed document contents to the standard output, which is recaptured by the web server.

While this technology seems simple and efficient enough at first sight, it comes with a few major drawbacks:

- A unique process is spawned for each request. Memory and other context information are lost from one request to another.

- Starting up a process can be resource-consuming for the system. Massive amount of simultaneous requests (each spawning a process) could quickly clutter a server.

- Designing an architecture where the web server and the gateway application would be located on different computers seems difficult, if not impossible.

Fast Common Gateway Interface (FastCGI)

The issues mentioned above render the CGI protocol relatively inefficient for servers that are subject to heavy load. The will to find solutions led Open Market to develop in the mid-90s an evolution of CGI—FastCGI. It has become a major standard over the past fifteen years and most web servers now offer the functionality—even proprietary server software such as Microsoft IIS.

Although the purpose remains the same, FastCGI offers significant improvements over CGI with the establishment of the following principles:

- Instead of spawning a new process for each request, FastCGI employs persistent processes that come with the ability to handle multiple requests.

- The web server and the gateway application communicate with the use of sockets such as TCP or POSIX Local IPC sockets. Consequently, both processes may be on two different computers on a network.

- The web server forwards the client request to the gateway and receives the response within a single connection; additional requests may also follow without having to create additional connections. Note that on most web servers, including Nginx and Apache, the implementation of FastCGI does not (or at least not fully) support multiplexing.

- Since FastCGI is a socket-based protocol, it can be implemented on any platform with any programming language.

Throughout this chapter, we will be setting up PHP and Python via FastCGI; though you will find the mechanism to be relatively similar in the case of other applications, such as Perl or Ruby on Rails.

Designing a FastCGI powered architecture is actually not as complex as one might imagine. As long as you have the web server and the processing application running, the only difficulty that remains is to establish the connection between both parties. The first step in that perspective is to configure the way Nginx will communicate with the FastCGI application. FastCGI compatibility with Nginx is introduced by the FastCGI module. This section details the directives that are made available by the module.

Main directives

The FastCGI module is included in the default Nginx build; you do not need to enable it manually at compile time. The following directives allow you to configure the way Nginx *passes* requests to the FastCGI application. Note that you will find a `fastcgi_params` file in the Nginx configuration folder that defines directive values that are valid for most situations.

Directive	Description

`fastcgi_pass`
 	
Context: `location`, `if`
	Specifies that the request should be passed to the FastCGI server, by indicating its location:
	
	• For TCP sockets, the syntax is: `fastcgi_pass hostname:port;`
	
	• For Unix Domain sockets, the syntax is: `fastcgi_pass unix:/path/to/fastcgi.socket;`
	
	• You may also refer to upstream blocks (read the following sections for more information): `fastcgi_pass myblock;`
	
	Examples:
	<pre>fastcgi_pass localhost:9000;
	fastcgi_pass 127.0.0.1:9000;
	fastcgi_pass unix:/tmp/fastcgi.socket;
	# Using an upstream block
	upstream fastcgi {
	  server 127.0.0.1:9000;
	  server 127.0.0.1:9001;
	}
	location ~* \.php$ {
	    fastcgi_pass fastcgi;
	}</pre>

Directive	Description

`fastcgi_param`
 	
Context: `http, server, location`
	Allows you to configure the request passed to FastCGI. Two parameters are strictly required for all FastCGI requests: `SCRIPT_FILENAME` and `QUERY_STRING`.
	
	Example:
	
	    `fastcgi_param SCRIPT_FILENAME`
	    `/home/website.com/www$fastcgi_script_`
	    `name;`
	    `fastcgi_param QUERY_STRING $query_`
	    `string;`
	
	As for POST requests, additional parameters are required: `REQUEST_METHOD`, `CONTENT_TYPE`, and `CONTENT_LENGTH`:
	
	    `fastcgi_param REQUEST_METHOD $re`
	    `quest_method;`
	    `fastcgi_param CONTENT_TYPE $content_`
	    `type;`
	    `fastcgi_param CONTENT_LENGTH $con`
	    `tent_length;`
	
	The `fastcgi_params` file that you will find in the Nginx configuration folder already includes all the necessary parameter definitions, except for the `SCRIPT_FILENAME` one that you have to specify for each of your FastCGI configurations.
	
	Syntax: `fastcgi_param PARAM value;`

`fastcgi_pass_header` Context: `http, server, location`	Specifies additional headers that should be passed to the FastCGI server. Syntax: `fastcgi_pass_header headername;` Example: `fastcgi_pass_header Authorization;`
`fastcgi_hide_header` Context: `http, server, location`	Specifies headers that should be hidden from the FastCGI server (headers that Nginx does not forward). Syntax: `fastcgi_hide_header headername;` Example: `fastcgi_hide_header X-Forwarded-For;`

Directive	Description
`fastcgi_index` Context: `http`, `server`, `location`	The FastCGI server does not support automatic directory indexes — if the requested URI ends with a /, Nginx appends the value of `fastcgi_index`. Syntax: `fastcgi_index filename;` Example: `fastcgi_index index.php;`
`fastcgi_ignore_client_abort` Context: `http`, `server`, `location`	This directive lets you define what happens if the client aborts their request to the web server. If the directive is turned on, Nginx ignores the abort request and finishes processing the request. If it's turned off, Nginx does not ignore the abort request. It interrupts the request treatment and aborts related communication with the FastCGI server. Syntax: `on` or `off` Default: `off`
`fastcgi_intercept_errors` Context: `http`, `server`, `location`	Defines whether or not Nginx should process the errors returned by the gateway or directly return error pages to the client. (Note: Error processing is done via the `error_page` directive of Nginx). Syntax: `on` or `off` Default: `off`
`fastcgi_read_timeout` Context: `http`, `server`, `location`	Defines the timeout for the response from the FastCGI application. If Nginx does not receive the response after this period, the `504 Gateway Timeout` HTTP error is returned. Syntax: Numeric value (in seconds) Default: 60 seconds
`fastcgi_connect_timeout` Context: `http`, `server`, `location`	Defines the backend server connection timeout. This is different than the read/send timeout — if Nginx is already connected to the backend server, the `fastcgi_connect_timeout` is not applicable. Syntax: Time value (in seconds) Default: 60 seconds

Directive	Description
`fastcgi_send_timeout` Context: `http, server, location`	This is the the timeout for sending data to the backend server. The timeout isn't applied to the entire response delay but rather between two write operations. Syntax: Time value (in seconds) Default value: 60

`fastcgi_split_path_info`
 	
Context: `location`
	A directive particularly useful for URLs of the following form: `http://website.com/page.php/param1/param2/`.
	
	The directive splits the path information according to the specified regular expression:
	
	`fastcgi_split_path_info ^(.+\.php)(.*)$;`
	
	This affects two variables:
	
	• `$fastcgi_script_name`: The filename of the actual script to be executed (in the example: `page.php`)
	
	• `$fastcgi_path_info`: The part of the URL that is after the script name (in the example: `/param1/param2/`)
	
	These can be employed in further parameter definitions:
	
	`fastcgi_param SCRIPT_FILENAME /home/website.com/www$fastcgi_script_name;`
	`fastcgi_param PATH_INFO $fastcgi_path_info;`
	
	Syntax: Regular expression

`fastcgi_store` Context: `http, server, location`	Enables a simple *cache store* where responses from the FastCGI application are stored as files on the storage device. When the same URI is requested again, the document is directly served from the cache store instead of forwarding the request to the FastCGI application. This directive enables or disables the cache store. Syntax: `on` or `off`

Directive	Description

`fastcgi_store_access`
 	
Context: `http, server,`
`location`
	This directive defines the access permissions applied to the files created in the context of the cache store.
	
	Syntax: `fastcgi_store_access [user:r|w|rw]`
	`[group:r|w|rw] [all:r|w|rw];`
	
	Default: `fastcgi_store_access user:rw;`

`fastcgi_temp_path`
 	
Context: `http, server,`
`location`
	Sets the path of temporary and cache store files.
	
	Syntax: File path
	
	Example:
	
	    `fastcgi_temp_path /tmp/nginx_fastcgi;`

`fastcgi_max_temp_file_`
`size`
 	
Context: `http, server,`
`location`
	Set this directive to 0 to disable the use of temporary files for FastCGI requests or to specify a maximum file size.
	
	Default value: 1 GB
	
	Syntax: Size value
	
	Example: `fastcgi_max_temp_file_size 5m;`

`fastcgi_temp_file_write_`
`size`
 	
Context: `http, server,`
`location`
	Sets the write buffer size when saving temporary files to the storage device.
	
	Syntax: Size value
	
	Default value: 2 * `proxy_buffer_size`

`fastcgi_buffers`
 	
Context: `http, server,`
`location`
	Sets the amount and size of buffers that will be used for reading the response data from the FastCGI application.
	
	Syntax: `fastcgi_buffers amount size;`
	
	Default: 8 buffers, 4 k or 8 k each, depending on platform
	
	Example:
	
	    `fastcgi_buffers 8 4k;`

`fastcgi_buffer_size`
 	
Context: `http, server,`
`location`
	Sets the size of the buffer for reading the beginning of the response from the FastCGI application, which usually contains simple header data.
	
	The default value corresponds to the size of 1 buffer, as defined by the previous directive (`fastcgi_buffers`).
	
	Syntax: Size value
	
	Example:
	
	    `fastcgi_buffer_size 4k;`

Directive	Description
`fastcgi_send_lowat` Context: `http`, `server`, `location`	An option allowing you to make use of the `SO_SNDLOWAT` flag for TCP sockets under FreeBSD only. This value defines the minimum number of bytes in the buffer for output operations. Syntax: Numeric value (size) Default value: 0

`fastcgi_pass_request_body`
 	
`fastcgi_pass_request_headers`
 	
Context: `http`, `server`, `location`
	Defines whether or not, respectively, the request body and extra request headers should be passed on to the backend server.
	
	Syntax: `on` or `off`;
	
	Default: `on`

`fastcgi_ignore_headers` Context: `http`, `server`, `location`	Prevents Nginx from processing one of the following four headers from the backend server response: `X-Accel-Redirect`, `X-Accel-Expires`, `Expires`, `Cache-Control`. Syntax: `fastcgi_ignore_headers header1 [header2...]`;

`fastcgi_next_upstream`
 	
Context: `http`, `server`, `location`
	When `fastcgi_pass` is connected to an upstream block, this directive defines the cases where requests should be abandoned and re-sent to the next upstream server of the block. The directive accepts a combination of values among the following:
	
	• `error`: An error occurred while communicating or attempting to communicate with the server
	• `timeout`: A timeout occurs during transfers or connection attempts
	• `invalid_header`: The backend server returned an empty or invalid response
	• `http_500`, `http_502`, `http_503`, `http_504`, `http_404`: In case such HTTP errors occur, Nginx switches to the next upstream
	• `off`: Forbids from using the next upstream server
	
	Examples:
	`fastcgi_next_upstream error timeout http_504;`
	`fastcgi_next_upstream timeout invalid_header;`

Directive	Description
`fastcgi_catch_stderr` Context: `http, server, location`	Allows you to intercept some of the error messages sent to `stderr` (Standard Error stream) and store them in the Nginx error log.
	Syntax: `fastcgi_catch_stderr filter;`
	Example: `fastcgi_catch_stderr "PHP Fatal error:";`

FastCGI caching

Once you have correctly configured Nginx to work with your FastCGI application, you may optionally make use of the following directives that will help you improve the overall server performance by setting up a cache system.

Directive	Description
`fastcgi_cache` Context: `http, server, location`	Defines a cache zone. The identifier given to the zone is to be reused in further directives
	Syntax: `fastcgi_cache zonename;`
	Example: `fastcgi_cache cache1;`
`fastcgi_cache_key` Context: `http, server, location`	This directive defines the cache key, in other words, what differentiates a cache entry from another. If the cache key is set to `$uri`, as a result, all requests with a similar `$uri` will correspond to the same cache entry. It's not enough for most dynamic websites; you also need to include the query string arguments in the cache key so that `/index.php` and `/index.php?page=contact` do not point to the same cache entry.
	Syntax: `fastcgi_cache_key key;`
	Example: `fastcgi_cache "$scheme$host$request_uri $cookie_user";`
`fastcgi_cache_methods` Context: `http, server, location`	Defines the HTTP methods eligible for caching. GET and HEAD are included by default and cannot be disabled. You may, for example, enable caching of POST requests.
	Syntax: `fastcgi_cache_methods METHOD;`
	Example: `fastcgi_cache_methods POST;`

Directive	Description
`fastcgi_cache_min_uses` Context: `http, server, location`	Defines the minimum amount of hits before a request is eligible for caching. By default, the response of a request is cached after one hit (next requests with the same cache key will receive the cached response). Syntax: Numeric value Example: `fastcgi_cache_min_uses 1;`
`fastcgi_cache_path` Context: `http, server, location`	Indicates the directory for storing cached files, as well as other parameters. Syntax: `fastcgi_cache_path path [levels=numbers keys_zone=name:size inactive=time max_size=size];` The additional parameters are: • `levels`: Indicates the depth of subdirectories (usually 1:2 is enough) • `keys_zone`: Lets you make use of the zone you previously declared with the `fastcgi_cache` directive, and indicate the size to occupy in memory • `inactive`: If a cached response is not used within the specified time frame, it's removed from the cache • `max_size`: Defines the maximum size of the entire cache Example: `fastcgi_cache_path /tmp/nginx_cache levels=1:2 zone=zone1:10m inactive=10m max_size=200M;`
`fastcgi_cache_use_stale` Context: `http, server, location`	Defines whether or not Nginx should serve stale cached data in certain circumstances (in regards to the gateway). If you use `fastcgi_cache_use_stale timeout`, and if the gateway times out, then Nginx will serve cached data. Syntax: `fastcgi_cache_use_stale [updating] [error] [timeout] [invalid_header] [http_500];` Example: `fastcgi_cache_use_stale error timeout;`

Directive	Description

`fastcgi_cache_valid`
 	
Context: `http, server, location`
	This directive allows you to customize the caching time for different kinds of response codes. You may cache responses associated to `404` error codes for 1 minute, and on the opposite cache, `200 OK` responses for 10 minutes or more. This directive can be inserted more than once:
	
	`fastcgi_cache_valid 404 1m;`
	`fastcgi_cache_valid 500 502 504 5m;`
	`fastcgi_cache_valid 200 10;`
	
	Syntax: `fastcgi_cache_valid code1 [code2...] time;`

Here is a full Nginx FastCGI cache configuration example, making use of most of the cache-related directives described above:

```
fastcgi_cache phpcache;
fastcgi_cache_key "$scheme$host$request_uri"; # $request_uri includes
the request arguments (such as /page.php?arg=value)
fastcgi_cache_min_uses 2; # after 2 hits, a request receives a cached
response
fastcgi_cache_path /tmp/cache levels=1:2 keys_zone=phpcache:10m inac
tive=30m max_size=500M;
fastcgi_cache_use_stale updating timeout;
fastcgi_cache_valid 404 1m;
fastcgi_cache_valid 500 502 504 5m;
```

Since these directives are valid for pretty much any virtual host configuration, you may want to save these in a separate file (`fastcgi_cache`) that you include at the appropriate place:

```
server {
    server_name website.com;
    location ~* \.php$ {
        fastcgi_pass 127.0.0.1:9000;
        fastcgi_param SCRIPT_FILENAME
/home/website.com/www$fastcgi_script_name;
        fastcgi_param PATH_INFO $fastcgi_script_name;
        include fastcgi_params;
        include fastcgi_cache;
    }
}
```

Upstream blocks

With the FastCGI module, and as you will discover in the next chapter with the Proxy module too, Nginx forwards requests to backend servers. It communicates with processes using either FastCGI or simply by behaving like a regular HTTP client. Either way, the backend server (a FastCGI application, another web server, and so on) may be hosted on a different server in the case of load-balanced architectures.

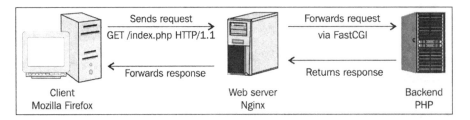

Now, the general issue with applications (such as PHP) is that they are quite resource-consuming, especially in terms of CPU. You may thus find yourself forced to balance the load across multiple servers, resulting in the following architecture:

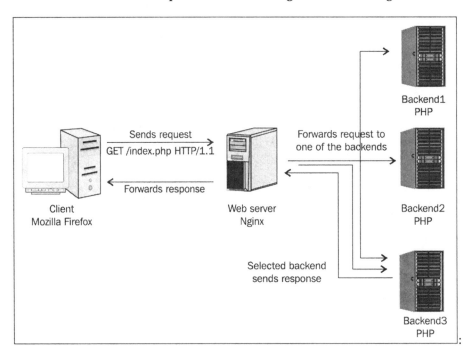

In this case, Nginx is connected to multiple backend servers. To establish such a configuration, a new module comes into play – the **Upstream module**.

Module syntax

This module allows you to declare named `upstream` blocks that define lists of servers.

```
upstream phpfpm {
    server 192.168.0.50:9000;
    server 192.168.0.51:9000;
    server 192.168.0.52:9000;
}
```

When defining the FastCGI configuration, connect to the `upstream` block:

```
server {
    server_name website.com;
    location ~* \.php$ {
        fastcgi_pass phpfpm;
        [...]
    }
}
```

In this case, requests eligible to FastCGI will be forwarded to one of the backend servers defined in the upstream block.

A question you might ask is how does Nginx decide which backend server is to be employed for each request? And the answer is simple—the default method of the Upstream module is round robin. However, this method is not necessarily the best. Two requests from the same visitor might be processed by two different servers, and that could be a problem for many reasons, for example, when PHP sessions are stored on the backend server and are not replicated across the other servers.

To ensure that requests from a same visitor always get processed by the same backend server, you may enable the `ip_hash` option when declaring the `upstream` block:

```
upstream phpfpm {
    ip_hash;
    server 192.168.0.50:9000;
    server 192.168.0.51:9000;
    server 192.168.0.52:9000;
}
```

This will distribute requests based on the visitors IP address employing a regular round robin algorithm. However, be aware that client IP addresses are sometimes subject to change for various reasons — dynamic IP refresh, proxy switching, Tor, and so on. Consequently, the ip_hash mechanism cannot fully guarantee that clients will always be involved to the same upstream server.

Server directive

The server directive that you place within upstream blocks accepts several parameters that influence the backend selection by Nginx:

- weight=n: Lets you indicate a numeric value that will affect the weight of the backend server. If you create an upstream block with two backend servers and set the weight of the first one to 2, it will be selected twice more often:

```
upstream php {
    server 192.168.0.1:9000 weight=2;
    server 192.168.0.2:9000;
}
```

This option is ignored if the upstream block is in the ip_hash mode.

- max_fails=n: Defines the number of communication failures that should occur (in the time frame specified with the fail_timeout parameter below) before Nginx considers the server inoperative.

- fail_timeout=n: Defines the time frame within which the maximum failure count applies. If Nginx fails to communicate with the backend server max_fails times over fail_timeout seconds, the server is considered inoperative.

- down: If you mark a backend server as down, the server is no longer used. This only applies when the ip_hash directive is enabled.

- backup: If you mark a backend server as backup, Nginx will not make use of the server until all other servers (servers not marked as backup) are down or inoperative.

These parameters are all optional and can be used altogether:

```
upstream phpbackend {
    server localhost:9000 weight=5;
    server 192.168.0.1 max_fails=5 fail_timeout=60s;
    server unix:/tmp/backend backup;
}
```

PHP with Nginx

We are now going to configure PHP to work together with Nginx via FastCGI. There are some very particular steps involved in the design of such a setup; the most bothersome being that you, most likely, cannot utilize your current build of PHP. This issue, among others, will be addressed throughout this section.

Architecture

Before starting the setup process, it's important to understand the way PHP will interact with Nginx. We have established that FastCGI is a communication protocol running through sockets, which implies that there is a client and a server. The client is obviously Nginx; as for the server, well, the answer is actually more complicated than just PHP.

By default, PHP supports the FastCGI protocol. The PHP binary processes scripts and is able to interact with Nginx via sockets. However, we are going to use an additional component to improve the overall process management.

There are several solutions available on the web, including actual PHP scripts opening sockets and supporting the FastCGI protocol. The solution we have here is **PHP-FPM** for *PHP FastCGI Process Manager*. It is currently acknowledged to be the most efficient solution in terms of features and performance, even though it may seem a little complex to set up.

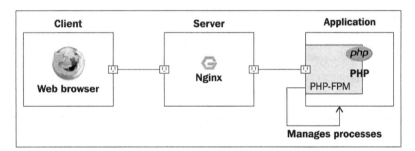

PHP-FPM takes FastCGI support to a whole new level; its numerous features are detailed in the next section.

PHP-FPM

As you can see in the previous figure, PHP-FPM is not actually a program *per se*. In its current form, it comes as a patch that you need to apply to the original PHP source code. The advantage of being completely integrated to PHP is that it reduces the possible memory and CPU overhead that could be the result of making use of a standalone application. The inconvenience is that you are going to have to build PHP specifically for it; you will not be able to utilize your current PHP setup.

PHP-FPM introduces new elements to your PHP structure:

- It automatically *daemonizes* PHP, turning it into a background process.
- It provides a command-line script for managing PHP processes. You may `start`/`stop`/`restart`/`reload` PHP-CGI processes that are listening to connections. The script highly resembles the regular *service* script: `php-fpm start`, `php-fpm stop`, `php-fpm reload`, and so on.
- Many more advantages, such as improved logging, IP address restrictions, and so on.

Setting up PHP and PHP-FPM

In this section, we will detail the process of downloading and compiling a fresh build of PHP, and more importantly, applying the PHP-FPM patch.

Downloading and extracting

You will need a fresh build of PHP. Supported versions of PHP, at the time of writing, range from 4.4.7 to 5.3.x. Visit the official website at `www.php.net` to download one of these versions. Then you will need to download the PHP-FPM patch corresponding to the exact version that you downloaded from `www.php-fpm.org`.

```
[root@website.com ~]# wget http://php.net/get/php-
5.3.0.tar.gz/from/www.php.net/mirror
```

```
[root@website.com ~]# wget http://php-fpm.org/downloads/php-5.3.0-
fpm-0.5.12.diff.gz
```

Once downloaded, extract the PHP archive with the `tar` command:

```
[root@website.com ~]# tar xzf php-5.3.0.tar.gz
```

Patching

The second archive that you downloaded is the PHP-FPM patch. It needs to be applied to the proper version of PHP. You downloaded PHP 5.3.0; you thus need the PHP-FPM patch for PHP 5.3.0. The following command reads the content of the patch and pipes it to the `patch` tool, which will apply the code changes on the specified directory:

```
[root@website.com ~]# gzip -cd php-5.3.0-fpm-0.5.12.diff.gz | patch -d
php-5.3.0 -p1
```

Upon executing this command, you should see a long list of patched files:

```
patching file configure

patching file configure.in

patching file libevent/aclocal.m4

[...]

patching file sapi/cgi/Makefile.frag

[root@website.com ~]#
```

Requirements

There are two main requirements for building PHP with PHP-FPM—the `libevent` and `libxml` development libraries. If these are not already installed on your system, you will need to install them with your system's package manager.

For Red Hat-based systems and other systems using Yum as the package manager:

```
yum install libevent-devel libxml2-devel
```

For Ubuntu, Debian, and other systems that use Apt or Aptitude:

```
aptitude install libxml2-dev libevent-dev
```

Building PHP

Once you have installed all the dependencies, you may start building PHP. Similar to other applications and libraries that were previously installed, you will basically need three commands: `configure`, `make`, and `make install`. Be aware that this will install a new instance of the application; if you already have PHP set up on your system, it will not override it, but instead be installed in a different location that is revealed to you during the `make install` command execution.

The first step (`configure`) is critical here as you will need to enable the PHP-FPM options in order for PHP to include the required functionality. There is a great variety of `configure` options that you can include in the `configure` command, some are necessary to enable important features such as database interaction, regular expressions, file compression support, web server integration, and so on. All the possible configure options are listed when you run this command:

```
[root@website.com php-5.3.0]# ./configure --help
```

A minimal command may be used, but be aware that a great deal of features will be missing. If you wish to include other components, additional dependencies may be needed, which are not documented here. In all cases, the `--enable-fpm` switch should be included:

```
[root@website.com php-5.3.0]# ./configure --enable-fpm
```

The next step is to build the application and install it at the same time:

```
[root@website.com php-5.3.0]# make all install
```

This process may take a while depending on your system specifications.

Post-install configuration

Begin by configuring your newly installed PHP, for example, copying the `php.ini` of your previous setup over the new one. The next step is to configure PHP-FPM—open up the `php-fpm.conf` file, by default, located in `/usr/local/etc/`.

The file contains some important configuration directives that we will reuse later:

- Edit the users and groups for the Unix socket and the processes
- Address and port on which PHP-FPM will be listening
- Amount of simultaneous requests that will be served
- IP address(es) allowed to connect to PHP-FPM

Running and controlling

Once you made the appropriate changes to the PHP-FPM configuration file, you may start it with the following command:

```
[root@website.com ~]# /usr/sbin/php-fpm start
```

If all goes according to plan, you should be greeted with the following message:

```
Starting php_fpm  done
```

Additionally, you may control the process with the following commands:

```
php-fpm stop; # Stops PHP-FPM

php-fpm quit; # Gracefully shuts down PHP-FPM

php-fpm restart; # Stops and starts PHP-FPM again

php-fpm reload; # Reloads configuration

php-fpm logrotate; # Performs a rotation of log files
```

Nginx configuration

If you have managed to start PHP-FPM, you are ready to tweak your Nginx configuration file to establish the connection between both parties. The following server block is a simple valid template on which you can base your own website configuration:

```
server {
    server_name .website.com; # server name, accepting www
    listen 80; # listen on port 80
    root /home/website/www; # our root document path
    index index.php; # default request filename: index.php

    location ~* \.php$ { # for requests ending with .php
    # specify the listening address and port that you configured
previously
        fastcgi_pass 127.0.0.1:9000;
        # the document path to be passed to PHP-FPM
        fastcgi_param SCRIPT_FILENAME $document_root$fastcgi_script_
name;
        # the script filename to be passed to PHP-FPM
        fastcgi_param PATH_INFO $fastcgi_script_name;
        # include other FastCGI related configuration settings
        include fastcgi_params;
    }
}
```

After saving the configuration file, reload Nginx: `/usr/local/nginx/sbin/nginx -s reload` or `service nginx reload`. Create a simple script at the root of your website to make sure PHP is being correctly interpreted:

```
[root@website.com ~]# echo "<?php phpinfo(); ?>" >/home/website/www/
index.php
```

Fire up your favorite web browser and load `http://localhost/` (or your website URL). You should be seeing something similar to the next screenshot—the PHP server information page.

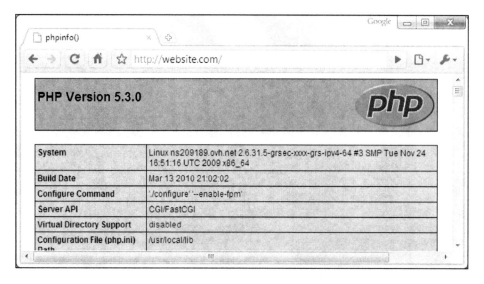

Note that you may run into the occasional `403 Forbidden` HTTP error if the file and directory access permissions aren't properly configured. If that is the case, make sure that you specified the correct user and group in the `php-fpm.conf` file and that the directory and files are readable by PHP.

Python and Nginx

Python is a popular object-oriented programming language available on many platforms, from Unix-based systems to Windows. It is also available for Java and the Microsoft .NET platform. If you are interested in configuring Python to work with Nginx, it's likely that you already have a clear idea of what Python does. We are going to use Python as server-side web programming language, with the help of the Django framework.

Django

Django is an open source web development framework for Python that aims at making web development simple and easy, as its slogan states—"The Web framework for perfectionists with deadlines". More information is available on the project website: `www.djangoproject.com`.

Among other interesting features such as a dynamic administrative interface, a caching framework, and unit tests, Django comes with a FastCGI manager. It's going to make things much simpler for us from the perspective of running Python scripts through Nginx.

Setting up Python and Django

We are going to install Python and Django on your Linux operating system, along with the prerequisites. The process is relatively smooth and mostly consists of running a couple of commands that rarely cause trouble.

Python

Python should be available on your package manager repositories. To install it, run the following commands. For Red Hat-based systems and other systems using Yum as the package manager:

```
yum install python python-devel
```

For Ubuntu, Debian, and other systems that use Apt or Aptitude:

```
aptitude install python python-dev
```

The package manager will resolve dependencies by itself.

Django

In order to install Django, we will use a different approach. We will be downloading the source directly from the Django SVN in order to make sure we get the latest version.

 SVN is an acronym for Subversion, a file management and revision system. Its main purpose is to maintain a collaborative working environment for development projects and to conserve historical versions of source code and other files. By connecting to an SVN repository, you are able to download specific versions of a project's source code.

The first step is thus to install Subversion, the tool that will allow us to synchronize with the Django repository. For Red Hat-based systems and other systems using Yum as the package manager, use:

```
yum install subversion
```

For Ubuntu, Debian, and other systems that use Apt or Aptitude:

```
aptitude install subversion
```

The package manager will resolve dependencies by itself.

Once Subversion is installed, we can download the source files into a dedicated folder, and install Django:

```
[root@website.com ~]# mkdir django && cd django
[root@website.com django]# svn co http://code.djangoproject.com/svn/
django/trunk/
[...]
[root@website.com django]# cd trunk
[root@website.com trunk]# python setup.py install
```

Finally, there is one last component required for running the Python FastCGI manager — the `flup` library, which provides the actual FastCGI protocol implementation. For Red Hat-based systems and other systems using Yum as the package manager (EPEL repositories must be enabled, otherwise you will need to build from source):

```
yum install python-flup
```

For Ubuntu, Debian, and other systems that use Apt or Aptitude:

```
aptitude install python-flup
```

Starting the FastCGI process manager

We will not detail how to start building a website with the Django framework here. Once that part is done, you will find a manage.py Python script that comes with the default project template. Move to the directory of this file, and run the following command:

```
[root@website.com www]# python manage.py runfcgi method=prefork
host=127.0.0.1 port=9000 pidfile=/var/run/ django.pid
```

If everything was correctly configured and the dependencies properly installed, running this command should produce no output, which is often a good sign; the FastCGI process manager is now running in the background waiting for connections. You can verify that the application is running with the ps command, for example, by executing ps aux | grep python. All we have to do now is to set up the virtual host in the Nginx configuration file.

Nginx configuration

The Nginx configuration is similar to the PHP one:

```
server {
    server_name .website.com;
    listen 80;
    root /home/website/www;
    index index.html;

    location / {
        fastcgi_pass 127.0.0.1:9000;
        fastcgi_param SCRIPT_FILENAME  $document_root$fastcgi_script_
name;
        fastcgi_param PATH_INFO $fastcgi_script_name;
        include fastcgi_params;
    }
}
```

Summary

Whether you use PHP, Python, or any other CGI application, you should now have a clear idea of how to get your scripts processed behind Nginx. There are all sorts of implementations on the web for mainstream programming languages and the FastCGI protocol, due to its well-acknowledged efficiency, is starting to take over server-integrated solutions such as Apache's mod_php, mod_wsgi and many others.

Though if you are unsure about connecting Nginx directly to those server applications, because you already have a well-functioning system architecture in place (for example, Apache with mod_php), you may want to consider the option offered in the next chapter—*Installing Nginx on top of your existing Apache setup.*

7
Apache and Nginx Together

If you are reading this book, chances are you already have some good knowledge of the Apache web server with its nearly 55 percent market share (as of early 2010 according to a Netcraft Survey). In fact, a lot of the administrators interested in Nginx are people who have encountered issues with the former regarding slow downs, it being complex to configure, unresponsive at times, security issues, and so on. Consequently, the first idea that comes to mind is to replace Apache with an alternative such as Nginx. However, there is a possibility that is not often considered, as it sounds a little far-fetched at first, namely, running both Nginx and Apache together. When you look into it, this solution offers a great deal of advantages, especially for administrators looking for a quick and efficient solution.

This chapter covers:

- An introduction to the reverse-proxy mechanism
- The advantages and disadvantages of the architecture
- Discovering the Proxy module of Nginx
- Configuring Nginx to work with Apache
- Reconfiguring Apache to work as a backend server
- Additional tweaks and notes

Nginx as reverse proxy

First, let's make it clear—the reverse proxy mechanism that we are going to describe in this chapter is not the optimal solution. It should be employed in problematic cases such as the following:

- When you already have Apache installed with complex configuration files that can hardly be ported to Nginx or you do not have the time or the will to completely switch to Nginx

- When your system operates a frontend system management panel such as Parallels Plesk, cPanel, or other solutions that generate Apache configuration files automatically

- When a functionality that your project or architecture requires is available with Apache but not with Nginx

In most other cases, a complete switch to Nginx is in order. Chapter 8 provides a good description of the process.

Understanding the issue

The reverse proxy mechanism mainly addresses one issue – the overall serving speed of Apache. Due to the massive amount of modules and other components that Apache loads in memory (for each HTTP request that it receives) your server may rapidly clutter when massive influxes of requests come in at the same time. One could say that Apache focuses on functionality at the expense of optimization and processing speeds. In practice, this results in excessive memory and CPU overhead. Oppositely, Nginx has proven to be both lightweight and stable, serving a larger amount of requests (using lesser RAM and CPU time in comparison to Apache).

What do we make of that? Before answering this question, it would be interesting to analyze the type of content that will be delivered by your server. Let us visit a regular web page that millions of people load every day: www.yahoo.com. While it's not fully representative of the World Wide Web, our analysis will be valid for a good number of websites and the Yahoo! homepage is the perfect illustration to the problem that we face.

When a regular user visits yahoo.com, the web browser actually has to download a great amount of data. Here are the different files that the browser downloads:

Media type	File/Request count	Total size	Total Gzipped Size
HTML source code	1	157.6 KB	52.5 KB
Javascript (.js) code files and libraries	6	382.1 KB	112.3 KB
Cascading Style Sheet (.css) files	3	256.8 KB	42.8 KB
Flash animations (.swf)	2	61.4 KB	61.4 KB
Images linked from CSS files (.png, .gif)	18	43.0 KB	43.0 KB
Regular images (.gif, .jpg)	11	73.3 KB	73.3 KB
TOTAL	41	974.2 KB	385.3 KB

These figures reflect a snapshot taken on March 20, 2010. Results may differ slightly according to your geographical location, date of visit, and other criteria.

The amount of data to download may not be too surprising—after all the 385.3 KB (make that 400~450 KB including cookie data and other overhead) can be transferred in less than a second with the fast Internet connections that are now being offered in many countries.

A much bigger problem, in our case, is the amount of requests that the server will have to handle. For all the first-time visitors, and for any web browser that does not use cached data to load this page, a minimum of 41 HTTP requests will be processed by the web server. Thankfully, a great portion of people will have most of the files cached, but that is never good if you have something to update. Besides, cached data is bound to expire one day or another.

Can your web server process 41 HTTP requests in less than a second? Can it process 41,000 (1000 page views/second)? Can it process 410,000? If so, you probably have the infrastructure to support such a load. Either way, you are better off with Nginx—as you have noticed, 40 out of the 41 requests are for static content—image files, CSS, JavaScript code files, and so on. Provided the speed at which Nginx serves those files, we could design an architecture that lets Nginx serve static files and Apache to handle dynamic content.

The reverse proxy mechanism

Somewhat like the FastCGI architecture described in the previous chapter, we are going to be running Nginx as a frontend server, in other words, in direct communication with the outside world; whereas Apache will be running as a backend server and will only exchange data with Nginx.

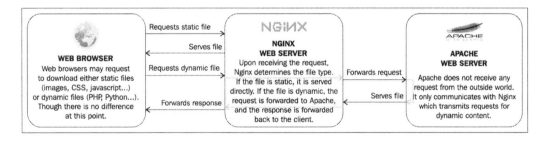

There are now two web servers running and processing requests:

- Nginx positioned as a frontend server (in other words, as reverse proxy) receives all the requests coming from the outside world. It filters them, either serving static files directly to the client or forwarding dynamic content requests to Apache.

- Apache runs as a backend server; it only communicates with Nginx. It may be hosted on the same computer as the frontend, in which case, the listening port must be edited to leave port 80 available to Nginx. Alternatively, you can employ multiple backend servers (using the `upstream` block, as seen in Chapter 6) on different machines and share the load.

To communicate and interact with each other, both processes will not be using FastCGI. Instead, as the name suggests, Nginx acts as a simple proxy server — it receives HTTP requests from client (acting as HTTP server) and forwards them to the backend server (acting as HTTP client). There is, thus, no new protocol or software involved. The mechanism is handled by the Proxy module of Nginx, detailed later in the chapter.

Advantages and disadvantages

The main purpose of setting up Nginx as frontend and giving Apache a simple backend role is to improve the *serving speed*. As we established, a great amount of requests coming from clients are for static files, and static files are served much faster by Nginx. The overall performance sharply improves both on the client side and server side.

On a lesser scale, Apache has experienced quite a number of *security* issues in the past, pushing forward new releases. You are forced to keep your system up to date in order to make sure you have a completely secure web server. But it would be reasonable to say that the more popular a web server is, the more likely bugs and security issues are to be discovered. Oppositely, the latest stable versions of Nginx have, so far, been apparently secure and the author had no other choice than to focus his rare updates on new functionality over security fixes.

Eventually, if you adopt this solution, you will find it particularly *easy* to set up as you nearly have no modification to make when it comes to Apache configuration. All it requires is a simple port change, but that isn't even necessary if you set up Nginx and Apache on different servers. Your setup works *as it is*, which is particularly useful if you already spent hours configuring Apache to work with server-side preprocessors such as PHP, Python, or others.

On the other hand, you are still deporting requests for dynamic content to Apache, which is, most of the time, slower than a combination of Nginx and FastCGI. The optimal solution would be to completely switch to Nginx and leave out Apache.

Besides, since Nginx is installed as the frontend, it implies that it receives *raw* requests from users. This implies that the URI comes in its original form, which can lead to confusion for Nginx; it will not be able to make the difference between static and dynamic content. You have two choices to solve this issue—either port your rewrite rules to Nginx or redirect any request that results in a 404 error to the Apache backend. To explain the latter, a request such as `/articles/43515-us-economy-strengthens.html` most likely does not correspond to any file on your system—it's meant to be rewritten. You may then check for the existence of such a file from within the Nginx configuration; if it doesn't exist, redirect the request to Apache.

Last but not the least, and this will be further discussed in the last section of this chapter, there may be some issues with control panel software such as Parallels Plesk, cPanel, and others. These panels are very useful for administrators, as they automate some of the most bothersome tasks like adding virtual hosts to the Apache configuration, creating e-mail accounts, configuring the DNS daemon, and many more. The two main issues being:

- These control panels allow you to apply changes on the web server configuration and based on your changes, they automatically generate valid configuration files for the server. Unfortunately, so far these control panels only offer Apache compatibility; they do not generate Nginx configuration files. So any change that you make will have no effect.

- Whether you completely replace Apache by Nginx or go for the reverse-proxy mechanism, Nginx usually ends up running on port 80. The control panel software generating configuration files is unaware of this fact and might be stubborn; when generating configuration files, it will systematically reset the Apache port to 80, creating conflicts with Nginx.

Both issues will be discussed again later in the chapter.

Nginx Proxy module

Similar to the previous chapter, the first step towards establishing the new architecture will be to discover the appropriate module. The default Nginx build comes with the Proxy module, which allows forwarding of HTTP requests from the client to a backend server. We will be configuring multiple aspects of the module:

- Basic address and port information on the backend server
- Caching, buffering, and temporary file options

- Limits, timeout, and error behavior
- Other miscellaneous options

All these options are available via directives that we will learn to configure throughout this section.

Main directives

This first set of directives will allow you to establish basic configuration such as the location of the backend server, information to be passed, and how it should be passed.

Directive	Description

proxy_pass
 	
Context: location, if
	Specifies that the request should be forwarded to the backend server by indicating its location:
	
	• For TCP sockets, the syntax is: proxy_pass http://hostname:port;
	
	• For Unix domain sockets, the syntax is: proxy_pass http://unix:/path/to/file.socket;
	
	• You may also refer to upstream blocks: proxy_pass http://myblock;
	
	• Instead of http://, you can use https:// for secure traffic. Additional URI parts as well as the use of variables are allowed.
	
	Examples:
	<pre>proxy_pass http://localhost:8080;
	proxy_pass http://127.0.0.1:8080;
	proxy_pass http://unix:/tmp/nginx.sock;
	proxy_pass https://192.168.0.1;
	proxy_pass http://localhost:8080/uri/;
	proxy_pass http://unix:/tmp/nginx.sock:/uri/;
	proxy_pass http://$server_name:8080;
	# Using an upstream block
	upstream backend {
	    server 127.0.0.1:8080;
	    server 127.0.0.1:8081;
	}
	location ~* \.php$ {
	    proxy_pass http://backend;
	}</pre>

Directive	Description
`proxy_method` Context: `http, server, location`	Allows overriding the HTTP method of the request to be forwarded to the backend server. If you specify POST, for example, all requests forwarded to the backend server will be POST requests. Syntax: `proxy_method method;` Example: `proxy_method POST;`
`proxy_hide_header` Context: `http, server, location`	By default, as Nginx prepares the response received from the backend server to be forwarded back to the client, it ignores some of the headers: `Date`, `Server`, `X-Pad`, and `X-Accel-*`. With this directive, you can specify an additional header line to be hidden from the client. You may insert this directive multiple times with one header name for each. Syntax: `proxy_hide_header header_name;` Example: `proxy_hide_header Cache-Control;`
`proxy_pass_header` Context: `http, server, location`	Related to the above directive, this directive forces some of the ignored headers to be passed on to the client. Syntax: `proxy_pass_header headername;` Example: `proxy_pass_header Date;`

`proxy_pass_ request_body`
 	
`proxy_pass_ request_headers`
 	
Context: `http, server, location`
	Defines whether or not respectively the request body and extra request headers should be passed on to the backend server.
	
	Syntax: on or `off`;
	
	Default: `on`

Directive	Description

`proxy_redirect`
 	
Context: `http, server,`
`location`
	Allows you to rewrite the URL appearing in the Location HTTP header on redirections triggered by the backend server.
	
	Syntax: `off`, `default`, or the URL of your choice
	
	• `off`: Redirections are forwarded *as it is*.
	
	• `default`: The value of the `proxy_pass` directive is used as the hostname and the current path of the document is appended. Note that the `proxy_redirect` directive must be inserted after the `proxy_pass` directive as the configuration is parsed sequentially.
	
	• URL: Replace a part of the URL by another.
	
	• Additionally, you may use variables in the rewritten URL.
	
	Examples:
	`proxy_redirect off;`
	`proxy_redirect default;`
	`proxy_redirect http://localhost:8080/`
	`http://example.com/;`
	`proxy_redirect http://localhost:8080/wiki/ /w/;`
	`proxy_redirect http://localhost:8080/ http://`
	`$host/;`

`proxy_next_`
`upstream`
 	
Context: `http, server,`
`location`
	When `proxy_pass` is connected to an upstream block, this directive defines the cases where requests should be abandoned and re-sent to the next upstream server of the block. The directive accepts a combination of values among the following:
	
	• `error`: An error occurred while communicating or attempting to communicate with the server
	
	• `timeout`: A timeout occurs during transfers or connection attempts
	
	• `invalid_header`: The backend server returned an empty or invalid response
	
	• `http_500`, `http_502`, `http_503`, `http_504`, `http_404`: In case such HTTP errors occur, Nginx switches to the next upstream
	
	• `off`: Forbids from using the next upstream server
	
	Examples:
	`proxy_next_upstream error timeout http_504;`
	`proxy_next_upstream timeout invalid_header;`

Caching, buffering, and temporary files

Ideally, as much as possible, you should reduce the amount of requests being forwarded to the backend server. The following directive will help you build a caching system, as well as control buffering options and the way Nginx handles temporary files.

Directive	Description
`proxy_buffer_size` Context: `http, server, location`	Sets the size of the buffer for reading the beginning of the response from the backend server, which usually contains simple header data. The default value corresponds to the size of 1 buffer, as defined by the directive above (`proxy_buffers`). Syntax: Numeric value (size) Example: `proxy_buffer_size 4k;`
`proxy_buffering` Context: `http, server, location`	Defines whether or not the response from the backend server should be buffered. If set to `on`, Nginx will store the response data in memory using the memory space offered by the buffers. If the buffers are full, the response data will be stored as a temporary file. If the directive is set to `off`, the response is directly forwarded to the client. Syntax: `on` or `off` Default: `on`
`proxy_buffers` Context: `http, server, location`	Sets the amount and size of buffers that will be used for reading the response data from the backend server. Syntax: `proxy_buffers amount size;` Default: 8 buffers, 4 k or 8 k each depending on platform Example: `fastcgi_buffers 8 4k;`
`proxy_busy_buffers_size` Context: `http, server, location`	When the backend-received data accumulated in buffers exceeds the specified value, buffers are flushed and data is sent to the client. Syntax: Numeric value (size) Default: 2 * `proxy_buffer_size`
`proxy_cache` Context: `http, server, location`	Defines a cache zone. The identifier given to the zone is to be reused in further directives. Syntax: `proxy_cache zonename;` Example: `proxy_cache cache1;`

Directive	Description
`proxy_cache_key` Context: `http`, `server`, `location`	This directive defines the cache key, in other words, it differentiates one cache entry from another. If the cache key is set to `$uri`, as a result, all requests with this `$uri` will work as a single cache entry. But that's not enough for most dynamic websites — you also need to include the query string arguments in the cache key, so that `/index.php` and `/index.php?page=contact` do not point to the same cache entry. Syntax: `proxy_cache_key key;` Example: `proxy_cache_key "$scheme$host$request_uri $cookie_user";`
`proxy_cache_path` Context: `http`	Indicates the directory for storing cached files, as well as other parameters. Syntax: `proxy_cache_path path [levels=numbers keys_zone=name:size inactive=time max_size=size];` The additional parameters are: • `levels`: Indicates the depth level of subdirectories (usually 1:2 is enough) • `keys_zone`: Lets you make use of the zone you previously declared with the `proxy_cache` directive and indicates the size to occupy in memory • `inactive`: If a cached response is not used within the specified time frame, it is removed from the cache • `max_size`: Defines the maximum size of the entire cache Example: `proxy_cache_path /tmp/nginx_cache levels=1:2 zone=zone1:10m inactive=10m max_size=200M;`
`proxy_cache_methods` Context: `http`, `server`, `location`	Defines the HTTP methods eligible for caching. GET and HEAD are included by default and cannot be disabled. You may (for example) enable caching of POST requests. Syntax: `proxy_cache_methods METHOD;` Example: `proxy_cache_methods POST;`

Directive	Description
`proxy_cache_min_uses` Context: `http, server, location`	Defines the minimum amount of hits before a request is eligible for caching. By default, the response of a request is cached after one hit (next requests with the same cache key will receive the cached response). Syntax: Numeric value Example: `proxy_cache_min_uses 1;`

`proxy_cache_valid`
 	
Context: `http, server, location`
	This directive allows you to customize the caching time for different kinds of response codes. You may cache responses associated with 404 error codes for 1 minute, and on the opposite cache, `200 OK` responses for 10 minutes or more. This directive can be inserted more than once:
	
	`proxy_cache_valid 404 1m;`
	`proxy_cache_valid 500 502 504 5m;`
	`proxy_cache_valid 200 10;`
	
	Syntax: `proxy_cache_valid code1 [code2...] time;`

`proxy_cache_use_stale` Context: `http, server, location`	Defines whether or not Nginx should serve stale cached data in certain circumstances (in regard to the gateway). If you use `proxy_cache_use_stale timeout`, and if the gateway times out, then Nginx will serve cached data. Syntax: `proxy_cache_use_stale [updating] [error] [timeout] [invalid_header] [http_500];` Example: `proxy_cache_use_stale error timeout;`
`proxy_max_temp_file_size` Context: `http, server, location`	Set this directive to 0 to disable the use of temporary files for requests eligible to proxy forwarding or specify a maximum file size. Syntax: Size value Default value: 1 GB Example: `proxy_max_temp_file_size 5m;`
`proxy_temp_file_write_size` Context: `http, server, location`	Sets the write buffer size when saving temporary files to the storage device Syntax: Size value Default value: 2 * `proxy_buffer_size`

`proxy_temp_path`
 	
Context: `http, server, location`
	Sets the path of temporary and cache store files.
	
	Syntax: `proxy_temp_path path [level1 [level2...]]`
	
	Examples:
	
	`proxy_temp_path /tmp/nginx_proxy;`
	`proxy_temp_path /tmp/cache 1 2;`

Limits, timeouts, and errors

The following directives will help you define the timeout behavior as well as various limitations regarding communications with the backend server.

Directive	Description
proxy_connect_ timeout Context: http, server, location	Defines the backend server connection timeout. This is different from the read/send timeout; if Nginx is already connected to the backend server, the proxy_connect_ timeout is not applicable. Syntax: Time value (in seconds) Example: proxy_connect_timeout 15;
proxy_read_timeout Context: http, server, location	The timeout for reading data from the backend server. This timeout isn't applied to the entire response delay but between two read operations instead. Syntax: Time value (in seconds) Default value: 60 Example: proxy_read_timeout 60;
proxy_send_timeout Context: http, server, location	This timeout for sending data to the backend server. The timeout isn't applied to the entire response delay but between two write operations instead. Syntax: Time value (in seconds) Default value: 60 Example: proxy_send_timeout 60;
proxy_ignore_ client_abort Context: http, server, location	If set to on, Nginx will continue processing the proxy request, even if the client aborts its request. In the other case (off), when the client aborts its request, Nginx also aborts its request to the backend server. Default value: off
proxy_intercept_ errors Context: http, server, location	By default, Nginx returns all error pages (HTTP status code 400 and higher) sent by the backend server directly to the client. If you set this directive to on, the error code is parsed and can be matched against the values specified in the error_page directive. Default value: off
proxy_send_lowat Context: http, server, location	An option allowing you to make use of the SO_SNDLOWAT flag for TCP sockets under FreeBSD only. This value defines the minimum number of bytes in the buffer for output operations. Syntax: Numeric value (size) Default value: 0

Other directives

Finally, the last set of directives available in the Proxy module is uncategorized and is as follows:

Directive	Description
`proxy_headers_hash_max_size` Context: `http, server, location`	Nginx uses hash tables for storing proxy headers in order to speed up the processing of requests. This directive defines the maximum size of the proxy headers hash table. If communications with your backend server use a total of more than 512 headers, you will have to increase this value. Syntax: Numeric value Default value: 512
`proxy_headers_hash_bucket_size` Context: `http, server, location`	Defines the maximum length of a header name in the proxy headers hash table. If one of your header names is longer than 64 characters, you will have to increase this value. Syntax: Numeric value Default value: 64
`proxy_ignore_headers` Context: `http, server, location`	Prevents Nginx from processing one of the following four headers from the backend server response: `X-Accel-Redirect, X-Accel-Expires, Expires,` and `Cache-Control`. Syntax: `proxy_ignore_headers header1 [header2...];`
`proxy_set_body` Context: `http, server, location`	Allows you to set a static request body for debugging purposes. Variables may be used in the directive value. Syntax: String value (any value) Example: `proxy_set_body test;`
`proxy_set_header` Context: `http, server, location`	This directive allows you to redefine header values to be transferred to the backend server. It can be declared multiple times. Syntax: `proxy_set_header Header Value;` Example: `proxy_set_header Host $host;`

Directive	Description
`proxy_store` Context: `http, server, location`	Specifies whether or not the backend server response should be stored as a file. Stored response files can be reused for serving other requests.
	Possible values: `on`, `off`, or a path relative to the document root (or alias). You may also set this to `on` and define the `proxy_temp_path` directive.

	Examples:
	`    proxy_temp_path on;`
	`    proxy_temp_path /temp/store;`

`proxy_store_access` Context: `http, server, location`	This directive defines file access permissions for the stored response files.
	Syntax: `proxy_store_access [user:[r|w|rw]] [group:[r|w|rw]] [all:[r|w|rw]];`
	Example: `proxy_store_access user:rw group: rw all:r;`

Variables

The Proxy module offers several variables that can be inserted in various locations, for example, in the `proxy_set_header` directive or in the logging-related directives such as `log_format`. The available variables are:

- `$proxy_host`: Contains the hostname of the backend server used for the current request.

- `$proxy_port`: Contains the port of the backend server used for the current request.

- `$proxy_add_x_forwarded_for`: This variable contains the value of the *X-Forwarded-For* request header, followed by the remote address of the client. Both values are separated by a comma. If the X-Forwarded-For request header is unavailable, the variable only contains the client remote address.

- `$proxy_internal_body_length`: Length of the request body (set with the `proxy_set_body` directive) or 0.

Configuring Apache and Nginx

After having reviewed the Proxy module, which allows us to establish our reverse-proxy configuration architecture, it's now time to put all these principles into practice. There are basically two main parts involved in the configuration, one relating to Apache and one relating to Nginx. The order in which you decide to apply those modifications does not make any difference whatsoever.

Note that while we have chosen to describe the process for Apache in particular, this method can be applied to any other HTTP server. The only point that differs is the exact configuration sections and directives that you will have to edit. Otherwise, the principle of reverse-proxy can be applied, regardless of the server software you are using.

Reconfiguring Apache

There are two main aspects of your Apache configuration that will need to be edited in order to allow both Apache and Nginx to work together at the same time. But let us first clarify where we are coming from, and what we are going towards.

Configuration overview

At this point, you probably have the following architecture set up on your server:

- A web server application running on port 80, such as Apache
- A dynamic server-side script processing application such as PHP, communicating with your web server via CGI, FastCGI, or as a server module

The new configuration that we are going towards will resemble the following:

- Nginx running on port 80
- Apache or another web server running on a different port, accepting requests coming from local sockets only
- The script processing application configuration will remain unchanged

As you can tell, only two main configuration changes will be applied to Apache as well as the other web server that you are running. Firstly, change the port number in order to avoid conflicts with Nginx, which will then be running as the frontend server. Secondly, (although this is optional) you may want to disallow requests coming from the outside and only allow requests forwarded by Nginx. Both configuration steps are detailed in the next sections.

Resetting the port number

Depending on how your web server was set up (manual build, automatic configuration from server panel managers such as cPanel, Plesk, and so on) you may find yourself with a lot of configuration files to edit. The main configuration file is often found in `/etc/httpd/conf/` or `/etc/apache2/`, and there might be more depending on how your configuration is structured. Some server panel managers create extra configuration files for each virtual host.

There are three main elements you need to replace in your Apache configuration:

- The Listen directive is set to listen on port 80 by default. You will have to replace that port by another such as 8080. This directive is usually found in the main configuration file.

- You must make sure that the following configuration directive is present in the main configuration file: NameVirtualHost A.B.C.D:8080, where A.B.C.D is the IP address of the main network interface on which server communications go through.

- The port you just selected needs to be reported in all your virtual host configuration sections, as described below.

The virtual host sections must be transformed from the following template

```
<VirtualHost A.B.C.D:80>
  ServerName   example.com
  ServerAlias  www.example.com
  [...]
</VirtualHost>
```

to the following:

```
<VirtualHost A.B.C.D:8080>
  ServerName   example.com:8080
  ServerAlias  www.example.com
[...]
</VirtualHost>
```

In this example, A.B.C.D is the IP address of the virtual host and example.com is the virtual host's name. The port must be edited on the first two lines.

Accepting local requests only

There are many ways you can restrict Apache to accept only local requests, denying access to the outside world. But first, why would you want to do that? As an extra layer positioned between the client and Apache, Nginx provides a certain comfort in terms of security. Visitors no longer have direct access to Apache, which decreases the potential risk regarding all security issues the web server may have. Globally, it's not necessarily a bad idea to only allow access to your frontend server.

The first method consists of changing the listening network interface in the main configuration file. The Listen directive of Apache lets you specify a port, but also an IP address, although, by default, no IP address is selected resulting in communications coming from all interfaces. All you have to do is replace the `Listen 8080` directive by `Listen 127.0.0.1:8080`; Apache should then only listen on the local IP address. If you do not host Apache on the same server, you will need to specify the IP address of the network interface that can communicate with the server hosting Nginx.

The second alternative is to establish per-virtual-host restrictions:

```
<VirtualHost A.B.C.D:8080>
   ServerName    example.com:8080
   ServerAlias   www.example.com
   [...]
   Order deny,allow
   allow from 127.0.0.1
   allow from 192.168.0.1
   deny all
</VirtualHost>
```

Using the `allow` and `deny` Apache directives, you are able to restrict the allowed IP addresses accessing your virtual hosts. This allows for a finer configuration, which can be useful in case some of your websites cannot be fully served by Nginx.

Once all your changes are done, don't forget to reload the server to make sure the new configuration is applied, such as `service httpd reload` or `/etc/init.d/httpd reload`.

Configuring Nginx

There are only a couple of simple steps to establish a working configuration of Nginx, although it can be tweaked more accurately as seen in the next section.

Enabling proxy options

The first step is to enable proxying of requests from your location blocks. Since the `proxy_pass` directive cannot be placed at the http or server level, you need to include it in every single place that you want to be forwarded. Usually, a `location / {` fallback block suffices since it encompasses all requests, except those that match `location` blocks containing a `break` statement.

Here is a simple example using a single static backend hosted on the same server:

```
server {
    server_name .example.com;
    root /home/example.com/www;
    [...]
    location / {
        proxy_pass http://127.0.0.1:8080;
    }
}
```

In the following example, we make use of an Upstream block allowing us to specify multiple servers, as described in Chapter 6:

```
upstream apache {
    server 192.168.0.1:80;
    server 192.168.0.2:80;
    server 192.168.0.3:80 weight=2;
    server 192.168.0.4:80 backup;
}

    server {
    server_name .example.com;
    root /home/example.com/www;
    [...]
    location / {
        proxy_pass http://apache;
    }
}
```

So far, with such a configuration, all requests are proxied to the backend server; we are now going to separate the content into two categories:

- Dynamic files: Files that require processing before being sent to the client, such as PHP, Perl, and Ruby scripts, will be served by Apache

- Static files: All other content that does not require additional processing, such as images, CSS files, static HTML files, and media, will be served directly by Nginx

We thus have to separate the content somehow to be provided by either server.

Separating content

In order to establish this separation, we can simply use two different location blocks—one that will match the dynamic file extensions and another one encompassing all the other files. This example passes requests for `.php` files to the proxy:

```
server {
    server_name .example.com;
    root /home/example.com/www;
    [...]
    location ~* \.php.$ {
      # Proxy all requests with an URI ending with .php*
      # (includes PHP, PHP3, PHP4, PHP5...)
        proxy_pass http://127.0.0.1:8080;
    }
    location / {
        # Your other options here for static content
        # for example cache control, alias...
        expires 30d;
    }
}
```

This method, although simple, will cause trouble with websites using URL rewriting. Most Web 2.0 websites now use links that hide file extensions such as `http://example.com/articles/us-economy-strengthens/`; some even replace file extensions with links resembling the following: `http://example.com/us-economy-strengthens.html`.

When building a reverse-proxy configuration, you have two options:

- Port your Apache rewrite rules to Nginx (usually found in the `.htaccess` file at the root of the website), in order for Nginx to know the actual file extension of the request and proxy it to Apache correctly.

- If you do not wish to port your Apache rewrite rules, the default behavior shown by Nginx is to return 404 errors for such requests. However, you can alter this behavior in multiple ways, for example, by handling 404 requests with the `error_page` directive or by testing the existence of files before serving them. Both solutions are detailed below.

Here is an implementation of this mechanism, using the `error_page` directive:

```
server {
    server_name .example.com;
    root /home/example.com/www;
    [...]
```

```
        location / {
            # Your static files are served here
            expires 30d;
            [...]
            # For 404 errors, submit the query to the @proxy
            # named location block
            error_page 404 @proxy;
        }

        location @proxy {
            proxy_pass http://127.0.0.1:8080;
        }
    }
```

Alternatively, making use of the `if` directive from the Rewrite module:

```
    server {
        server_name .example.com;
        root /home/example.com/www;
        [...]
        location / {
          # If the requested file extension ends with .php,
          # forward the query to Apache
          if ($request_filename ~* \.php.$) {
            break; # prevents further rewrites
            proxy_pass http://127.0.0.1:8080;
          }
          # If the requested file does not exist,
          # forward the query to Apache
          if (!-f $request_filename) {
            break; # prevents further rewrites
            proxy_pass http://127.0.0.1:8080;
          }
          # Your static files are served here
          expires 30d;
        }
    }
```

There is no real performance difference between both solutions, as they will transfer the same amount of requests to the backend server. You should work on porting your Apache rewrite rules to Nginx if you are looking to get optimal performance.

Advanced configuration

For now, we have only made use of one directive offered by the Proxy module. There are many more features that we can employ to optimize our design. The table below lists a handful of settings that are valid for most of your reverse-proxy configurations, although they need to be verified individually. And since they can be employed multiple times, you can place them in a separate configuration file that you will include in your location blocks.

Start by creating a `proxy.conf` text file that you place in the Nginx configuration directory. Insert the directives described below in that file. Then for each location of your `if` blocks that forward requests to a backend server or upstream block, insert the following line after the `proxy_pass` directive:

```
include proxy.conf;
```

Suggested values for some of the settings:

Setting	Description
proxy_redirect off;	It lets Nginx forward redirections to the client "as it is" without processing the response itself.
proxy_set_header Host $host;	The Host HTTP header in the request forwarded to the backend server defaults to the proxy hostname, as specified in the configuration file. This setting lets Nginx use the original Host from the client request instead.
proxy_set_header X-Real-IP $remote_addr;	Since the backend server receives a request from Nginx, the IP address it communicates with is not that of the client. Use this setting to forward the actual client IP address into a new header, X-Real-IP.
proxy_set_header X-Forwarded-For $proxy_add_x_forwarded_for;	Similar to the header above, except that if the client already uses a proxy on his/her own end, the actual IP address of the client should be contained in the X-Forwarded-For request header. Using $proxy_add_x_forwarded_for ensures that both the IP address of the communicating socket and possibly the original IP address of the client (behind a proxy) gets forwarded to the backend server.
client_max_body_size 10m;	Limits the maximum size of the request body to 10 megabytes. Actually, this setting is referenced here to make sure that you adjust the value to the same level as your backend server. Otherwise a request that is correctly received and processed by Nginx may not be successfully forwarded to the backend.

Setting	Description
`client_body_buffer_size 128k;`	Defines the minimum size of the memory buffer that will hold a request body. Past this size, the content is saved in a temporary file. Adjust it according to the expected size of requests your visitors will be sending, similar to `client_max_body_size`.
`proxy_connect_timeout 15;`	If you are working with a backend server on a local network, make sure to keep this value reasonably low (15 seconds here, but it depends on the average load). The maximum value for this directive is 75 seconds anyway.
`proxy_send_timeout 15;`	Make sure you define a timeout for write operations (timeout between two write operations during a communication to the backend server).
`proxy_read_timeout 15;`	Similar to the directive above, except for read operations.

Many other directives may be configured here. However, default values are appropriate for most setups.

Additional steps

There are a few more additional steps that you may be interested in if you want to perfect your reverse-proxy architecture. Three main issues are discussed here — the issue of IP addresses and how to ensure that the backend server retrieves the correct one, how to handle HTTPS requests with such a setup, and finally a few words about server control panels (cPanel, Plesk, and others).

Forwarding the correct IP address

Nowadays, a good portion of websites make use of the visitor's IP address for all kinds of reasons:

- Storing the IP address of a visitor posting a comment on a blog or a discussion forum
- Geotargeted advertising or other services
- Limiting services to specific IP address ranges

It is thus important for those websites to ensure that the web server correctly receives the IP address of the visitor.

As explained before, since Apache, or more generally, the backend server uses the IP address of the socket it communicates with, the IP that will appear in our design will always be the IP of the server hosting Nginx. We discussed a solution already — inserting the `proxy_set_header X-Real-IP $remote_addr;` directive in the configuration in order to forward the client IP address in the `X-Real-IP` header.

Unfortunately, that is not enough as some web applications are not configured to make use of the `X-Real-IP` header. The client remote address needs to be replaced somehow by that value. When it comes to Apache, a module was written to do just that: `mod_rpaf`. Details on how to install and configure it are not discussed here; you may find more documentation over at the official website: `http://stderr.net/apache/rpaf/`.

SSL issues and solutions

If your website is going to serve secure web pages, you have to somehow allow visitors to connect to your infrastructure via SSL on port 443. Two solutions are possible at this point — either you do not make use of Nginx at all and keep your Apache SSL configuration unmodified or you configure Nginx to accept communications on port 443.

The first solution is clearly the simplest — do not change the port of your virtual hosts as configured in Apache. Your website should still be fully accessible from the outside, unless your backend server is hosted on another computer on the local network.

The alternative is to configure Nginx to accept secure connections via the SSL module, as described in Chapter 5. Once your `server` block is correctly configured, you can establish a proxied configuration to forward secure requests to your Apache server. Note that if your backend server is hosted on the same machine, you will have to edit the configuration in order to avoid port conflicts between the frontend and backend.

Server control panel issues

A lot of server administrators rely on control panel software to simplify many aspects of their work — managing hosted domains, e-mail accounts, network settings, and much more. Advanced software solutions such as Parallels Plesk or cPanel are able to generate configuration files for many server applications (web, e-mail, database, and so on) on-the-fly. Unfortunately, they all only support Apache as a unique web server application; Nginx is unsupported at the moment.

If you followed the steps of the reverse-proxy configuration process, you noticed that at some point, the Apache configuration files had to be manually edited. We replaced the listening port and edited or inserted some configuration directives. Obviously, when the control panel software generates configuration files, it is unaware of the manual changes we made, therefore it erases our modifications. When you restart Apache, you are greeted with error messages and conflicts.

At this point, there is no other solution than to apply the changes again after each configuration rebuild. With the growing popularity of Nginx, developers will hopefully implement full Nginx support in their software, or at least allow editing those configuration settings required to use Nginx as a reverse proxy.

Summary

Configuring Nginx as reverse proxy for our architecture introduces a lot of advantages and can be configured. However, a few obstacles might stand in your way, especially if you are running control panel software solutions to manage your services. Moreover, you do not get to make the most of Nginx as you are not using it for all your requests.

If you are seeking to find an even more efficient solution, you may want to look into completely replacing Apache by Nginx. The next chapter will detail this process, step-by-step, from virtual hosts to rewrite rules to FastCGI.

8

From Apache to Nginx

Every experienced system administrator will tell you the same story—when your web infrastructure works fine and client requests are served at a good speed, the last thing you want to do is modify the architecture that you have spent days, weeks, or even months putting together. The thing is, as your website grows more popular, problems tend to occur inevitably (and said problems are not as documented as mainstream ones), regardless of the effort you originally involved in server configuration. Then eventually you have to start looking for solutions. In that extent, there are multiple reasons why you would want to completely adopt Nginx at the expense of your previous web server. Whether you decided that Nginx could be more efficient as a unique server rather than working as a reverse-proxy or simply because you want to get rid of Apache once and for all, this chapter will guide you through the complete process of replacing the latter by the former.

This chapter covers:

- An in-depth comparison between Apache and Nginx
- A full guide to porting your Apache configuration
- How to port your Apache rewrite rules to Nginx
- Rewrite rule walkthroughs for a few popular web applications

Nginx versus Apache

This section will provide answers to the main questions that one would ask about Nginx—how does it stand apart from the other servers? How does it compare to Apache? Whether you were using Apache before or considered it as a replacement for your current web server, why should you decide to adopt Nginx at the expense of the web server that empowers nearly half of the Internet websites worldwide?

Features

With the reverse-proxy configuration that was elaborated in the previous chapter, the presence or absence of specific features wasn't much of a problem, given the fact that Nginx would simply have to differentiate between static and dynamic content, and in consequence, serve static file requests and forward dynamic file requests to a backend server.

However, when you start to consider Nginx as a possible full replacement for your current web server, you better make sure of what's in the box. If your projected architecture requires specific components, the first thing you would usually do is check the application features. The table below lists a couple of major features and describes how Nginx performs in comparison to Apache.

Core and functioning

Features	Nginx	Apache
Request management How does the web server process requests?	**Event-driven architecture** Requests are accepted using asynchronous sockets and aren't processed in separate threads, in order to reduce memory and CPU overhead.	**Synchronous sockets, threads, and processes** Each request is in a separate thread or process and uses synchronous sockets.
Programming language Which language was the web server written in?	C The C language is notably low-level and offers more accurate memory management.	C and C++ Although Apache was written in C, many modules were designed with C++.
Portability Which operating systems are supported?	Multiplatform Nginx runs under Windows, GNU/Linux, Unix, BSD, Mac OS X, and Solaris.	Multiplatform Apache runs under Windows, GNU/Linux, Unix, BSD, Mac OS X, Solaris, Novell NetWare, OS/2, TPF, OpenVMS, eCS, AIX, z/OS, HP-UX, and so on.
Year of birth How long ago did the development start?	2002 While Nginx is younger than Apache, it was intended for a more modern era.	1994 Apache is one of the numerous open source projects initiated in the 90s that contributed to making the World Wide Web what it is today.

General functionality

This section mainly focuses on differences between Apache and Nginx rather than listing all sorts of features that have already been covered in previous chapters.

Feature	Nginx	Apache
HTTPS support	**Supported as module**	**Supported as module**
Can the web server deliver secure web pages?	If you want HTTPS support, you need to make sure to compile Nginx with the proper module.	Apache comes with HTTPS support via a module included by default.
Virtual Hosting	**Supported natively**	**Supported natively**
Can the web server host multiple websites on the same computer?	Nginx natively supports virtual hosting, but is not configured by default to accept per-virtual-host configuration files (more details further in this chapter).	Apache natively supports virtual hosting and offers the possibility to include one configuration file per folder (`.htaccess`).
CGI Support	**FastCGI only**	**CGI and FastCGI**
Does the web browser support CGI and FastCGI?	Nginx supports FastCGI via a module that is included by default at compile time.	Both protocols are exploitable via modules that can be loaded into Apache.
Module system	**Static module system**	**Dynamic module system**
How does the web server handle modules?	Modules must be included at compile time.	Modules can be loaded and unloaded dynamically from configuration files.

Generally speaking, Apache has a lot more to offer notably with a much larger number of modules available. Most of its functionality, even core for the application core, is modularized. At this time, the official Apache module website references over 500 modules for various version branches, versus a little more than 80 for Nginx. This state of facts is mainly caused by the reasons described just below.

Flexibility and community

This is another criterion for establishing an honest comparison between two applications of that family. In today's computer science industry, one cannot simply regard the raw functionality of an application without considering questions such as:

- Where am I going to get help if I get stuck?
- Am I going to find documentation about the features offered?
- Are more modules going to be implemented in the future?
- Is the project still active and being updated by its developers?
- Has the server security been tested by a large enough number of administrators?

These questions generally answer themselves when the server gets popular enough. In the case of Apache, saying that it is a mainstream application would be an understatement. Documentation is easily found; developers have released hundreds of modules over the years, and it has received regular updates for the past fifteen years.

What about Nginx, how does it stand on those matters? That is definitely a sensitive issue. To begin with, there are some solid websites centralizing information such as the official wiki. If you have a problem with Apache, a simple search engine query suffices to find multiple articles answering the exact question you have been asking yourself. If you have a problem with Nginx though, you will likely have to resort to newsgroups or mailing lists of web forums.

On the updates and security side though, Nginx is frequently updated by its author Igor Sysoev. Those updates rarely include security fixes as the server has been built on solid and reliable foundations from the start. Although it doesn't serve as many websites as Apache does, Nginx still empowers some of the most popular online platforms such as SourceForge, WordPress, ImageShack, and more. This contributes to conferring it an undeniable legitimacy in the domain of high-performance web servers.

Performance

While features and community-related matters are important in general, the aspect that can make all the difference is performance. Administrators naturally tend to favor the server that will provide optimal comfort for the end user, characterized by minimal page load times and maximum RPS (Requests Per Second) rate.

Chapter 3 provided a first approach of HTTP server performance testing. The same tests can be applied to Apache in order to establish direct performance comparisons. In fact, many admin bloggers and technicians have already done so, and the general trend is unquestionably in favor of Nginx on all aspects:

- The RPS rate is generally much higher with Nginx, sometimes twice higher than Apache's. In other words, Nginx is able to serve twice as many pages as Apache in the same lapse of time.

- Response times are lower on Nginx—as the request count grows, Apache becomes slower and slower to serve pages.

- Apache tends to use slightly more bandwidth than Nginx for serving the same requests. This can be interpreted in two ways—either Apache generates more traffic overhead, or it is able to transfer data at a faster rate by better occupying the available bandwidth (it's still unsure as to which of these assumptions is the most valid).

In conclusion on the field of performance, Nginx wins hands down. It's clearly the main reason why so many have switched to the lightweight Russian web server.

Usage

The reason why Nginx is so far ahead of Apache performance-wise is because it's precisely the reason it was written for. Originally, Igor Sysoev created Nginx to power an extremely high-traffic Russian website (`www.rambler.ru`), which received hundreds of millions of requests every day. This was probably not part of the original plans of the Apache designers when they initiated the project back in the early 90s.

More generally, it is said that Nginx was designed to address the **C10k problem**. This problem designates a common observation according to which the current state of computer technology and network scalability only allows a computer (from the mainstream industry) to maintain up to 10,000 simultaneous network connections, due to operating system and software limitations. While that number isn't representative anymore due to the progress of the technology, at the time, the issue was considered very seriously and it triggered the development of major web servers such as Lighttpd, Cherokee, and obviously Nginx.

Conclusion

There is one famous quote going around the Nginx community that summarizes the situation pretty accurately:

> *"Apache is like Microsoft Word, it has a million options but you only need six. Nginx does those six things, and it does five of them 50 times faster than Apache."* Chris Lea, ChrisLea.com

Other notable testimonies help build the reputation of Nginx:

> *"I currently have Nginx doing reverse proxy of over tens of millions of HTTP requests per day (that's a few hundred per second) on a **single server**. At peak load, it uses about 15 MB RAM and 10 percent of my CPU on my particular configuration (FreeBSD 6). Under the same kind of load, Apache falls over (after using 1000 or so processes and god knows how much RAM), Pound falls over (too many threads, and using 400 MB+ of RAM for all the thread stacks), and Lighty leaks more than 20 MB per hour (and uses more CPU, but not significantly more)."* Bob Ippolito, MochiMedia.com

If you are in the market for high scale projects with limited resources at your disposal, Nginx comes in as a great solution. Apache is a good option to get your projects started when your knowledge of web servers and hosting is limited, but as soon as you meet success, you, your server, and your visitors may eventually find it inconsistent.

Porting your Apache configuration

That's it. You've had enough of Apache. You finally decided to make a complete switch to Nginx. There are quite a few steps ahead of you now, the first of which being to adapt your previous configuration in a way to ensure that your existing websites work 1:1 after the switch.

Directives

This first section will summarize some of the common Apache configuration directives and attempt to provide equivalent or replacement solutions from Nginx. The list follows the order of the default Apache configuration file.

Apache directive	Nginx equivalent
ServerTokens	**server_tokens**
Apache allows you to configure the information transmitted in request headers regarding the server OS and software name and versions.	In Nginx, you may enable or disable transmission of server information by using the `server_tokens` directive from the main HTTP module.
ServerRoot	**--prefix build-time option**
Lets you define the root directory of the server, which will contain the configuration and logs directory.	With Nginx, this option is defined at compile time with the `--prefix` switch of the configure script or at execution time with the -p command line option.
PidFile	**pid**
Defines the path of the application pid file.	The exact equivalent directive is `pid`.
TimeOut	**Multiple directives**
This directive defines three elements — the maximum execution time of a GET request, the maximum allowed delay between two TCP packets in POST and PUT requests, and the maximum allowed delay between two TCP 'ACK' packets.	There are multiple directives allowing a similar behavior: • `send_timeout`: Defines the maximum allowed delay between two read operations by the client • `client_body_timeout`: Defines the timeout for reading client request • `bodyclient_header_timeout`: Defines the timeout for reading client request headers
KeepAlive, MaxKeepAliveRequests, KeepAliveTimeout These three directives control the keep-alive behavior of Apache.	**keepalive_timeout, keepalive_requests** These two directives are the direct equivalents to the Apache ones, except that if you want to completely disable keep-alives, set `keepalive_timeout` or `keepalive_requests` to 0.
Listen	**listen**
Defines the interface and port on which Apache will listen for connections.	In Nginx, this directive is only defined at the virtual host level (`server` block).
LoadModule	**--with_****_module**
With this directive, Apache offers the possibility to load modules dynamically.	Nginx cannot load modules dynamically; these need to be included at compile time. Once incorporated in Nginx, they cannot be disabled.

Apache directive	Nginx equivalent
Include	**include**
File inclusion directive supports wildcards.	The `include` directive of Nginx is identical.
User, Group	**user**
Allows you to define the user and group under which the daemon will be running.	The user directive of Nginx lets you specify both the user and the group.
ServerAdmin, ServerSignature	**No equivalent**
Lets you specify the e-mail address of the server administrator and a signature message to be displayed on error and diagnostic pages.	As of version 0.7.66, there is no equivalent for Nginx. Error pages do not show the e-mail address of the server administrator or other information.
UseCanonicalName	**No direct equivalent**
Defines how Apache constructs self-referential URLs.	Although there is no direct equivalent for this Apache directive, the construction of self-referential URLs can be defined via module-specific settings (proxy, FastCGI, and so on).
DocumentRoot	**root**
Defines the root directory from which Apache will serve files. The directive can be used at the server and virtual host levels.	The root directive can be inserted to define the document root at all levels: `http`, `server`, `location`, and `if` blocks.
DirectoryIndex, IndexOptions, IndexIgnore	**index, autoindex, random_index, fancyindex** (third party)
Define directory index and file listing options.	Nginx also offers a good variety of options for managing indexes.
AccessFileName	**No equivalent**
Defines the filename of `.htaccess` files that are included dynamically on page execution.	Nginx, as of version 0.7.66, has no such feature as `.htaccess` files. Read sections further below for more information.
TypesConfig, DefaultType	**types, default_type**
Defines MIME type options.	Equivalent directives exist in Nginx, although with a different syntax.
HostNameLookups	**No equivalent**
Allows looking up of hostnames for client IP addresses for logging or access control purposes.	As of Nginx 0.7.66, there is no equivalent functionality.

Apache directive	Nginx equivalent
ErrorLog, LogLevel, LogFormat, CustomLog	**access_log, log_format**
Logging activation and format settings	Nginx also allows a large variety of options, but they are combined in fewer directives.
Alias, AliasMatch, ScriptAlias	**alias**
Directory aliasing options.	The `alias` equivalent directive is offered by Nginx, but nothing for the other two.

Modules

As we have discovered earlier in Chapter 2, modules in Nginx cannot be loaded dynamically and must be included at compile time. Additionally, they cannot be disabled at runtime since they are completely compiled and integrated in the main binary. Consequently, you should carefully consider your choice of modules when you build Nginx.

> If you are worried about the impact on performance of the modules you selected, you should be aware that the only noticeable differences will come from "filter modules", the name given to modules that apply a filter to the content of requests and/or responses and thus are always activated. Examples of filter modules: Addition, Charset, Gzip, SSI, and more. In the case of non-filter modules (such as Autoindex, FastCGI, Stub Status, and others), if none of their directives are used, the module handler is never executed.

The table below lists some module that Apache and Nginx have in common. Note that there might be equivalent modules, but they do not necessarily provide the exact same functionality and directives are likely to be different in all cases. You should check the documentation of these modules in their respective chapter.

Apache Module	Nginx Module	Status	Configure switch
mod_auth_basic	auth_basic	Included by default	--without-http_auth_basic_module
mod_autoindex	autoindex	Included by default	--without-http_autoindex_module
mod_charset_lite	charset	Included by default	--without-http_charset_module
mod_dav	dav	Optional	--with-http_dav_module

Apache Module	Nginx Module	Status	Configure switch
`mod_deflate`	`gzip`	Included by default	`--without-http_gzip_module`
`mod_expires`	`headers`	Included by default	Cannot be disabled
`mod_fcgid`	`fastcgi`	Included by default	`--without-http_fastcgi_module`
`mod_headers`	`Headers`	Included by default	Cannot be disabled
`mod_include`	`ssi`	Included by default	`--without-http_ssi_module`
`mod_log_config`	`log`	Included by default	Cannot be disabled
`mod_proxy`	`proxy`	Included by default	`--without-http_proxy_module`
`mod_rewrite`	`rewrite`	Included by default	`--without-http_rewrite_module`
`mod_ssl`	`ssl`	Optional	`--with-http_ssl_module`
`mod_status`	`stub_status`	Optional	`--with-http_stub_status_module`
`mod_substitute`	`sub`	Optional	`--with-http_sub_module`
`mod_uid`	`userid`	Included by default	`--without-http_userid_module`

Virtual hosts and configuration sections

Just like Nginx allows you to define configuration settings at various levels
(`http`, `server`, `location`, `if`), Apache also has its own sections. The section
list is described below along with a configuration example.

Configuration sections

The table below provides a translation of Apache sections into Nginx configuration
blocks. Some Apache sections have no direct Nginx equivalent, but for most cases,
identical behavior can be reproduced in a slightly different syntax.

Apache section	Nginx section	Description
Default	`http`	The settings placed at the root of the Apache configuration files correspond to the settings placed at the root of the Nginx configuration file and also those placed in the `http` block (as opposed to other blocks such as `mail` or `imap` used for mail server proxying functionality).
`<VirtualHost>`	`server`	Apache settings placed in the `<VirtualHost>` sections should be placed in the `server` blocks of the Nginx configuration file.
`<Location>` `<LocationMatch>`	`location`	The behavior of the `<Location>` and `<LocationMatch>` (regular expression) can be reproduced with the Nginx `location` block.
None	`if`	Nginx offers dynamic conditional structure with the `if` block. There is no exact equivalent in Apache. The closest equivalence is the `RewriteCond` directive from the Rewrite module.
`<Directory>` `<DirectoryMatch>` `<Files>` `<FilesMatch>`	None	Apache allows you to apply settings to specific locations of the local file system while Nginx only offers per-URI settings.
`<IfDefine>`	None	Applies a set of directives if the specified condition is true on startup. This feature is not available on Nginx.
`<IfModule>`	None	Applies a set of directives on startup if the specified module is loaded. Since Nginx does not support dynamic module loading, this feature is not available.
`<Proxy>` `<ProxyMatch>`	None	Applies a set of directives to proxied resources by specifying a wildcard URI or a regular expression. This section has no equivalent on Nginx.

Creating a virtual host

In Apache, virtual hosts are optional. You are allowed to define server settings at the root of the configuration file:

```
Listen 80
ServerName example.com
ServerAlias www.example.com
DocumentRoot "/home/example.com/www"
[...]
```

However, this behavior is useful only if you are going to host one website on the server, or if you want to define the default settings for incoming requests that do not match other virtual host access rules.

In Nginx, however, all the websites you will be hosting must be placed in a `server` block which allows the creation of a virtual host, equivalent of the `<VirtualHost>` section in Apache. The table below describes the translation of an Apache `<VirtualHost>` section to an Nginx `server` block:

Apache virtual host	Nginx virtual host equivalent
`<VirtualHost 12.34.56.78:80>`	`server {`
`ServerName    example.com:80`	`listen 12.34.56.78:80;`
`ServerAlias   www.example.com`	`server_name example.com www.example.com;`
`UseCanonicalName Off`	# No equivalent.
`SuexecUserGroup user group`	# No equivalent.
`ServerAdmin   "admin@example.com"`	# No equivalent.
`DocumentRoot /home/example.com/www`	`root /home/example.com/www;`
`CustomLog /home/example.com/logs/access_log cust`	`access_log /home/example.com/logs/access_log cust;`
	# Note that the `cust` format must be declared beforehand with `log_format`.
`ErrorLog /home/example.com/logs/error_log`	`error_log /home/example.com/logs/error_log;`
`<Location /documents/>`	`location /documents/ {`
`  Options +Indexes`	`    autoindex on;`
`</Location>`	`}`
`<IfModule mod_ssl.c>`	# there is no equivalent for IfModule.
`SSLEngine off`	`ssl off;`
`</IfModule>`	

Apache virtual host	Nginx virtual host equivalent

`<Directory /home/example.com/`
`www>`
 	
`  <IfModule mod_fcgid.c>`
`  <Files ~ (\.php)>`
`    SetHandler fcgid-script`
`    FCGIWrapper /usr/bin/php-`
`cgi .php`
`    Options +ExecCGI`
`    allow from all`
`  </Files>`
`  </IfModule>`
`  Options -Includes -ExecCGI`
`</Directory>`
	# There is no equivalent to the Directory section. The location block only applies per-URI settings. The location block applies settings for all requests relative to the virtual host root directory. We use it to apply settings to the .php files.
	
	`location ~ \.php {`
	`  # Insert your FCGI settings`
	`    fastcgi_pass 127.0.0.1:9000;`
	`    fastcgi_param SCRIPT_FILENAME`
	`/home/example.com/`
	`www$fastcgi_script_name;`
	`    fastcgi_param PATH_INFO`
	`$fastcgi_script_name;`
	`    include fastcgi_params; # Your`
	`additional FastCGI settings`
	`}`
	
	# Other directives have no direct equivalent or are not necessary with Nginx.

`</VirtualHost>`	`}`

This translation guide is valid for regular virtual hosts, serving non-secure web pages. There are a few differences when creating a secure virtual host using SSL. The table below focuses on the SSL-related directives, although directives from the table above can still be used.

Apache virtual host	Nginx virtual host
`<VirtualHost 12.34.56.78:443>`	`server {`
`ServerName example.com:443`	`listen 12.34.56.78:443;`
`ServerAlias www.example.com`	`server_name example.com www.example.com;`
`SSLEngine on`	`ssl on;`
`SSLVerifyClient none`	`ssl_verify_client off;`
`SSLCertificateFile /home/example.com/cert/certchL9435`	`ssl_certificate /home/example.com/cert/cert.pem;`
	`ssl_certificate_key /home/example.com/cert/cert.key;`

Apache virtual host	Nginx virtual host

`<Directory /home/example.com/`
`www>`
 	
      `SSLRequireSSL`
 	
`</Directory>`
`</VirtualHost>`
	# There is no equivalent required with Nginx.
	
	`}`

htaccess files

This section approaches the tricky problem of `.htaccess` files and the underlying thematic of shared hosting. There is indeed no such mechanism in Nginx, which among other reasons, renders shared hosting difficult to achieve.

Reminder on Apache .htaccess files

`.htaccess` files are small independent configuration files that webmasters are allowed to place in every single directory of their website. Upon receiving a request accessing a particular directory, Apache checks for the presence of such a file and applies it to the request context. This allows webmasters to apply separate settings at multiple levels:

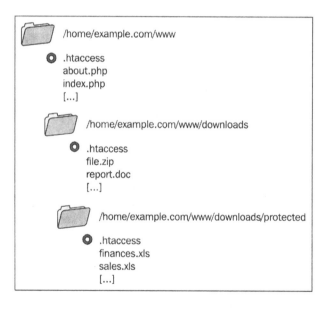

In the context of a client request for `/downloads/protected/finances.xls`, all three `.htaccess` files would be applied in the following order:

1. `/home/example.com/www/.htaccess`
2. `/home/example.com/www/downloads/.htaccess`
3. `/home/example.com/www/downloads/protected/.htaccess`

The settings precedence is given to the last `.htaccess` file read—if the same setting is defined in `/www/.htaccess` and `/www/downloads/.htaccess`, the latter file has priority over the former.

Nginx equivalence

Unfortunately, there is no such mechanism in Nginx. We can, however, find replacement solutions by making the most of directives that we have at our disposal.

There are three major uses for `.htaccess` files in Apache:

- Creating access and authentication rules for specific directories
- Defining rewrite rules at the top level (usually not directory-specific)
- Setting flags for modules such as `mod_php`, `mod_perl`, or `mod_python`

When it comes to the latter, the use of flags is only achievable when the preprocessors are set up as Apache modules. If your server runs PHP through CGI or FastCGI, flags will not be recognized and generate a `500 Internal Server Error`. In our case, connecting Nginx to such applications can only be done via FastCGI or HTTP; consequently flags are not allowed.

Depending on how you declare your virtual hosts, there are two solutions for implementing an htaccess-like behavior or at least something remotely similar.

The first solution, if you are going to list all virtual hosts from a unique configuration file, is to insert an `include` directive in the server block that refers to an extra configuration file located in the `/www/` directory. But let us not forget that this configuration file should be hidden and not downloadable by clients:

```
server {
    listen 80;
    server_name .example.com;
    root /home/example.com/www;
    [...]
    # Include extra configuration files
    location / {
```

```
        include /home/example.com/www/.ngconf*;
    }


    # Deny access if someone tries to download the file
    location ~ \.ngconf {
        return 404;
    }
}
```

This will include any file with a name starting with .ngconf from the /www/ directory of the virtual host. Note the * in the include directive: if you specify a filename without a wildcard, Nginx will consider the configuration to be invalid if the file is missing. If you use the wildcard, the absence of such a file does not generate any error.

The .ngconf file would then include directives related to the virtual host itself:

```
autoindex off; # Disable directory listing
location /downloads/ {
    autoindex on; # Allow directory listing in /downloads/
}
[...]
```

This solution seems relatively secure for web hosting providers, as this only allows webmasters to define location-related settings (preventing important changes such as using a different port, different host name, and more). However, be aware that if a webmaster creates invalid .ngconf files, Nginx will refuse to reload until the issue is fixed.

Alternatively, you could decide to place virtual host declarations within separate files located in the root directory of each virtual host. In which case, you would only need the following directive in the main Nginx configuration file:

```
include /home/*/www/.ngconf;
```

The .ngconf file then has to contain the complete virtual host declaration, including the port and server name. This solution should only be considered for servers that you entirely manage by yourself; you should never allow external webmasters to have so much control over your server.

That being said, there is still one major difference between Apache and Nginx:

- Apache applies settings from .htaccess files every time a client request is processed
- Nginx applies settings from .ngconf files only when you reload the configuration (such as service nginx reload)

At this moment, there is no work around for this last issue; Nginx does not allow on-the-fly configuration changes.

Rewrite rules

The most common source of worries during an HTTP server switch is the rewrite rules. Unfortunately, Nginx is not directly compatible with the Apache rewrite rules in two regards:

- Usually, rewrite rules are placed within .htaccess files, as discussed in the previous section. Nginx offers no such mechanism, so rewrite rules will have to be placed in a different location.

- The syntax of the rewrite instructions and conditions is quite different and will need to be adapted.

This section will approach some of the issues encountered when porting rules to Nginx, and then will provide some prewritten rules for a couple of major web applications.

General remarks

Before studying practical examples, let us begin with a couple of important remarks regarding rewrite rules in Nginx.

On the location

With all that has been said and written about Nginx, we can safely say that it's not the most appropriate web server for web hosting companies that do shared hosting. The lack of .htaccess files renders it practically impossible to host websites that have their own server settings, among which are rewrite rules. While a replacement solution has been offered in the previous section, it's not optimal as it requires a configuration reload after each change, and to crown it all, reloading is only possible if the entire configuration contains no error.

The consequence of this first issue is that you will have to relocate the rewrite rules. They will have to be placed directly in the server or location blocks of your virtual host, regardless of which file contains the virtual host configuration. With Apache, rewrite rules would be located somewhere such as /home/example.com/ www/.htaccess; while with Nginx, you need to incorporate them in the virtual host configuration file, for example, /usr/local/nginx/conf/nginx.conf.

On the syntax

There are two major Apache directives that are important when it comes to porting rewrite rules to Nginx; other directives either have no equivalent, are not supported on purpose, or their behavior is already incorporated in the offered Nginx equivalences:

- `RewriteCond` allows you to define conditions that should be matched for the URL to be rewritten

- `RewriteRule` performs the actual URL rewrite by specifying a regular expression pattern, the rewritten URL, and a set of flags

The first of those directives, `RewriteCond`, is equivalent to Nginx's `if`. It is used for verifying conditions before applying a rewrite rule; the example below ensures that the requested file does not exist (`!-f` flag) before rewriting the URL:

```
RewriteCond %{REQUEST_FILENAME} !-f
RewriteRule . /index.php [L]
```

The Nginx equivalent, using `if` and `rewrite`, would be:

```
if (!-f $request_filename) {
    rewrite . /index.php last;
}
```

It gets a little more complicated when you want to rewrite under multiple conditions: the Nginx `if` statement only supports one condition in the expression and does not allow imbrications of `if` blocks. How does one reproduce a behavior like the one below?

```
RewriteCond %{REQUEST_FILENAME} !-f # File must not exist
RewriteCond %{REQUEST_FILENAME} !-d # Directory must not exist
RewriteRule . /index.php [L] # Rewrites URL
```

There is a simple logical workaround for this particular issue—we will be using multiple `if` blocks, in which we affect a variable. After the two initial `if` blocks, a third comes in to check if the variable was affected by the first two:

```
set $check "";
# If the specified file does not exist, set $check to "A"
if (!-f $request_filename) {
    set $check "A";
}
# If the specified directory does not exist, set $check to $check + B
if (!-d $request_filename) {
    set $check "${check}B";
```

```
    }
    # If $check was affected in both if blocks, perform the rewrite
    if ($check = "AB") {
        rewrite . /index.php last
    }
```

Note that for those two particular rewrite conditions (-f to test file existence; -d to test directory existence), Nginx already offers a solution that combines both tests: -e. So a quicker solution would have been:

```
    if (!-e $request_filename) {
        rewrite . /index.php last;
    }
```

In addition to testing file and directory existence, -e also checks if the specified filename corresponds to an existing symbolic link.

For more information on the Rewrite module in general, please refer to Chapter 5.

RewriteRule

The RewriteRule Apache directive is the direct equivalent to rewrite in Nginx. However, there is a subtle difference — URIs in Nginx begin with the / character. Nevertheless, the translation remains simple:

```
    RewriteRule ^downloads/(.*)$ download.php?url=$1 [QSA]
```

The preceding Apache rule is transformed into the following:

```
    rewrite ^/downloads/(.*)$ /download.php?url=$1;
```

Note that the [QSA] flag tells Apache to append the query arguments to the rewritten URL. However, Nginx does that by default. To prevent Nginx from appending query arguments, insert a trailing ? to the substitution URL:

```
    rewrite ^/downloads/(.*)$ /download.php?url=$1?;
```

The RewriteRule Apache directive allows additional flags; these can be matched against the ones offered by Nginx, described in Chapter 5.

WordPress

WordPress is probably a familiar name to you — as of September 2009, the immensely popular open source blogging application was being used by over 200 million websites worldwide. Powered by PHP and MySQL, it's compatible with Nginx *out of the box*. Well, this statement would be entirely true if it weren't for rewrite rules.

The web application comes with a `.htaccess` file to be placed at the root of the website:

```
# BEGIN WordPress
<IfModule mod_rewrite.c>
RewriteEngine On
RewriteBase /
RewriteCond %{REQUEST_FILENAME} !-f
RewriteCond %{REQUEST_FILENAME} !-d
RewriteRule . /index.php [L]
</IfModule>
# END WordPress
```

This first example is relatively easy to understand and to translate to Nginx. In fact, most of the rewriting process consists of three steps:

1. Checking if the requested URI corresponds to an existing file, in which case, it is served normally.

2. Checking if the requested URI corresponds to a directory, in which case, it is served normally.

3. Rewrite to `index.php`; WordPress will then analyze the URI by itself from within the PHP script (by checking the `$_SERVER["REQUEST_URI"]` variable).

Since there are not a lot of complex rules to take care of, the URLs being decomposed by the PHP script itself, the translation to Nginx is rather easy. Here is a full example of a Nginx virtual host, stripped out of all unrelated directives:

```
server {
    listen 80;
    server_name blog.example.com;
    root /home/example.com/blog/www;
    index index.php;
    location / {
    # If requested URI does not match any existing file, directory or
symbolic link, rewrite the URL to index.php
        if (!-e $request_filename) {
            rewrite ^ /index.php last;
        }
    }
    # For all PHP requests, pass them on to PHP-FPM via FastCGI
    # For more information, consult chapter 6
    location ~ \.php$ {
        fastcgi_pass 127.0.0.1:9000;
```

```
        fastcgi_param SCRIPT_FILENAME
/home/example.com/blog/www$fastcgi_script_name;
        fastcgi_param PATH_INFO $fastcgi_script_name;
        include fastcgi_params; # include extra FCGI params
    }
}
```

MediaWiki

As its name suggests, MediaWiki is the web engine that empowers the famous Wikipedia online open encyclopedia. It is currently an open source software and anyone can download and install it on their local server. The application can also be used as CMS (Content Management Software), and large companies such as Novell have found it to be a reliable solution.

Contrary to WordPress, MediaWiki does not come with a prewritten .htaccess file for prettying up URLs. Instead, the official MediaWiki website offers a wide variety of methods; all documented in the form of wiki articles. Webmasters can implement solutions that go as far as modifying the main Apache configuration file. However, there are simpler solutions that require no such thing. No particular Apache solution has been retained here, as three simple Nginx rewrite rules suffice to do the trick.

- The first one redirects default requests (for example, / as request URI) to /wiki/Main_Page.

- The second one rewrites all the URIs of the /wiki/abcd form into the actual URL /w/index.php?title=abcd, without forgetting to append the rest of the parameters to the request URL.

- The third one ensures that requests to /wiki get redirected to the home page /w/index.php.

Here is a full virtual host configuration example, including the rewrite rules:

```
server {
    listen 80;
    server_name wiki.example.com;
    root /home/example.com/wiki/www;
    location / {
        index index.php;
        rewrite ^/$ /wiki/Main_Page permanent;
    }
    # 2 rewrite rules
    rewrite ^/wiki/([^?]*)(?:\?(.*))? /w/index.php?title=$1&$2;
    rewrite ^/wiki /w/index.php;
```

```
        # Your FCGI configuration here
        location ~ \.php$ {
            fastcgi_pass    127.0.0.1:9000;
            fastcgi_index   index.php;
            fastcgi_param   SCRIPT_FILENAME
/home/example.com/wiki/www$fastcgi_script_name;
            include fastcgi_params;
        }
    }
```

vBulletin

Discussion forums started blooming in the 2000s and a lot of popular web applications have appeared such as vBulletin, phpBB, or Invision Board. Most of these forum software platforms have jumped in the bandwagon and now boast full SEO-friendly URL support. Unfortunately, rewrite rules often come in the form of .htaccess files; indeed, the vBulletin developers have chosen to provide rewrite rules for Apache 2 and IIS, unsurprisingly forgetting Nginx. Let's teach them a lesson; the table below describes a solution for converting their Apache rewrite rules to Nginx.

Apache rule	Nginx rule
`RewriteEngine on`	`# Not necessary.`

`RewriteCond %{REQUEST_FILENAME}`
`-s [OR]`
`RewriteCond %{REQUEST_FILENAME}`
`-l [OR]`
`RewriteCond %{REQUEST_FILENAME}`
`-d`
`RewriteRule ^.*$ - [NC,L]`
	# Do not rewrite if the requested URI corresponds to an existing file, directory, or link on the system.
	
	`if (-e $request_filename) {`
	`        break;`
	`}`

`RewriteRule ^threads/.* showth` `read.php [QSA]`	`rewrite ^/threads/.*$` `/showthread.php last;`
`RewriteRule ^forums/.* forum` `display.php [QSA]`	`rewrite ^/forums/.*$` `/forumdisplay.php last;`
`RewriteRule ^members/.* mem` `ber.php [QSA]`	`rewrite ^/members/.*$` `/members.php last;`
`RewriteRule ^blogs/.* blog.php` `[QSA]`	`rewrite ^/blogs/.*$ /blog.php` `last;`
`ReWriteRule ^entries/.* en` `try.php [QSA]`	`rewrite ^/entries/.*$` `/entry.php last;`

Apache rule	Nginx rule

`RewriteCond %{REQUEST_FILENAME}`
`-s [OR]`
`RewriteCond %{REQUEST_FILENAME}`
`-l [OR]`
`RewriteCond %{REQUEST_FILENAME}`
`-d`
`RewriteRule ^.*$ - [NC,L]`
	# For some reason, the same set of rules appears twice in the .htaccess file provided by vBulletin. You do not need to insert the Nginx equivalent a second time.

`RewriteRule`
`^(?:(.*?)(?:/|$))(.*|$)$`
`$1.php?r=$2 [QSA]`
	`rewrite`
	`^/(?:(.*?)(?:/|$))(.*|$)$`
	`/$1.php?r=$2 last;`

Summary

Switching from Apache to Nginx may seem complex at first. There are many steps involved in the process, and you may face unsolvable problems if you are not confident and well-prepared. You need to be aware of the current limitations of Nginx: no on-the-fly configuration changes, and thus no .htaccess or a similar feature. Nginx does not have nearly as many modules as Apache does, at least not yet. Last but not least, you have to convert all your rewrite rules for your websites to be functional under Nginx. So yes, it does take quite a bit of work. But this is a small price to pay to get a server that will ensure long-term stability and scalability. You and your visitors will not regret it, as it generally comes with improved loading and response speeds.

Directive Index

The table below lists directives from all of the available first-party Nginx modules. Each directive comes with a brief description, the module providing the directive (marked with a "*" if the module is not included by default), and the chapter and section where you will find more information. Directives are sorted alphabetically.

Directive	Module
`accept_mutex`: Enables or disables the use of an accept mutex	Events
Chapter 3, Events module section	
`accept_mutex_delay`: Sets the delay of the accept mutex	Events
Chapter 3, Events module section	
`access_log`: Defines access log settings	Log
Chapter 5, Website access and logging section	
`add_after_body`: Adds content after response body	Addition*
Chapter 5, Content and encoding section	
`add_before_body`: Adds content before response body	Addition*
Chapter 5, Content and encoding section	
`add_header`: Adds arbitrary headers to responses	Headers
Chapter 5, Content and encoding section	
`alias`: Sets a directory alias	HTTP Core
Chapter 4, Paths and documents section	
`allow`: Allows an IP address or address range to access a resource	Access
Chapter 5, Limits and restrictions section	

Directive	Module
`ancient_browser`: Affects `$ancient_browser` if the request user agent matches a specified string	Browser
Chapter 5, About your visitors section	
`ancient_browser_value`: Sets the value to be affected to `$ancient_browser`	Browser
Chapter 5, About your visitors section	
`auth_basic`: Sets a text message to be displayed in basic authentication dialogs	Auth Basic
Chapter 5, Limits and restrictions section	
`auth_basic_user_file`: Defines the file containing usernames and passwords for basic authentication	Auth Basic
Chapter 5, Limits and restrictions section	
`autoindex`: Enables automatic directory indexes	Autoindex
Chapter 5, Website access and logging section	
`autoindex_exact_size`: Shows file sizes in bytes for automatic directory indexes	Autoindex
Chapter 5, Website access and logging section	
`autoindex_localtime`: Enables or disables adjusting file dates to match server local time	Autoindex
Chapter 5, Website access and logging section	
`break`: Prevents further URL rewrites	Rewrite
Chapter 5, Rewrite module directives section	
`charset`: Sets `charset` value in Content-Type HTTP header	Charset
Chapter 5, Content and encoding section	
`charset_map`: Defines character re-encoding tables	Charset
Chapter 5, Content and encoding section	
`charset_types`: Defines MIME types eligible for charset re-encoding	Charset
Chapter 5, Content and encoding section	
`client_body_buffer_size`: Specifies the buffer size for client request body	HTTP Core
Chapter 4, Client requests section	

Directive	Module
`client_body_in_file_only`: Forces Nginx to store the client request body as a file in all cases	HTTP Core
Chapter 4, Client requests section	
`client_body_in_single_buffer`: Defines whether or not the body of client requests should be stored in a single buffer	HTTP Core
Chapter 4, Client requests section	
`client_body_temp_path`: Sets the path for storing temporary client request body files	HTTP Core
Chapter 4, Client requests section	
`client_body_timeout`: Sets inactivity timeout for reading client request body	HTTP Core
Chapter 4, Client requests section	
`client_header_buffer_size`: Sets the size of buffers allocated to request headers	HTTP Core
Chapter 4, Client requests section	
`client_header_timeout`: Sets inactivity timeout for reading client request headers	HTTP Core
Chapter 4, Client requests section	
`client_max_body_size`: Sets the maximum size for client request body	HTTP Core
Chapter 4, Client requests section	
`connection_pool_size`: Defines the size of the pool memory space to be allocated to connections	HTTP Core
Chapter 4, Socket and host configuration section	
`connections`: Deprecated (see `worker_connections`)	Events
Chapter 3, Events module section	
`create_full_put_path`: Enables or disables recursive directory creation (creates full path) for PUT requests	DAV*
Chapter 5, Other miscellaneous modules section	
`daemon`: Enables or disables daemon mode	Core
Chapter 3, Core module directives section	
`dav_access`: Defines access permissions at the current level	DAV*
Chapter 5, Other miscellaneous modules section	

Directive	Module
`fastcgi_cache_key`: Sets the key for caching FastCGI-processed requests	FastCGI
Chapter 6, FastCGI caching section	
`fastcgi_cache_methods`: Sets eligible HTTP methods for FastCGI caching	FastCGI
Chapter 6, FastCGI caching section	
`fastcgi_cache_path`: Configures FastCGI caching options for a specified zone	FastCGI
Chapter 6, FastCGI caching section	
`fastcgi_cache_use_stale`: Defines whether or not stale cache data should be used in certain circumstances	FastCGI
Chapter 6, FastCGI caching section	
`fastcgi_cache_valid`: Sets caching validity period for specific response codes	FastCGI
Chapter 6, FastCGI caching section	
`fastcgi_catch_stderr`: Allows you to intercept some of the error messages sent to `stderr` and store them in the Nginx error log	FastCGI
Chapter 6, Main directives section	
`fastcgi_connect_timeout`: Defines the backend server connection timeout	FastCGI
Chapter 6, Main directives section	
`fastcgi_hide_header`: Skips FastCGI headers	FastCGI
Chapter 6, Main directives section	
`fastcgi_ignore_client_abort`: Sets FastCGI module behavior when clients abort requests	FastCGI
Chapter 6, Main directives section	
`fastcgi_ignore_headers`: Prevents Nginx from processing one of the following four headers from the backend server response: *X-Accel-Redirect, X-Accel-Expires, Expires, Cache-Control*	FastCGI
Chapter 6, Main directives section	
`fastcgi_index`: Specifies directory index for FastCGI	FastCGI
Chapter 6, Main directives section	

Directive	Module
`fastcgi_store`: Defines FastCGI cache store settings	FastCGI
Chapter 6, Main directives section	
`fastcgi_store_access`: Sets FastCGI cache store access permissions	FastCGI
Chapter 6, Main directives section	
`fastcgi_temp_file_write_size`: Sets the write buffer size when saving temporary files to the storage device	FastCGI
Chapter 6, Main directives section	
`fastcgi_temp_path`: Sets directory path for FastCGI temporary files	FastCGI
Chapter 6, Main directives section	
`flv`: Enables seeking in FLV files	FLV*
Chapter 5, Content and encoding section	
`geo`: Defines a map of values based on the client's IP address	Geo
Chapter 5, About your visitors section	
`geoip_city`: Sets the path to your IP-to-city database	Geo IP*
Chapter 5, About your visitors section	
`geoip_country`: Sets the path to your IP-to-country database	Geo IP*
Chapter 5, About your visitors section	
`google_perftools_profiles`: Sets path of Google-perftools profiles file	Google Perftools*
Chapter 5, Other miscellaneous modules section	
`gzip_buffers`: Defines the size of buffers for storing a Gzipped response	Gzip
Chapter 5, Content and encoding section	
`gzip_comp_level`: Defines the compression level for Gzipped responses	Gzip
Chapter 5, Content and encoding section	
`gzip_disable`: Disables Gzip compression for requests with a user-agent matching the specified regular expression	Gzip
Chapter 5, Content and encoding section	
`gzip_hash`: Sets the amount of memory that should be allocated for the internal compression state (memLevel argument)	Gzip
Chapter 5, Content and encoding section	

Directive	Module
`gzip_http_version`: Enables Gzip compression for the specified HTTP version	Gzip
Chapter 5, Content and encoding section	
`gzip_min_length`: Sets a minimum length for responses to be eligible to Gzip compression	Gzip
Chapter 5, Content and encoding section	
`gzip_no_buffer`: Enabling this directive disables buffering for Gzipped responses	Gzip
Chapter 5, Content and encoding section	
`gzip_proxied`: Enables or disables Gzip compression for the body of responses received from a proxy	Gzip
Chapter 5, Content and encoding section	
`gzip_static`: Enables pre-compressed response module	Gzip static*
Chapter 5, Content and encoding section	
`gzip_types`: Sets MIME types eligible for Gzip compression	Gzip
Chapter 5, Content and encoding section	
`gzip_vary`: Enables or disables including the *Vary HTTP* header in the response	Gzip
Chapter 5, Content and encoding section	
`gzip_window`: Sets the size of the window buffer (*windowBits* argument) for Gzipping operations	Gzip
Chapter 5, Content and encoding section	
`if_modified_since`: Defines how Nginx handles the If-Modified-Since HTTP header	HTTP Core
Chapter 4, Paths and documents section	
`ignore_invalid_headers`: When disabled Nginx returns a `400 Bad Request` HTTP error, in case request headers are misformed	HTTP Core
Chapter 4, Client requests section	
`image_filter`: Applies transformations on images	Image Filter*
Chapter 5, Content and encoding section	
`image_filter_buffer`: Sets the maximum file size for images	Image Filter*
Chapter 5, Content and encoding section	

Directive	Module
`image_filter_jpeg_quality`: Sets JPEG quality for image filter output	Image Filter*
Chapter 5, Content and encoding section	
`include`: Includes an external configuration file	Core
Chapter 3, Core module directives section	
`index`: Sets the default filename(s) for directory indexes	Index
Chapter 5, Website access and logging section	
`internal`: Restricts a location block to internal sub-requests and redirects	HTTP Core
Chapter 4, Limits and restrictions section	
`keepalive_requests`: Maximum amount of requests served over a single keep-alive connection	HTTP Core
Chapter 4, Client requests section	
`keepalive_timeout`: Amount of seconds Nginx waits before closing a keep-alive connection	HTTP Core
Chapter 4, Client requests section	
`large_client_header_buffers`: Sets size of buffers for client request with larger headers	HTTP Core
Chapter 4, Client requests section	
`limit_conn`: Limits the amount of connections per zone	Limit Zone
Chapter 5, Limits and restrictions section	
`limit_except`: Sets the allowed HTTP methods	HTTP Core
Chapter 4, Limits and restrictions section	
`limit_rate`: Limits transfer rate per connection	HTTP Core
Chapter 4, Limits and restrictions section	
`limit_rate_after`: Limits transfer rate after a specified limit	HTTP Core
Chapter 4, Limits and restrictions section	
`limit_req`: Limits the amount of requests per zone	Limit Req
Chapter 5, Limits and restrictions section	
`limit_req_zone`: Defines a zone to be used with `limit_req`	Limit Req
Chapter 5, Limits and restrictions section	
`limit_zone`: Defines a zone to be used with `limit_conn`	Limit Zone
Chapter 5, Limits and restrictions section	

Directive	Module
`lingering_time`: Defines behavior when a client submits a request that exceeds the maximum allowed size	HTTP Core
Chapter 4, Client requests section	
`lingering_timeout`: Amount of time that Nginx should wait between two read operations before closing the client connection	HTTP Core
Chapter 4, Client requests section	
`listen`: Specifies settings for listening sockets	HTTP Core
Chapter 4, Socket and Host configuration section	
`lock_file`: Sets the path of the lock file	Core
Chapter 3, Core module directives section	
`log_format`: Defines format of access log entries	Log
Chapter 5, Website access and logging section	
`log_not_found`: Enables or disables logging of 404 errors	HTTP Core
Chapter 4, Other directives section	
`log_subrequest`: Enables or disables including details about sub-requests in the logfiles	HTTP Core
Chapter 4, Other directives section	
`map`: Defines a map of values to be matched against a variable; the result is stored in another variable	Map
Chapter 5, About your visitors section	
`map_hash_bucket_size`: Sets the maximum size of a map entry	Map
Chapter 5, About your visitors section	
`map_hash_max_size`: Sets the maximum amount of entries in a map	Map
Chapter 5, About your visitors section	
`master_process`: Enables or disables master process	Core
Chapter 3, Core module directives section	
`memcached_buffer_size`: Sets memcached data buffer size	Memcached
Chapter 5, Content and encoding section	
`memcached_connect_timeout`: Sets memcached connect timeout	Memcached
Chapter 5, Content and encoding section	
`memcached_next_upstream`: Sets conditions for switching to the next upstream server for memcached configurations	Memcached
Chapter 5, Content and encoding section	

Directive	Module
`memcached_pass`: Configures memcached access	Memcached
Chapter 5, Content and encoding section	
`memcached_read_timeout`: Sets memcached data read operations timeout	Memcached
Chapter 5, Content and encoding section	
`memcached_send_timeout`: Sets memcached data send operations timeout	Memcached
Chapter 5, Content and encoding section	
`merge_slashes`: Enables or disables merging of double slashes in URLs	HTTP Core
Chapter 4, Other directives section	
`min_delete_depth`: Defines a minimum URI depth for deleting files or directories when processing the DELETE command	DAV*
Chapter 5, Other miscellaneous modules section	
`modern_browser`: Affects the `$modern_browser` if the request user agent matches specified string	Browser
Chapter 5, About your visitors section	
`modern_browser_value`: Sets the value to be affected to `$modern_browser`	Browser
Chapter 5, About your visitors section	
`msie_padding`: Enables response padding for MSIE browsers	HTTP Core
Chapter 4, Other directives section	
`msie_refresh`: Enables MSIE-specific redirects for the MSIE browser family	HTTP Core
Chapter 4, Other directives section	
`multi_accept`: Enables or disables accepting multiple connections from the queue at once	Events
Chapter 3, Events module section	
`open_file_cache`: Defines open file cache store settings	HTTP Core
Chapter 4, File processing and caching section	
`open_file_cache_errors`: Defines whether or not file errors should be cached in the open file cache store	HTTP Core
Chapter 4, File processing and caching section	

Directive	Module
`open_file_cache_min_uses`: Defines the minimum amount of uses for a file to remain in the cache	HTTP Core
Chapter 4, File processing and caching section	
`open_file_cache_valid`: Sets the cache verification interval	HTTP Core
Chapter 4, File processing and caching section	
`open_log_file_cache`: Configures the cache of log file descriptors	Log
Chapter 5, Website access and logging section	
`override_charset`: Overrides charset for documents received via proxy or FastCGI	Charset
Chapter 5, Content and encoding section	
`pid`: Sets the path of the pid file	Core
Chapter 3, Core module directives section	
`port_in_redirect`: Enables or disables including port number for internal redirects	HTTP Core
Chapter 4, Socket and host configuration section	
`post_action`: Defines a *post-completion action*, a URI that will be called by Nginx after the request has been completed	HTTP Core
Chapter 4, Other directives section	
`postpone_gzipping`: Defines a minimum data threshold to be reached before starting the Gzip compression	HTTP Core
Chapter 5, Content and encoding section	
`postpone_output`: Postpones the sending of the response; this directive defines the size of data to be sent in each packet	HTTP Core
Chapter 4, Socket and host configuration section	
`proxy_buffer_size`: Sets the size of backend response buffer	Proxy
Chapter 7, Caching, buffering, and temporary files section	
`proxy_buffering`: Enables or disables backend response buffering	Proxy
Chapter 7, Caching, buffering, and temporary files section	
`proxy_buffers`: Sets amount and size of buffers for backend communications	Proxy
Chapter 7, Caching, buffering, and temporary files section	

Directive	Module
`proxy_busy_buffers_size`: Sets size of buffers for busy backend servers	Proxy
Chapter 7, Caching, buffering, and temporary files section	
`proxy_cache`: Defines a proxy cache zone	Proxy
Chapter 7, Caching, buffering, and temporary files section	
`proxy_cache_key`: Sets the key for caching proxied requests	Proxy
Chapter 7, Caching, buffering, and temporary files section	
`proxy_cache_methods`: Sets eligible HTTP methods for proxy caching	Proxy
Chapter 7, Caching, buffering, and temporary files section	
`proxy_cache_min_uses`: Sets amount of times a cache entry should be used before being protected from cache sweeping	Proxy
Chapter 7, Caching, buffering, and temporary files section	
`proxy_cache_path`: Configures proxy caching options for a specified zone	Proxy
Chapter 7, Caching, buffering, and temporary files section	
`proxy_cache_use_stale`: Defines whether or not stale cache data should be used in certain circumstances	Proxy
Chapter 7, Caching, buffering, and temporary files section	
`proxy_cache_valid`: Sets caching validity period for specific response codes	Proxy
Chapter 7, Caching, buffering, and temporary files section	
`proxy_connect_timeout`: Sets timeout for connecting to the backend	Proxy
Chapter 7, Limits, timeouts, and errors section	
`proxy_headers_hash_bucket_size`: Sets the maximum size of entries in the headers hash table	Proxy
Chapter 7, Other directives section	
`proxy_headers_hash_max_size`: Sets the maximum amount of entries in the headers hash table	Proxy
Chapter 7, Other directives section	
`proxy_hide_header`: Skips specified header for reverse proxying	Proxy
Chapter 7, Main directives section	

Directive	Module
`proxy_ignore_client_abort`: Sets proxy module behavior when clients abort requests	Proxy
Chapter 7, Limits, timeouts, and errors section	
`proxy_ignore_headers`: Prevents Nginx from processing specified headers	Proxy
Chapter 7, Other directives section	
`proxy_intercept_errors`: Defines whether or not backend generated errors should be returned 'as is'	Proxy
Chapter 7, Limits, timeouts, and errors section	
`proxy_max_temp_file_size`: Sets maximum size for temporary files	Proxy
Chapter 7, Caching, buffering, and temporary files section	
`proxy_method`: Allows additional HTTP methods for reverse proxying	Proxy
Chapter 7, Main directives section	
`proxy_next_upstream`: Defines upstream server skipping conditions	Proxy
Chapter 7, Main directives section	
`proxy_pass`: Enables reverse proxying to a backend server by specifying its location	Proxy
Chapter 7, Main directives section	
`proxy_pass_header`: Disables skipping of specified header for reverse proxying	Proxy
Chapter 7, Main directives section	
`proxy_pass_request_body`: Allows request body to be passed to backend	Proxy
Chapter 7, Main directives section	
`proxy_pass_request_header`: Allows extra request headers to be passed to backend	Proxy
Chapter 7, Main directives section	
`proxy_read_timeout`: Sets read timeout for backend communications	Proxy
Chapter 7, Limits, timeouts, and errors section	
`proxy_redirect`: Enables or disables handling of redirects generated by backend	Proxy
Chapter 7, Main directives section	

Directive	Module
`proxy_send_lowat`: Allows you to make use of the `SO_SNDLOWAT` flag for TCP sockets for communications with backends, under FreeBSD only	Proxy
Chapter 7, Limits, timeouts, and errors section	
`proxy_send_timeout`: Sets write timeout for backend communications	Proxy
Chapter 7, Limits, timeouts, and errors section	
`proxy_set_body`: Sets request body for debugging purposes	Proxy
Chapter 7, Other directives section	
`proxy_set_header`: Sets extra header data for debugging purposes	Proxy
Chapter 7, Other directives section	
`proxy_store`: Enables cache store for proxy communications	Proxy
Chapter 7, Other directives section	
`proxy_store_access`: Sets cache store access permissions	Proxy
Chapter 7, Other directives section	
`proxy_temp_file_write_size`: Sets write buffer size when writing temporary files	Proxy
Chapter 7, Caching, buffering, and temporary files section	
`proxy_temp_path`: Sets directory path for proxy temporary files	Proxy
Chapter 7, Caching, buffering, and temporary files section	
`random_index`: Enables or disables selecting a random file to be served as directory index	Random Index*
Chapter 5, Website access and logging section	
`real_ip_header`: Sets the HTTP header to be used for the replacement IP address	Real IP*
Chapter 5, About your visitors section	
`recursive_error_pages`: Enables or disables the use of recursive error pages with the error_page directive	HTTP Core
Chapter 4, Paths and documents section	
`request_pool_size`: Defines the size of the pool memory space to be allocated to requests	HTTP Core
Chapter 4, Socket and host configuration section	

Directive	Module
`reset_timedout_connection`: Enables or disables erasing connection information after timeouts	HTTP Core
Chapter 4, Socket and host configuration section	
`resolver`: Sets the IP address of the DNS server	HTTP Core
Chapter 4, Other directives section	
`resolver_timeout`: Sets the timeout for resolving hostnames	HTTP Core
Chapter 4, Other directives section	
`return`: Interrupts request and returns specified code	Rewrite
Chapter 5, Rewrite module directives section	
`rewrite`: Rewrites a URL	Rewrite
Chapter 5, Rewrite module directives section	
`rewrite_log`: Enables or disables issuing log messages from the rewrite engine at the `notice` log level	Rewrite
Chapter 5, Rewrite module directives section	
`root`: Sets the document root of a virtual host or virtual path	HTTP Core
Chapter 4, Paths and documents section	
`satisfy`: Defines resource access conditions	HTTP Core
Chapter 4, Limits and restrictions section	
`secure_link_secret`: Sets the secret word for the secure URL	Secure Link*
Chapter 5, SSL and security section	
`send_lowat`: Enables or disables the use of the `SO_SNDLOWAT` TCP socket flag under BSD systems for communications with the client	HTTP Core
Chapter 4, Socket and host configuration section	
`send_timeout`: The number of seconds after last packet received before Nginx closes a client connection	HTTP Core
Chapter 4, Client requests section	
`sendfile`: Enables or disables the use of the sendfile kernel call to handle file transmissions	HTTP Core
Chapter 4, Socket and Host Configuration section	
`sendfile_max_chunk`: Maximum size of data to be used for each call to sendfile	HTTP Core
Chapter 4, Socket and Host Configuration section	
`server`: Declares a server entry in an upstream block	Upstream
Chapter 6, Upstream blocks section	

Directive	Module
`server_name`: Sets the virtual host server names	HTTP Core
Chapter 4, Socket and Host Configuration section	
`server_name_in_redirect`: Enables or disables server name for internal redirects	HTTP Core
Chapter 4, Socket and Host Configuration section	
`server_names_hash_bucket_size`: Sets the maximum size of a server name in the hash table	HTTP Core
Chapter 4, Socket and Host Configuration section	
`server_names_hash_max_size`: Sets the maximum amount of server names in the hash table	HTTP Core
Chapter 4, Socket and Host Configuration section	
`server_tokens`: Enables or disable server information display	HTTP Core
Chapter 4, Other directives section	
`set`: Sets the value of a variable	Rewrite
Chapter 5, Rewrite module directives section	
`set_real_ip_from`: Defines a trusted server by declaring its IP address	Real IP*
Chapter 5, About your visitors section	
`source_charset`: Sets source charset for documents	Charset
Chapter 5, Content and encoding section	
`ssi`: Activates server-side includes	SSI
Chapter 5, SSI module directives and variables section	
`ssi_ignore_recycled_buffers`: Prevents Nginx from making use of recycled buffers	SSI
Chapter 5, SSI module directives and variables section	
`ssi_min_file_chunk`: Defines buffering and storage settings for SSI requests	SSI
Chapter 5, SSI module directives and variables section	
`ssi_silent_errors`: Defines whether or not SSI errors should be silent	SSI
Chapter 5, SSI module directives and variables section	
`ssi_types`: Defines MIME types eligible for SSI parsing	SSI
Chapter 5, SSI module directives and variables section	

Directive	Module
`ssi_value_length`: Defines the maximum size for SSI tag values	SSI
Chapter 5, SSI module directives and variables section	
`ssl`: Enables HTTPS for a virtual host	SSL*
Chapter 5, SSL and security section	
`ssl_certificate`: Sets the path of the PEM certificate file	SSL*
Chapter 5, SSL and security section	
`ssl_certificate_key`: Sets the path of the PEM secret key file	SSL*
Chapter 5, SSL and security section	
`ssl_ciphers`: Sets ciphers to be used by the SSL engine	SSL*
Chapter 5, SSL and security section	
`ssl_client_certificate`: Sets the path of the client PEM certificate file	SSL*
Chapter 5, SSL and security section	
`ssl_dhparam`: Sets the path of the DH file	SSL*
Chapter 5, SSL and security section	
`ssl_engine`: Specifies the name of the desired SSL engine	Core
Chapter 3, Core module directives section	
`ssl_prefer_server_ciphers`: Defines whether or not the server ciphers should be preferred over the client servers	SSL*
Chapter 5, SSL and security section	
`ssl_protocols`: Sets protocols to be used by the SSL engine	SSL*
Chapter 5, SSL and security section	
`ssl_session_cache`: Configures SSL session cache settings	SSL*
Chapter 5, SSL and security section	
`ssl_session_timeout`: Sets the timeout for SSL sessions	SSL*
Chapter 5, SSL and security section	
`ssl_verify_client`: Enables or disables verifying client certificates	SSL*
Chapter 5, SSL and security section	
`ssl_verify_depth`: Sets certificate verification depth	SSL*
Chapter 5, SSL and security section	
`stub_status`: Enables or disables stub status information	Stub Status*
Chapter 5, Other miscellaneous modules section	

Directive	Module
sub_filter: Searches and replaces text in the response	Substitution*
Chapter 5, Content and encoding section	
sub_filter_once: Defines whether or not sub_filter should search and replace only one occurrence	Substitution*
Chapter 5, Content and encoding section	
sub_filter_types: Defines MIME types to be affected by the search and replace filter	Substitution*
Chapter 5, Content and encoding section	
tcp_nodelay: Enables or disables TCP_NODELAY socket option for keep-alive connections	HTTP Core
Chapter 4, Socket and Host configuration section	
tcp_nopush: Enables or disables TCP_NOPUSH (BSD) or TCP_CORK (Linux) socket option for keep-alive connections	HTTP Core
Chapter 4, Socket and Host configuration section	
thread_stack_size: Sets the size of the thread stack	Core
Chapter 3, Core module directives section	
timer_resolution: Interval for synchronizing the internal clock	Core
Chapter 3, Core module directives section	
try_files: Attempts to serve files; if none found, jump to a named block	HTTP Core
Chapter 4, Paths and documents section	
types: Matches MIME types with file extensions	HTTP Core
Chapter 4, MIME types section	
types_hash_bucket_size: Defines the maximum size of an entry in the MIME types hash table	HTTP Core
Chapter 4, MIME types section	
types_hash_max_size: Defines the maximum amount of entries in the MIME types hash table	HTTP Core
Chapter 4, MIME types section	
underscores_in_headers: Allows or disallows underscores in HTTP header names	HTTP Core
Chapter 4, Other directives section	

Directive	Module
`worker_connections`: Defines the amount of simultaneous connections per worker process	Events
Chapter 3, Events Module section	
`worker_cpu_affinity`: Defines affinity of worker processes with CPU cores	Core
Chapter 3, Core module directives section	
`worker_priority`: Sets the priority of worker processes	Core
Chapter 3, Core module directives section	
`worker_processes`: Sets the amount of worker processes	Core
Chapter 3, Core module directives section	
`worker_rlimit_core`: Sets the size of core files for worker processes	Core
Chapter 3, Core module directives section	
`worker_rlimit_nofile`: Sets the amount of file a worker process can use simultaneously	Core
Chapter 3, Core module directives section	
`worker_rlimit_sigpending`: Defines the amount of signals a worker process can queue	Core
Chapter 3, Core module directives section	
`worker_threads`: Enables threading (not recommended)	Core
Chapter 3, Core module directives section	
`working_directory`: Sets the working directory for worker processes	Core
Chapter 3, Core module directives section	
`xml_entities`: Specifies a DTD file containing symbolic element definitions	XSLT*
Chapter 5, Content and encoding section	
`xslt_stylesheet`: Specifies the XSLT template file path with its parameters	XSLT*
Chapter 5, Content and encoding section	
`xslt_types`: Sets MIME types, on which transformations should be applied	XSLT*
Chapter 5, Content and encoding section	

B
Module Reference

This appendix summarizes the available Nginx modules, as of stable version 0.7.66. For each module, a brief description is provided as well as some particular characteristics and a reference to the chapter where you will be able to find more information. The modules are listed in alphabetical order.

Modules marked with a * are optional modules, which are not included when you build Nginx without extra configure switches. The appropriate configure switch to enable or disable modules is detailed with each module.

Access

Allows you to grant or deny access to a resource, based on an IP address or address range.

Key directives: `allow, deny`

Configure switch: `--without-http_access_module` disables the module.

Chapter 5, Limits and restrictions section

Addition*

Lets you specify content that should be added before or after the response body.

Key directives: `add_before_body, add_after_body`

Configure switch: `--with-http_addition_module` enables the module.

Chapter 5, Content and encoding section

Auth_basic module

Lets you set up basic authentication settings on a specified location.

Key directives: `auth_basic, auth_basic_user_file`

Configure switch: `--without-http_auth_basic_module` enables the module.

Chapter 5, Limits and restrictions section

Autoindex

Enables automatic file listing for directories without an index file.

Key directive: `autoindex`

Configure switch: `--without-http_autoindex_module` disables the module.

Chapter 5, Website access and logging section

Browser

Parses the *User-Agent* HTTP header and assigns variables in consequence.

Key directives: `modern_browser, ancient_browser`

Configure switch: `--without-http_browser_module` disables the module.

Chapter 5, About your visitors section

Charset

Provides page content recoding functionality.

Key directives: `charset, override_charset`

Configure switch: `--without-http_charset_module` disables the module.

Chapter 5, Content and encoding section

Core

Provides core functionality such as daemonization and socket processing.

Key directives: `worker_processes, user`

Configure switch: This module is enabled by default and cannot be disabled.

Chapter 3, Core module section

DAV*

Enables WebDAV (Web-based Distributed Authoring and Versioning) support.

Key directives: `dav_methods, dav_access`

Configure switch: `--with-http_dav_module` enables the module.

Chapter 5, Other miscellaneous modules section

Empty GIF

Allows serving an empty GIF file directly from memory.

Key directive: `empty_gif`

Configure switch: `--without-http_empty_gif_module` disables the module.

Chapter 5, Content and encoding section

Events

Allows you to select and configure the connection event model.

Key directive: `worker_connections`

Configure switch: This module is enabled by default and cannot be disabled.

Chapter 3, Events module section

FastCGI

Enables FastCGI support.

Key directives: `fastcgi_pass`, `fastcgi_param`

Configure switch: `--without-http_fastcgi_module` disables the module.

Chapter 6, FastCGI module section

FLV*

Enables seeking in FLV files.

Key directive: `flv`

Configure switch: `--with-http_flv_module` enables the module.

Chapter 5, Content and encoding section

Geo

Affects a variable based on a map of values affected to IP addresses or address ranges.

Key directive: `geo`

Configure switch: `--without-http_geo_module` disables the module.

Chapter 5, About your visitors section

Geo IP*

Enables support for MaxMind's GeoIP databases.

Key directives: `geoip_country`, `geoip_city`

Configure switch: `--with-http_geoip_module` enables the module.

Chapter 5, About your visitors section

Google-perftools*

Enables Google Performance Tools profiling support.

Key directive: `google_perftools_profiles`

Configure switch: `--with-google_perftools_module` enables the module.

Chapter 5, Other miscellaneous modules section

Gzip

Allows compression of the response body with the Gzip compression algorithm.

Key directives: `gzip, gzip_comp_level`

Configure switch: `--without-http_gzip_module` disables the module.

Chapter 5, Content and encoding section

Gzip Static*

Enables serving of pre-compressed response files.

Key directive: `gzip_static`

Configure switch: `--with-http_gzip_static_module` enables the module.

Chapter 5, Content and encoding section

Headers

Allows defining arbitrary HTTP response headers.

Key directives: `add_header, expires`

Configure switch: This module is included by default and cannot be disabled.

Chapter 5, Content and encoding section

HTTP Core

Provides core HTTP functionality.

Key directives: `listen`, `server_name`, and so on

Configure switch: `--without-http` disables all HTTP-related functionality.

Chapter 4, HTTP Core module section

Image Filter*

Provides image transforming functionality via GDLib.

Key directive: `image_filter`

Configure switch: `--with-http_image_filter_module` enables the module.

Chapter 5, Content and encoding section

Index

Allows defining a file to be used as the directory index.

Key directive: `index`

Configure switch: This module is included by default and cannot be disabled.

Chapter 5, Website access and logging section

Limit Requests

Allows limiting of requests for a defined zone.

Key directives: `limit_req`, `limit_req_zone`

Configure switch: `--without-http_limit_req_module` disables the module.

Chapter 5, Limits and restrictions section

Limit Zone

Allows limiting of connections for a defined zone.

Key directives: `limit_zone, limit_conn`

Configure switch: `--without-http_limit_zone_module` disables the module.

Chapter 5, Limits and restrictions section

Log

Provides access log customization functionality.

Key directives: `access_log, log_format`

Configure switch: This module is included by default and cannot be disabled.

Chapter 5, Website access and logging section

Map

Affects a variable based on a defined map of keys and values.

Key directive: `map`

Configure switch: `--without-http_map_module` disables the module.

Chapter 5, About your visitors section

Memcached

Provides directives for interacting with *memcached* (memory cache daemon).

Key directive: `memcached_pass`

Configure switch: `--without-http_memcached_module` disables the module.

Chapter 5, Content and encoding section

Proxy

Provides reverse proxying functionality.

Key directives: `proxy_pass`, `proxy_set_header`, and so on

Configure switch: `--without-http_proxy_module` disables the module.

Chapter 7, Proxy module section

Random index*

Allows selecting a random file as the directory index.

Key directive: `random_index`

Configure switch: `--with-http_random_index_module` enables the module.

Chapter 5, Website access and logging section

Real IP*

Allows retrieving the real client IP from headers when using Nginx as the backend.

Key directives: `set_real_ip_from`, `real_ip_header`

Configure switch: `--with-http_realip_module` enables the module.

Chapter 5, About your visitors section

Referer

Allow establishing a whitelist of HTTP referrers.

Key directive: `valid_referers`

Configure switch: `--without-http_referer_module` disables the module.

Chapter 5, About your visitors section

Rewrite

Provides URL rewriting functionality.

Key directives: `rewrite, if, return, break,` and more

Configure switch: `--without-http_rewrite_module` disables the module.

Chapter 5, Rewrite module section

Secure Link*

Provides link validation based on a hash to be located in the URL.

Key directive: `secure_link_secret`

Configure switch: `--with-http_secure_link_module` enables the module.

Chapter 5, SSL and security section

SSI

Provides Server Side Includes functionality.

Key directives: `ssi, ssi_types`

Configure switch: `--without-http_ssi_module` disables the module.

Chapter 5, SSI module section

SSL*

Enables HTTP over SSL support.

Key directives: `ssl, ssl_certificate,` and more

Configure switch: `--with-http_ssl_module` enables the module.

Chapter 5, SSL and security section

Stub status*

Provide server status information functionality.

Key directive: `stub_status`

Configure switch: `--with-http_stub_status_module` enables the module.

Chapter 5, Other miscellaneous modules section

Substitution*

Allows replacing content in a web page.

Key directives: `sub_filter, sub_filter_once`

Configure switch: `--with-http_sub_module` enables the module.

Chapter 5, Content and encoding section

Upstream

Allows setting up of load-balanced architecture.

Key directives: `upstream, server`

Configure switch: `--without-http_upstream_ip_hash_module` disables the `ip_hash` directive only. The upstream module itself is included by default and cannot be disabled.

Chapter 6, Upstream module section

User ID

Allows setting up cookies identifying visitors.

Key directives: `userid, userid_domain`

Configure switch: `--without-http_userid_module` disables the module.

Chapter 5, About your visitors section

XSLT*

Allows applying XSLT templates on the response body.

Key directives: `xslt_stylesheet`, `xml_entities`

Configure switch: `--with-http_xslt_module` enables the module.

Chapter 5, Content and encoding section

C
Troubleshooting

Even if you read every single word of this book with utmost attention, you are unfortunately not sheltered from all kinds of issues, ranging from simple configuration errors to the occasional unexpected behavior of one module or another. In this appendix, we attempt to provide solutions for some of the common problems encountered by administrators who just got started with Nginx.

The appendix covers:

- A basic guide containing general tips on Nginx troubleshooting
- How to solve some of the most common install issues
- Dealing with 403 Forbidden HTTP errors
- Why your configuration does not apply correctly
- A few words about the if block behavior

General tips on troubleshooting

Before we begin, whenever you run into some kind of problem with Nginx, you should make sure to follow the recommendations given below, as they are generally a good source of solutions.

Checking access permissions

A lot of errors that Nginx administrators are faced with are caused by invalid access permissions. At two stages, you are offered to specify a user and group for the Nginx worker processes to run:

- When configuring the build with the configure command, you are allowed to specify a user and group that will be used by default (refer to Chapter 2).
- In the configuration file, the user directive allows you to specify a user and group. This directive overrides the value that you may have defined during the configure step.

If Nginx is supposed to access files that do not have the correct permissions, in other words, which cannot be read (and by extension cannot be written, for directories that hold temporary files for example) by the specified user and group, Nginx will not be able to serve files correctly.

Testing your configuration

A common mistake is often made by administrators showing a little too much self-confidence — after having modified the configuration file (often without a backup), they reload Nginx to apply the new configuration. If the configuration file contains syntax or semantic errors, the application will refuse to reload. Even worse, if Nginx was stopped, such as after a complete server reboot, it will refuse to start at all. In all those cases, remember to follow these recommendations:

- Always keep a backup of your working configuration files
- Before reloading or restarting Nginx, test your configuration with this simple command: `nginx -t` to test your current configuration files or `nginx -t -c /path/to/config/file.conf`
- Reload your server instead of restarting it — preferring `service nginx reload` over `service nginx restart` (`nginx -s reload` instead of `nginx -s stop && nginx`)

Have you reloaded the service?

You would be surprised to learn how often this happens — the most complicated situations have the simplest solutions. Before tearing your hair out, before rushing to the forums or IRC asking for help, start with the most simple of verifications.

You just spent two hours creating your virtual host configuration; you saved the files properly and fired up your web browser to check the results. But remember that one additional step — Nginx, unlike Apache, does not support on-the-fly configuration changes in `.htaccess` files or similar. So take a moment to make sure you did reload Nginx with `service nginx reload`, `/etc/init.d/nginx reload` or `/usr/local/nginx/sbin/nginx -s reload` without forgetting to test your configuration beforehand!

Checking logs

There is usually no need to look for the answer to your problems on the Internet — chances are that the answer is already given to you by Nginx in the logfiles. There are two variations of log files you may want to check — first, the access logs. These contain information about requests themselves: the request method and URI, the HTTP response code issued by Nginx, and more, depending on the log format you defined.

More importantly for troubleshooting, the error log is a goldmine of information. Depending on the level you defined (see `error_log` directive for more details), Nginx will provide details on its inner functioning. For example, you will be able to see request URI translated to actual file system path; this can be a great help for debugging rewrite rules. The error log should be located in the `/logs/` directory of your Nginx setup, by default `/usr/local/nginx/logs`.

Install issues

There are typically three sources of errors when attempting to install Nginx or to run it for the first time:

- Some of the prerequisites are missing or an invalid path to the source was specified. More details about prerequisites can be found in Chapter 2.

- After having installed Nginx correctly, you cannot use the SSL-related directives to host a secure website. Have you made sure to include the SSL module correctly during the configure step? More details in Chapter 2.

- Nginx refuses to start and outputs a message similar to `[emerg] 3629#0: open() "/path/to/logs/access.log" failed (2: No such file or directory)`. In this case, one of the files that Nginx tries to open, such as logfiles, cannot be accessed. This could be caused by invalid access permissions or by invalid directory path, for example, when specifying log files to be stored in a directory that does not exist on the system.

403 Forbidden custom error page

If you decided to use `allow` and `deny` directives to respectively allow or deny access to a resource on your server, clients who are being denied access will usually fall back on a `403 Forbidden` error page. You carefully set up a custom, user-friendly 403 error page for your clients to understand why they are denied access. Unfortunately, you cannot get that custom page to work; clients still get the default Nginx 403 error page.

```
server {
    [...]
    allow 192.168.0.0/16;
    deny all;
    error_page 403 /error403.html;
}
```

The problem is simple—Nginx also denies access to your custom 403 error page! In such a case, you need to override the access rules in a location block specifically matching your page. You could use the following to allow access to your custom 403 error page only:

```
server {
    [...]
    location / {
        error_page 403 /error403.html;
        allow 192.168.0.0/16;
        deny all;
    }
    location = /error403.html {
        allow all;
    }
}
```

If you are going to have more than just one error page, you could specify a location block matching all error page filenames:

```
server {
    [...]
    location / {
        error_page 403 /error403.html;
        error_page 404 /error404.html;
        allow 192.168.0.0/16;
        deny all;
    }
    location ~ "^/error[0-9]{3}\.html$" {
        allow all;
    }
}
```

All your visitors are now allowed to view your custom error pages.

Location block priorities

The problem frequently occurs when using multiple location blocks in the same server block—configuration does not apply as you thought it would.

As an example, say you want to define a behavior to be applied to all image files that are requested by clients:

```
location ~* \.(gif|jpg|jpeg|png)$ {
    # matches any request for GIF/JPG/JPEG/PNG files
    proxy_pass http://imageserver; # proxy pass to backend
}
```

Later on, you decide to enable automatic indexing of the /images/ directory. You thus decide to create a new location block, matching all requests starting with /images/:

```
location ^~ /images/ {
    # matches any request that starts with /images/
    autoindex on;
}
```

With this configuration, when a client requests to download /images/square.gif, Nginx will apply the second location block only. Why not the first one? The reason being that location blocks are processed in a specific order. For more information about location block priorities, refer to the *Chapter 4, HTTP configuration*, under *Location block* section.

If block issues

In some situations, if not most, you should avoid using if blocks. There are two main issues occurring, regardless of the Nginx build you are using.

Inefficient statements

There are some cases where if is used inappropriately, in a way that risks saturating your storage device with useless checks.

```
location / {
    # Redirect to index.php if the requested file is not found
    if (!-e $request_filename) {
        rewrite ^ index.php last;
    }
}
```

With such a configuration, every single request received by Nginx will trigger a complete verification of the directory tree for the requested filename, thus requiring multiple storage disk access system calls. If you test /usr/local/nginx/html/hello.html, Nginx will check /, /usr, /usr/local, /usr/local/nginx, and so on. In any case, you should avoid resorting to such a statement, for example, by filtering the file type beforehand (for instance, by making such a check, only if the requested file matches specific extensions):

```
location / {
    # Filter file extension first
    if ($request_filename !~ "\.(gif|jpg|jpeg|png)" {
        break;
    }
```

```
        if (!-f $request_filename) {
            rewrite ^ index.php last;
        }
    }
```

Unexpected behavior

The `if` block should ideally be employed for simple situations, as its behavior might be surprising in some cases. Apart from the fact that `if` statements cannot be imbricated, the following situations may present issues:

```
# Two consecutive statements with the same condition:
location / {
    if ($uri = "/test.html") {
        add_header X-Test-1 1;
        expires 7;
    }
    if ($uri = "/test.html") {
        add_header X-Test-1 1;
    }
}
```

In this case, the first `if` block is ignored and only the second one is processed. However, if you insert a Rewrite module directive in the first block, such as `rewrite`, `break`, or `return`, the block will be processed and the second one will be ignored.

There are many other cases where the use of `if` causes problems:

- Having `try_files` and `if` statements in the same location block is not recommended; the `try_files` directive will, in most cases, be ignored.

- Some directives are theoretically allowed within the `if` block but can create serious issues, for instance, `proxy_pass` and `fastcgi_pass`. You should keep those within `location` blocks.

- You should avoid using `if` blocks within a `location` block that captures regular expression patterns from its modifier.

The origin of these problems comes from the fact that while the Nginx configuration is established in a declarative language, directives from the *Rewrite module* such as `if`, `rewrite`, `return`, or `break` make it look like actual scripting. In general, you should try to avoid using directives from other modules within `if` blocks as much as possible.

Index

Symbols

About Packt Publishing

Packt, pronounced 'packed', published its first book "*Mastering phpMyAdmin for Effective MySQL Management*" in April 2004 and subsequently continued to specialize in publishing highly focused books on specific technologies and solutions.

Our books and publications share the experiences of your fellow IT professionals in adapting and customizing today's systems, applications, and frameworks. Our solution based books give you the knowledge and power to customize the software and technologies you're using to get the job done. Packt books are more specific and less general than the IT books you have seen in the past. Our unique business model allows us to bring you more focused information, giving you more of what you need to know, and less of what you don't.

Packt is a modern, yet unique publishing company, which focuses on producing quality, cutting-edge books for communities of developers, administrators, and newbies alike. For more information, please visit our website: www.packtpub.com.

About Packt Open Source

In 2010, Packt launched two new brands, Packt Open Source and Packt Enterprise, in order to continue its focus on specialization. This book is part of the Packt Open Source brand, home to books published on software built around Open Source licences, and offering information to anybody from advanced developers to budding web designers. The Open Source brand also runs Packt's Open Source Royalty Scheme, by which Packt gives a royalty to each Open Source project about whose software a book is sold.

Writing for Packt

We welcome all inquiries from people who are interested in authoring. Book proposals should be sent to author@packtpub.com. If your book idea is still at an early stage and you would like to discuss it first before writing a formal book proposal, contact us; one of our commissioning editors will get in touch with you.

We're not just looking for published authors; if you have strong technical skills but no writing experience, our experienced editors can help you develop a writing career, or simply get some additional reward for your expertise.

Lighttpd

ISBN: 978-1-847192-10-3   Paperback: 236 pages

Installing, compiling, configuring, optimizing, and securing this lightning-fast web server

1. Install, configure, and work with Lighttpd

2. Migrate from Apache to Lighttpd

3. Set up Ruby on Rails, WordPress, MediaWiki etc.

4. Understand and harness Lua/FastCGI

5. Write custom modules/plugins for the Lighttpd API

Cacti 0.8 Network Monitoring

ISBN: 978-1-847195-96-8   Paperback: 132 pages

Monitor your network with ease!

1. Install and setup Cacti to monitor your network and assign permissions to this setup in no time at all

2. Create, edit, test, and host a graph template to customize your output graph

3. Create new data input methods, SNMP, and Script XML data query

4. Full of screenshots and step-by-step instructions to monitor your network with Cacti

Please check **www.PacktPub.com** for information on our titles

Learning Nagios 3.0

ISBN: 978-1-847195-18-0   Paperback: 316 pages

A comprehensive configuration guide to monitor and maintain your network and systems

1. Secure and monitor your network system with open-source Nagios version 3

2. Set up, configure, and manage the latest version of Nagios

3. In-depth coverage for both beginners and advanced users

Hacking Vim 7.2

ISBN: 978-1-849510-50-9   Paperback: 244 pages

Ready-to-use hacks with solutions for common situations encountered by users of the Vim editor

1. Create, install, and use Vim scripts to extend Vim's functionality

2. Personalize your work-area to fit your workflow

3. Optimize your Vim editor to be faster and more responsive

4. Packed with tips and tricks based on the author's practical experience

Please check **www.PacktPub.com** for information on our titles

CPSIA information can be obtained at www.ICGtesting.com
Printed in the USA
268997BV00004B/24/P